'I love this book, and wish I'd written it! The authors describe Bronfenbrenner's theory in its most up-to-date version, and do so in very accessible language. They clearly explain the theory's relevance for early childhood scholars and educators, and do so using a wealth of examples drawn from their own observations in classrooms and from research. Children's typically occurring activities and interactions with peers and teachers feature throughout, and the authors show how the children's own characteristics and the environment (including the classroom setup, the children's home background, and the broader socio-cultural context) influence those activities and interactions. The authors also invite their readers to reflect on their own experiences in light of the relevant theoretical concepts, and at the end of all but the first and last chapters appear carefully considered "implications" and "key concepts" for practice.'

—**Jonathan Tudge**, Department of Human Development
and Family Studies, UNC-Greensboro, USA

'Although Bronfenbrenner was one of our great public intellectuals, his legacy has been understood in terms of a static systems model which explains, rather than challenges, inequality and disadvantage. In this new book, this legacy is revealed instead as a complex and dynamic account of relationships and interactions. The authors explore how Bronfenbrenner developed his description of the network of influences which shape children's lives, emphasising the processes, rather than the contexts, within which development takes place. In unravelling this interplay between people and places they show how transformative processes can be set in motion by early childhood practitioners in their daily work with young children and their families.'

—**Liz Brooker**, Emeritus Reader, University College London
Institute of Education, UK

'In a necessarily short endorsement it is hard to capture the wealth of thinking in this highly readable book. Far from static, Bronfenbrenner's work is presented as dynamic, evolving and rich. Powerful concepts, which the authors present accessibly but accompanied by provocative and reflective questions for early years practitioners, will be a call to make linkages to practice. In promoting the applications of a bio-ecological approach to early years, the authors are encouraging a form of practitioner-activism, which sees small children as active in their own learning and development in collaboration with others around them and together in the environments in which they spend their lives. A great contribution to the early years field.'

—**Professor Aline-Wendy Dunlop**, University of Strathclyde, UK

INTRODUCING BRONFENBRENNER

Children learn in contexts, and the spaces, places and people they come into contact with have a deep influence on their development. Urie Bronfenbrenner's bioecological model of development places the child at the centre of this complex network, and his influence has been extensive in early childhood education. This book presents an introduction to Bronfenbrenner's model of development, drawing on practice-based research to identify and animate key elements of his model's impact. It illustrates how his model can help bring quality to early learning environments and incorporates it into daily work with young children.

As well as providing a glossary of key terms, *Introducing Bronfenbrenner* covers areas such as:

*   a bioecological perspective on educational transition;
*   early education as a dynamic process;
*   nurturing children's learning and development;
*   reflecting the bioecological in early years practice.

Using a variety of vignettes, practical examples of good practice and case studies, *Introducing Bronfenbrenner* is an essential guide to his work. It will be of interest to professionals working with children in early childhood settings and to undergraduate students training to become early childhood professionals.

Professor Nóirín Hayes is a developmental psychologist. She is Visiting Professor at the School of Education, Trinity College Dublin and Professor [Emeritus], Dublin Institute of Technology.

Dr Leah O'Toole lectures in Psychology at Marino Institute of Education, an Associated College of Trinity College Dublin.

Dr Ann Marie Halpenny is Lecturer in Psychology in the School of Languages, Law and Social Sciences at Dublin Institute of Technology. She has previously published with Routledge.

Introducing Early Years Thinkers
Series editor Sandra Smidt

Smidt (2014) *Introducing Freire*
The famous Brazilian educator Paulo Freire has influenced educators, teachers and students in a broad tapestry of contexts and countries, as he challenged conventional thinking on how teachers ought to teach and learners ought to learn. By making his ideas accessible and relevant, this insightful and thought-provoking text draws out the relevance and topicality of Freire's work and applies this to a wide range of educational settings, from adult education, through schools, to early years settings.

Halpenny and Pettersen (2013) *Introducing Piaget*
Jean Piaget was one of the most significant contributors to our current understanding of how children think and learn, from birth through to adolescence. In this comprehensive and accessible new book, Ann Marie Halpenny and Jan Pettersen capture the key concepts and principles of Piaget's fascinating work on children's thinking, and explore how thinking evolves and develops from infancy through the early years and beyond. This exciting new book is an invaluable resource for teachers, practitioners and students with an interest in learning and development in the early years.

Smidt (2012) *Introducing Malaguzzi*
Loris Malaguzzi is recognised as the founder of the extraordinary programmes of preschool education that developed after the war in Reggio Emilia, Italy. In this engaging text, Sandra Smidt examines how Malaguzzi's philosophy developed out of his personal experiences of growing up in post-fascist Italy. His ideas are explored and illustrated throughout by examples relating to everyday early years practice.

Smidt (2011) *Introducing Bruner*
Sandra Smidt takes the reader on a journey through the key concepts of Jerome Bruner, a significant figure in the field of early education whose work has spanned almost a century. His wide-ranging and innovative principles of early learning and teaching are unpicked here using everyday language and the links between his ideas and those of other key thinkers of the twentieth and twenty-first centuries are revealed.

Smidt (2008) *Introducing Vygotsky*
Exploring the key concepts of Lev Vygotsky, one of the twentieth century's most influential theorists in the field of early education, *Introducing Vygotsky* emphasises the social nature of learning and examines the importance of issues such as culture, history, language, and symbols in learning. This accessible text is illustrated throughout with examples drawn from real-life early years settings.

INTRODUCING BRONFENBRENNER

A Guide for Practitioners and Students in Early Years Education

Nóirín Hayes, Leah O'Toole and Ann Marie Halpenny

Routledge
Taylor & Francis Group

LONDON AND NEW YORK

First published 2017
by Routledge
2 Park Square, Milton Park, Abingdon, Oxon OX14 4RN

and by Routledge
711 Third Avenue, New York, NY 10017

Routledge is an imprint of the Taylor & Francis Group, an informa business

© 2017 Nóirín Hayes, Leah O'Toole and Ann Marie Halpenny

British Library Cataloguing in Publication Data
A catalogue record for this book is available from the British Library

Library of Congress Cataloging in Publication Data
Names: Hayes, Noirin, author. | O'Toole, Leah, author. | Halpenny, Ann Marie, author.
Title: Introducing Bronfenbrenner : a guide for practitioners and students in early years education / Noirin Hayes, Leah O'Toole and Ann Marie Halpenny.
Description: Abingdon, Oxon ; New York, NY : Routledge, 2017. | Series: Introducing early years thinkers
Identifiers: LCCN 2016042195| ISBN 9781138182813 (hardback) | ISBN 9781138182820 (pbk.) | ISBN 9781315646206 (ebook)
Subjects: LCSH: Early childhood education—Psychological aspects. | Developmental psychology. | Environmental psychology. | Nature and nurture. | Bronfenbrenner, Urie, 1917–2005.
Classification: LCC LB1139.23 .H394 2017 | DDC 372.21—dc23
LC record available at https://lccn.loc.gov/2016042195

ISBN: 978-1-138-18281-3 (hbk)
ISBN: 978-1-138-18282-0 (pbk)
ISBN: 978-1-315-64620-6 (ebk)

Typeset in Bembo and Stone Sans
by Florence Production Ltd, Stoodleigh, Devon, UK

CONTENTS

1
INTRODUCING BRONFENBRENNER

Children grow and develop in the midst of society; the people, places, objects and ideas they encounter form the basis of their learning and development. The role of early childhood experiences and the importance of those who work in early childhood settings is now well established and understood. Much of this understanding is due to the work of Urie Bronfenbrenner (1917–2005). Although his name may not be as familiar as that of Vygotsky or Piaget, he has had a profound effect on the way we think about child development and our approaches to working with young children and their families.

Urie Bronfenbrenner was born on 29 April, 1917 in Moscow to a Jewish family of professionals. His father, Alexander, was a pathologist. This was a time of revolution in Russia, and despite the Bronfenbrenners being comfortably off, it was not a safe place in which to raise a Jewish family. In 1922, Alexander escaped from Russia through Odessa and on to Romania. From there, he proceeded to the United States where he found a medical position at a hospital in Pennsylvania. A year later, in 1923, his wife, Eugenie, and their son, Urie, crossed from Russia to Tallin in Estonia and, from there, travelled on to join him.

Urie settled in to his new country and was one of many immigrant children attending his local primary school. He and his father both learned to speak fluent English, but his mother continued to speak Russian and taught Urie to appreciate the language and literature of his place of birth. Later, the family moved to upstate New York where Alexander was appointed to head a laboratory studying the characteristics and causes of what was then referred to as 'feeble-mindedness'. As he grew, Urie assisted his father in the laboratory, "running experiments and nurturing his incipient interest in psychology" (Panken, 2005, p. 10).

Following his schooling, Uri Bronfenbrenner studied psychology at Cornell University, graduating in 1938. Having completed his Masters in Developmental Psychology at Harvard University, he then studied at the University of Michigan where he received his PhD. The focus of his doctoral research was the development of children within their peer group, setting him on course to invest the rest of his long life researching child development. During World War II, he was a field psychologist at various military hospitals, and in 1948, he returned to Cornell University as Professor of Psychology and Human Development.

Bronfenbrenner was a prolific author and scholar activist who believed that it is the responsibility of academic scholars to engage directly with policymakers and professionals and to use academic work to ameliorate the problems of society. He wrote many non-theoretical papers reporting research on the lives of children and their families (Rosa and Tudge, 2013), and using these research studies and his understanding of the dynamic nature of development, he sought to persuade policymakers of the importance of family support and early childhood education. His particular ambition was to develop understanding of the complexity of human development and build this understanding into policy, practice and research. He did not shy away from addressing wider societal issues and their impacts on children and families. He became involved in public policy, and he frequently acted as an expert witness on child development, testifying before committees and the US Congress. In his commentaries on social issues, he drew attention to the changing nature of family life in the US. He was particularly concerned about the developmental impacts of increased urbanisation and of children spending extended periods of time in the care of others. Referencing the emerging research evidence from fields of psychology, sociology, education and health, he noted that the support and involvement of the entire society is necessary to raise children successfully. In particular, he recognised and valued the important role that state-supported early childhood education and care could play in achieving this objective. While this is a view that few would dispute now, it was radical in the United States of the 1960s, where independence and self-reliance were highly valued and the state saw little or no role for itself in providing family support services.

In fact, Bronfenbrenner's views on early child development and education were out of line with many other academics commenting at the time. For instance, in 1970, he participated in a forum at the White House on the subject Children and Parents. When the final report was submitted, he added a minority report in disagreement with it. He later wrote that the report failed "to convey the urgency and severity of the problem confronting the nation's families and their children" and did not "alert the reader to the critical role played by business and industry – both private and public – in determining the lifestyle of the American family" (Bronfenbrenner, 1970/2005b, p. 211). These concerns about the wider influence of society on children's development and the position of children in society provided the foundations on which his later work was based.

Many of the views articulated by Bronfenbrenner in his early policy presentations and articles are echoed in our current theorising and understanding of the importance of early child development and education (Siraj and Mayo, 2014). He played a critical role in advancing the public's recognition of the importance of early childhood education both for the sake of the child and to add value to the family and society at large.

Although rarely presented as a key theorist in early childhood education, his work has underpinned much progress internationally in early education, and his model of development is one that has informed research, curriculum design and professional education. For instance, deriving from research in the UK by the Effective Provision of Pre-school and Primary Education (EPPE) project (Melhuish *et al.*, 2008; Sylva *et al.*, 2004), we now recognise the importance of early learning environments, both the home and early years settings, to children's early development. This echoes Bronfenbrenner's views as far back as 1967 when he wrote that research points to the home background as "the most important element in determining how well the child did in school" (Bronfenbrenner, 1967/2005, p. 203). Similarly, on the limitations of targeted early educational support, he cited findings indicating that "if a lower-class[1] child had schoolmates who came from advantaged homes, he did reasonably well; but if all the other children also came from deprived backgrounds, he did poorly" (1967/2005, pp. 203–204). He also noted that for middle-class children in a mainly lower-class school, "the performance of the advantaged children remains unaffected. It is as though good home background had immunized them" (1967/2005, p. 204).

His work looked beyond individual development to take account of wider influencing factors and the context, or ecology, of development. He drew support for his integrated ecological perspective on development not only from his own academic work but also from the experiences he gathered through his academic exchange visits to the Union of Socialist Soviet Republics (USSR). Although Bronfenbrenner did not consider himself to be Russian, he spoke the language fluently and was interested in the Soviet Union; he spent almost two decades of his career researching and writing about the country of his birth. It was in the USSR that Vygotsky was born and had worked. It is interesting to note that Vygotsky (1896–1934), who although born in what is now Belarus, spent his working life in Moscow, also recognised the importance of context to learning and development, emphasising the role of culture in driving human development. His attention to the critical role of the social context to individual learning and development can be seen as a precursor to Bronfenbrenner's later ecological model of development (Parrish, 2014). While Vygotsky's views differed from Bronfenbrenner, who highlighted the vital role of interactions as driving development, it does not put the two theorists in opposition but, rather, highlights their differing emphases.

Post-World War II relations between the US and the USSR were strained in what was termed the Cold War. Many political efforts were made to bridge the divide between the democratic, capitalist US and the communist USSR. Given Bronfenbrenner's fluency in the Russian language, he was able to avail himself of a number of scholar exchange opportunities so that he could investigate and write on the differences between childrearing and family practices across both countries. Bronfenbrenner left a vast collection of unpublished reports, field notes, letters and commentaries, and a review of these by Panken (2005) sheds light on both the man and the Cold War as the context for US/USSR relations.

The culmination of his work in the USSR was the publication in 1970 of his book *Two Worlds of Childhood: US and USSR*. This book drew out the differences between children's experiences in the USSR and in the US, highlighting the impact of different cultural experiences. Bronfenbrenner was impressed by the good behaviour of children in the USSR: "They are well-mannered, attentive, and industrious. . . . they reveal a strong motivation to learn, a readiness to serve society" (1970, p. 227). He concluded that, generally speaking, the children of the USSR conform to "a more homogeneous set of standards" (1970, p. 229) than their counterparts in the US. One explanation he provided for this was the collective upbringing of young children in the USSR where there was harmony between the values of the family and society. This, he believed, eased children's transition into and adjustment to society. He noted that, by contrast, US society "emerges as one that gives decreasing prominence to the family as a socialising agent" (1970, p. 230). He voiced concern that since World War II, *de facto* responsibility for the upbringing of children had shifted to other settings, such as schools, which may not see this as their role. While he made it clear that this was no reflection on the affection or concern parents have for their children, he argued that it does decrease the "power of the family in the lives of children" (1970, pp. 229–230).

Deriving from this cross-cultural study, Bronfenbrenner argued that American parents were spending less time raising their children as they had to work to survive. The result, he argued, was that many children were growing up without enough contact with adults and were, therefore, separated from society. This interrupted the socialisation process so that children learned from each other rather than from responsible adults. To rebalance the situation, he proposed increased government investment in social programmes offering support to families, such as providing childcare, and saw this as an investment in the future.

Lyndon B. Johnson declared a 'war on poverty' when he became President of the United States in 1963 following the assassination of President J. F. Kennedy. He established the preschool intervention Head Start with the aim of counteracting many of the educational problems faced by poor children by giving them a short educational input before they started primary school. The idea of intervening early in the educational lives of poorer children led President Johnson to establish the Office of Economic Opportunity. This office put together a committee of experts to plan a project that would help communities meet the needs of disadvantaged preschool children. Two early childhood educators were appointed to this design committee: Edward Zigler (who has written a history of the development of Head Start [Zigler and Muenchow, 1992]) and Urie Bronfenbrenner (Neugebauer, 2010). The establishment of Head Start was announced in 1965. In its original design, it was an eight-week summer preschool programme, staffed by volunteers, for over five hundred thousand low-income children who were due to enter primary school in September of 1965. It was later offered as a year-long preschool programme. Gradually, the name Head Start came to refer to a wide range of early interventions meeting the needs of disadvantaged young children and their families.

In reflecting on Head Start, Bronfenbrenner noted that "the principal purpose of the programs is not remedial education but giving children and their families, from all levels of society, a sense of dignity, purpose and meaningful activities" (1967/2005, p. 208). Head Start has been researched and expanded and has grown extensively over the years in both the length of the intervention and the age at which children are targeted. It remains the standard early intervention programme in the US (https://www.nhsa.org).

Throughout his career, Bronfenbrenner exhibited an intense interest in the family, family support and the social policy context in the US (Rosa and Tudge, 2013). He wrote many papers and articles linking his theoretical position on human development to implications for policy and for practice. He also considered that there was an absence of sound 'real-world' research to inform policy and practice. He developed his model of development as a framework within which to locate research, particularly that emphasising all the elements affecting individual development in context.

Bronfenbrenner's ecological model of human development

Early and influential psychological studies developed their knowledge through researching the individual in isolation and paid relatively little attention to the dynamic impact of the context within which development occurred. Criticising this approach, Bronfenbrenner wrote that "much of developmental psychology is the science of the strange behaviour of children in strange situations with strange adults for the briefest possible period of time" (1977, p. 513). This laboratory-based approach to studying child development changed with the growth of interest in the ecological approach, which took account of the actual environments and systems within which human beings live, the relationships between individuals and these systems, and the relationships between the systems themselves.

Reflecting this shift, more recent research in psychology, sociology and education has moved away from the traditional approach to studying children in isolation. Increasingly, attention is given to understanding childhood in a wider sociocultural context where children are seen as active participants. Bronfenbrenner's work has been central to this shift (Bronfenbrenner, 1979, 1995; Bronfenbrenner and Morris, 1998, 2006[2]). Writing in the Foreword of *Making Human Beings Human: Bioecological Perspectives on Human Development*, Richard Lerner observes that the growth and acceptance of dynamic, integrated and holistic approaches to considering human development in context "owe their origin, persuasive articulation, and refinement to the singularly creative, theoretically elegant, empirically rigorous, and humane and democratic scholarly contributions of Urie Bronfenbrenner" (in Bronfenbrenner, 2005, pp. ix–x).

Given the improved understanding of the integrated and dynamic nature of learning and development and the value of considering many theoretical positions when studying development, Bronfenbrenner saw the need for a developmental framework within which to consider psychological theories of learning and theories of educational practice. This required a level of complexity to accommodate the variety of factors influencing learning while, at the same time, providing a framework within which these factors can be considered, reconciled and responded to in pedagogical practice, policy and planning. Bronfenbrenner's ecological model of human development presents such a framework. Although the model was detailed in his 1979 book, its roots can be found as far back as his doctoral thesis, submitted in 1942 (Bronfenbrenner, 1942/2005, p. 22).

In the 1970s, Bronfenbrenner (1967/2005, 1977, 1979) began to refine his ideas as he recognised that good practice in understanding child development, including early educational practice, required a deep understanding of the developing child in context, which, he argued, required a complex 'ecological' theory of development. He used the word 'ecological' to capture the embedded and holistic nature of human development. His most influential book, *The Ecology of Human Development: Experiments by Nature and Design* (1979), described such a model. The ecological approach to understanding development recognises that individuals are embedded in and affected by different levels of context: both macro (the large scale, at a distance) and micro (small/local, close by). In considering studies on human development, Bronfenbrenner (1977) was critical of the fact that researchers studied development out of context. For him, development was a function of the interplay between the individual and his/her environment. Therefore, he insisted on locating development within environmental systems. He defined the 'ecology of human development' as involving

> the scientific study of the progressive, mutual accommodation between an active, growing human being and the changing properties of the immediate settings in which the developing person lives, as this process is affected by relations between these settings, and by the larger contexts in which the settings are embedded.
>
> (1979, p. 21)

From the very beginning and through its various iterations, his model has addressed both the structural or biological aspects of development alongside the process or sociocultural dimensions (Bronfenbrenner, 1979, 1989a; Bronfenbrenner and Ceci, 1994; Bronfenbrenner and Morris, 1998, 2006). An additional feature of the model is its emphasis on the dynamic, bidirectional relationships between people and context. Siraj and Mayo recognise Bronfenbrenner's model as having value across disciplines as it "bridges the social and psychological aspects of human development" (2014, p. 16). In his original model, Bronfenbrenner located the developing child within a series of four systems, which he called the 'microsystem', the 'mesosystem', the 'exosystem' and the 'macrosystem'. These systems, or levels, are organised from those closest, or proximal, to the child to those whose influence is indirect or distal (Greene and Moane, 2000). Reflecting his Russian background, Bronfenbrenner referred to these systems as 'nested' each within the next like a set of Russian dolls (the matryoshka dolls). Later, recognising the importance and influence of time (and history) in development, he included a fifth system, which he called the 'chronosystem'. Studying individual development through the lens of this model allows early years practitioners to contextualise child development and to take account of the overlapping and interacting nature of the different levels. The model has been influential in both early educational practice and curriculum development, most notably in its use by the New Zealand Ministry of Education in the development and implementation of their early years curriculum *Te Whāriki* (Ministry of Education, New Zealand, 1996).

The child's closest and most familiar microsystem is the family, but there are other microsystems, including settings close to the child such as day care, preschool and school. The mesosystem refers to communication and interactions between the various elements of the individual's microsystems. In early education, this would include the relationship between family members and early years practitioners. The third level in the ecological system model, the exosystem, refers to more distant influences, factors external to the children and adults but impacting on them nonetheless, such as educational policy or curriculum design. The macrosystem represents the influence of even more distant factors, such as societal values and the cultural view of the child. Finally, the chronosystem refers to the influence of time on development. This takes account of time from the individual's perspective but also takes into account historical time; it is of relevance to early years practitioners when, for instance, considering issues of transitions.

The ecological model of human development was appealing and very quickly became accepted as a useful framework within which to study development, being taken up by psychologists, sociologists and teachers. It began to feature in textbooks, and the idea of nested systems seems to have provided a very useful visual guide in accounting for the myriad factors that affect development. In fact, Bronfenbrenner wrote of "an instance of what might be called 'the failure of success'" (1992/2005, p. 107). Having argued over the years that research in developmental psychology had failed to take sufficient account of the context within which development occurred, he now found it to be in danger of losing sight of the developing child, with "a surfeit of studies on 'context without development'" (1992/2005, p. 108).

Over time, the model went through periods of change. Rosa and Tudge (2013) identify three specific phases of development from the original *Ecological Model of Human Development* in 1979 to the final iteration as the *Bioecological Model of Human Development* in 1998/2006. Reflecting on the relatively limited attention that is given to the later, more powerful version of the model of development in research and practice, Rosa and Tudge (2013) argue that this may actually be a result of the success of the earlier version. It may be that the first presentation of the model, introducing the concepts of different levels or systems of context, had such a powerful impact across disciplines – notwithstanding its limitations, recognised most thoroughly by Bronfenbrenner himself – that his later work suffered. Rosa and Tudge write that:

There is really no reason for continuing to treat Bronfenbrenner's theory as one of contextual influences on development, or ignoring the focus, during the third and final phase, on proximal processes and the use of the PPCT [Process–Person–Context–Time] model as a guide for research using the bioecological theory.

(2013, p. 256)

The bioecological model of human development

Due to over-attention to the specific systems of development at the expense of the position and influence of the developing individual, Bronfenbrenner reconsidered the title of his model in order to foreground the individual. In his article "Ecological systems theory", his definition of the ecology of development includes the addition of the text in italics:

> The ecology of human development is the study of the progressive, mutual accommodation, *throughout the life course*, between an active, growing human being and the changing properties of the immediate settings in which the developing person lives, as this process is affected by the relations between these settings, and by the larger contexts in which the settings are embedded.
> (Bronfenbrenner, 1992/2005, p. 107; emphasis in the original)

The emphasis is added by Bronfenbrenner to highlight the importance of the individual over time. The new title for the model, the 'bioecological model' of human development, was proposed in 1994 by Bronfenbrenner and Ceci. In all the iterations of his model of development from the initial presentation of his ecological model in 1979 to its most recent configuration as the bioecological model (Bronfenbrenner and Morris, 1998; 2006), Bronfenbrenner has identified the need for researchers and practitioners to pay close attention to the individual developing in a complexity of interacting systems. The bioecological model, which in its title highlights the importance of the developing individual,

> represents a marked shift in the centre of gravity of the model, in which features of the earlier version are first called into question, but then recombined, along with new elements, into a more complex and more dynamic structure. . . . the model presented, while still evolving, is now called the bioecological model.
> (Bronfenbrenner and Morris, 1998, pp. 993–994)

One of the driving forces behind the development of the bioecological model was a challenge to developmental psychologists posed by the American psychologist Anne Anastasi as far back as 1958. In a paper titled "Heredity, environment, and the question 'how?'", she identified the need for developmental psychology to uncover the mechanisms through which the genetic code of an individual (the genotype) is transformed into observable characteristics and behaviour (the phenotype). While not attempting to definitively answer this very complex challenge, Bronfenbrenner, with his colleague Stephen Ceci wrote a paper in which they addressed some of Anastasi's questions and proposed the first draft of the bioecological model of development (Bronfenbrenner and Ceci, 1993). They made a critical distinction between 'environment' and 'process', with the latter occupying a central, driving position in development and having a meaning that is quite specific to the model. In fact, process is at the core of the revised model. The construct of process (P) encompasses particular forms of interaction between organism and environment, often termed nature and nurture. They called these processes the 'proximal processes' to emphasise the fact that they are located within the microsystems of development and operate over time; they are posited as the primary mechanisms producing human development. The power of these processes to influence development varies based on characteristics of the person (P), of immediate and remote environmental contexts (C) and the time periods (T) in which they take place. To capture the integrated nature of the various elements, the model is characterised as the PPCT model, and it is through proximal processes that an individual's genetic potential is made visible in their behaviours and actions. They suggest that the investigation of proximal processes, and their developmental consequences under different environmental conditions provides developmental psychologists with an indirect strategy for testing the role of both genetics and environment in contributing to individual differences in psychological growth.

Elaborating on the role of process in development, Bronfenbrenner and Morris (1998, 2006) argue that human development, especially in the early years, takes place through processes of progressively more complex reciprocal interactions between an active and evolving biopsychological human organism (the child) and the persons, objects and symbols in the immediate external environment. To be effective, these interactions must be of high quality and occur on a fairly regular basis over extended periods of time. Examples of enduring patterns of proximal process can be seen in early years settings, including feeding or comforting a baby, playing with a young child, child–child activities, group or solitary play, engaging in conversation and dialogue, reading, learning new skills, athletic activities, problem-solving, caring for others in distress, making plans, performing complex tasks and acquiring new knowledge and know-how (Bronfenbrenner and Morris, 1998, p. 996).

The bioecological model and early education

In identifying proximal processes as key to development, Bronfenbrenner and Morris (1998, 2006) provide us with a clear focus for early years practice, and more recent research supports their view by illustrating the importance of interaction and relationships to healthy child development. Positive, high-quality, interactive early learning experiences facilitate the development of generative or positive dispositions as opposed to disruptive or negative ones. Bronfenbrenner and Morris note that the model introduces:

[c]oncepts and criteria . . . that differentiate between those features of the environment that foster versus interfere with the development of proximal processes. Particularly significant in the latter sphere is the growing hecticness, instability and chaos in the principal settings in which human competence and character are shaped – in the family, child-care arrangements, school, peer groups and neighbourhoods.

(1998, p. 995)

The concept of proximal processes has important implications for early education, highlighting the power of interactions and the important role of the adult. Through reflective observation of the child, adults can come to understand the characteristics of the child and the environment, which will facilitate positive development and learning. Drawing on many different studies of child development with children of different ages, Bronfenbrenner and Morris (1998, 2006) describe the positive, generative dispositions valued by Western culture. One example of generative disposition given is the extent to which the child tends to engage and persist in progressively more complex activities. For example, given a facilitating environment, children will elaborate, restructure and create new features in an environment, not only physical and social but also symbolic. Another class of developmentally generative disposition they describe reflects the increased capacity and active propensity of children, as they grow older, to conceptualise their experiences. This, Bronfenbrenner and Morris argue, contributes to the development of "directive belief systems" (2006, p. 811) about oneself as an active agent both in relation to the self and to environment. This is particularly important and relevant to early years practice as these personal belief systems, emerging in early childhood, are the foundations for self-directed learning, attention and problem-solving. The manner in which adults respond to, guide and support children's development can profoundly impact on the adult the child becomes.

Different theories of development shed light on different aspects of development, with varying suggestions and challenges for educational principles and practices. The value of a model such as the bioecological one is that it provides a framework, allowing us to visualise complex dynamics in different contexts and reflect on the various different factors impacting on the development of children. However, system models, such as that proposed by Bronfenbrenner, have been criticised as being too preoccupied with individualism and ignoring the power of interactions and discourse between parents, teachers and children in early education (Dahlberg *et al.*, 1999; Downes, 2014; Penn, 1997). These criticisms seem particularly misplaced in relation to the bioecological model of development, which actively stresses the importance of good-quality interactions, relationships and communication, of the process through locating the construct of proximal processes as the central factor driving development. The quality of these proximal processes is mediated by social interactions and this provides a link between the structural (biological) factors influencing development and the processes which support it.

Bronfenbrenner's model presents a valuable framework of development within which to link psychological and educational theory to early educational curriculum and practice from both a research and pedagogical point of view. It is a model with sufficient detail to allow attention to all the complex systems of early educational experience whilst, at the same time, highlighting the reality, dynamism and complexity of everyday life. This book provides those working in early childhood with a comprehensive introduction to the work of Bronfenbrenner and its relevance to contemporary early educational practice. It illustrates how the model acts as a framework within which the quality of early educational pedagogy can be understood and enhanced. The chapters are presented in two sections. The first section, chapters 1 to 5, introduces the bioecological model and discusses different theoretical aspects of the model. The second section, chapters 6 to 10, focuses more on the practical application of the model in early years settings. The reader should note that male and female pronouns are used in alternate chapters in order to facilitate a gender-balanced approach.

This introductory chapter, Chapter 1, provides a brief overview of Bronfenbrenner's life, highlighting key biographical details and drawing attention to his many achievements within the field of developmental psychology, early education and in the wider social context.

Chapter 2 explores the development of the bioecological model, discussing Bronfenbrenner's well-known concepts of microsystem, mesosystem, exosystem, macrosystem and chronosystem, as well as elaborating on the more up-to-date version of the model which emphasises the interaction of 'process', 'person', 'context' and 'time'.

Chapter 3 focuses on process through exploring the nature and power of the concept of the proximal processes. It illustrates that relationships are vital for children's development emotionally, socially and cognitively and explains how building good relationships should be a central concern for early years practice.

Bronfenbrenner argues that we must understand process, person, context and time if we are to understand the child. Chapter 4 develops the idea that children's development through relationships must be understood in context.

Chapter 5 draws on practice-based research (specifically regarding educational transitions) to identify and animate key elements of the model impacting on early educational pedagogy and practice, while providing the reader with an enhanced understanding of why the model is so powerful and how it can be realised in practice.

In Chapter 6 the concept of children as active, interested and influential agents shaping their own learning in early childhood settings is explored. Drawing on key principles within Bronfenbrenner's theory, the importance of building a pedagogy that promotes and respects children and child-initiated practice in early childhood is reinforced.

In Chapter 7, we consider how best to provide a rich and stimulating learning environment that contributes to children's positive development and wellbeing. The chapter will discuss features of good-quality early learning environments and the potential impact of both indoors and outdoors environments and materials.

In Chapter 8, Bronfenbrenner's emphasis on development as a dynamic process is explored regarding pedagogy in early education which values the moment for its immediate developmental contribution but which also acknowledges its potential in respect of later development.

Chapter 9 explores how best to develop the skills of observation and reflection, both of which are central to a nurturing pedagogy. They enhance practice and planning, are manifest in well-managed and yet reasonably flexible practice, and assist in the provision of a learning environment that includes children and supports and extends children's learning.

The final chapter presents an opportunity to review the theory and practice sections of the book, to reflect on the key aspects contributing to good-quality early years practice and to consider how best to utilise this knowledge in enhancing early years practice.

Notes

1   As Bronfenbrenner's work spanned over 50 years, you will find that some of his language sounds quaint to our ears and some of his characterisations (of class, race, gender, etc.) are quite out of date, seeming to represent deficit models at times. Despite this, the points underlying what he said are what are of interest.
2   We use these two articles interchangeably. The work was originally published in 1998 and the slightly revised version was published posthumously in 2006.

2

THE BIOECOLOGICAL MODEL OF HUMAN DEVELOPMENT

Introduction

Bronfenbrenner identified some interesting concepts regarding the multifaceted systems of influence on children's lives. This chapter highlights the significant ways in which he continued to develop and update his theory up to the time of his death in 2005. While much emphasis has been placed on Bronfenbrenner's systems of contextual influences, developed in his earlier theorising, less attention has been paid to the important role the individual plays in her own development and the central importance of proximal processes – reciprocal interactions between the child and her environment:

> Especially in its early phases, but also throughout the life course, human development takes place through processes of progressively more complex reciprocal interaction between an active, evolving biopsychological human organism and the persons, objects, and symbols in its immediate external environment. To be effective, the interaction must occur on a fairly regular basis over extended periods of time. Such enduring forms of interaction in the immediate environment are referred to as proximal processes.
>
> (Bronfenbrenner and Morris, 2006, p. 797)

The aim of this chapter is to unpack the implications of Bronfenbrenner's model of human development for understanding early childhood. The chapter also tracks some of the new directions that he brought to his model over time. We also consider some current reflections on Bronfenbrenner's theory and its implications for early years practice.

Before outlining the theory, let's consider an interpretation of the term 'ecological' as it is used in the theory. According to Bronfenbrenner, "[e]cology implies an adjustment between organism and environment" (1975, p. 439). Later, he wrote a more complete definition:

The ecology of human development involves the scientific study of the progressive, mutual accommodation between an active, growing human being and the changing properties of the immediate settings in which the developing person lives, as this process is affected by relations between these settings, and by the larger contexts within which the settings are embedded.

(Bronfenbrenner, 1979, p. 21)

Bronfenbrenner was interested in "how environments change, and the implications of this change for the human beings who live and grow in these environments" (1975, p. 439). Using an ecological approach, he explored the interrelations between the developing person and the changing micro and macro contexts in which development is embedded. In early years learning, this implies that development is influenced by changing micro contexts, like family, friends and communities surrounding the child, and also by changes within the macro contexts – the broader social and cultural context in which they are growing. This approach also foregrounds ongoing change and adjustment in development and the importance of recognising the progressive and dynamic nature of development, reflected in a later emphasis on proximal processes.

The development of Bronfenbrenner's work can be characterised in three phases, moving from his initial emphasis on the role of context in development to recognising the active role of the child to the final phase where he captured the

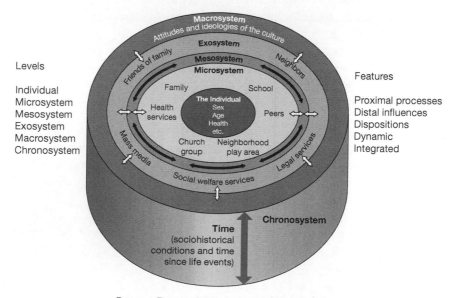

FIGURE 2.1 Bioecological model of development

Source: Adapted from Santrock (2007)

dynamic nature of development in his Process–Person–Context–Time (PPCT) model of development, drawing attention to proximal processes and demonstrating how they are influenced by the context in which they occur. Importantly, Bronfenbrenner gave much greater prominence to the characteristics of the developing child in his later work. The model is represented in Figure 2.1.

Nested systems of influence: development in context

The first 'version' of an ecological model of human development conceived of development of the individual within the environment characterised as four systems: microsystem, mesosystem, exosystem and macrosystem. The most direct influences, closest to the child (e.g. family, friends), are envisaged as being embedded or nested within those located more remotely from the individual (e.g. political systems, cultural contexts). Significantly, the child is located at the centre of the model. Microsystems include aspects of the environment impacting on the daily life of the child. Parents, siblings, extended family members, early years practitioners and settings and other children within daycare settings comprise the microsystems that exert primary and direct influence on children's lives.

In early years practice, the child as learner and the learning environment are closely connected. The child develops language abilities in settings where adults talk to children and to each other; the child learns to explore in settings where exploration is valued and the curriculum reflects these values.

REFLECTION

Think about the microsystems of the children you work with. Can you identify some of them? Who are the main actors within them? How do these microsystems affect the quality of children's experiences?

Bronfenbrenner called the second level of influence the mesosystem. This describes the level of context that takes account of interconnections between two or more settings (such as school, peer group and family) and acknowledges their impact on the child. In short, the mesosystem is a system of two or more microsystems. This is a very powerful concept, showing how behaviour in any one setting is influenced by experiences not just within that setting, but in the full range of settings experienced by the child. "[A]n individual's relationships in every setting are impacted by relationships in other settings in that individual's life. There is . . . a chain of activity that individuals drag with them across microsystems" (Slesnick *et al.*, 2007, p. 1238).

Parental involvement in the early years context provides a good illustration of two microsystems (home and early years setting) interacting with each other. Links between home and early years setting are important. The environment, routines and people within a home provide opportunities for the spontaneous learning that should be a feature of all early years contexts (Mitchell *et al.*, 2008). A mesosystem could include a meeting between a parent (from the child's family microsystem) and practitioner (from the microsystem of the early years setting). Connections like those between practitioners and parents may facilitate greater understanding of the child's exosystem and macrosystem, especially with regard to parents' occupations, family culture and other important details in their lives (Neal and Neal, 2013).

REFLECTION

To what extent do you facilitate partnership with parents in your setting? Can you identify other important mesosystem communications that can contribute to best practice in early childhood education?

In the exosystem, Bronfenbrenner highlighted less visible and more distant influences on the child's life, such as decisions made by the manager of a setting, the quality of the parents' workplace, social media and informal social networks. The exosystem also encompasses conditions influencing the wellbeing of the adults in children's lives. Exosystems include settings that influence the child but in which the child does not directly participate. For example, a child's parent may be experiencing stress within their workplace and this may influence the quality of their interactions with the child. A further example of an exosystem is the education policymaking community; an individual child generally does not play a role, yet educational policies nonetheless influence the child's educational experiences. For example, the increasing international pattern of providing a universal free preschool year may allow greater access for young children to preschool education and thus influence the microsystems in which they interact.

REFLECTION

What role does the family context of the child play in helping you understand her learning and development? Does the local neighbourhood influence how children develop? Does the community within which your setting is located influence how you respond to children?

Finally, macrosystems encompass those influences that take place at a cultural level; for example, sociocultural beliefs about the value of early childhood care and education and about the rights and responsibilities of children (National Council for Curriculum Assessment [NCCA], 2009). Although children are not in direct contact with macrosystems, the decisions generated at this level significantly influence their lives. Additionally, each cultural community that children belong to makes its own specific demands (Ministry of Education, New Zealand, 1996).

REFLECTION

How does cultural context influence the design of the setting, the pedagogical principles underpinning practice and the routines that evolve from these principles? How does the cultural context in which you grew up influence your practice with young children? Is your practice inclusive and reflective of the diversity of children's backgrounds?

In addition to the four core systems, Bronfenbrenner (1986a, 1986b) later introduced the chronosystem, reflecting change or continuity across time and influencing each of the other systems (Neal and Neal, 2013). Transitions like the move from preschool to primary school are part of the chronosystem while also being part of the mesosystem. The historical time in which a child develops also influences the nature and quality of her experiences. Children growing up in the 1950s and 1960s had a very different experience of technology than children born in this century. The chronosystem also has relevance regarding the particular values and attitudes to childhood evident at a particular historical time. Childhood is shaped by the circumstances in which children grow, and the beliefs and attitudes of historical time influence the roles that children are allowed to take. Typically in the early part of the twentieth century, children were not afforded an active role in their learning and development. In the late twentieth century and the early twenty-first century, the role children play in their learning and development has evolved from a peripheral, passive one to being more central and active. We elaborate on the chronosystem later in this chapter, detailing some of the subsystems associated with this level of context – macrotime, mesotime and microtime.

REFLECTION

How does the historical time in which you are working influence the nature and content of your practice? To what extent does ICT play a role in children's learning and development in your setting?

Context without development? Focus on the active role of the developing child

In a second phase, broadly between 1980 and 1994, Bronfenbrenner renamed his model a 'bioecological model' of human development to better reflect the active role the child plays in shaping her development and to provide greater emphasis on biological influences (Tudge *et al.*, 2009). Avoiding the implication that context impacts solely *on* the child, Bronfenbrenner moved his theory on to reflect a more dynamic process whereby the context or environment impacts *with* and *through* the child's participation.

In this phase, Bronfenbrenner expanded on his descriptions of the different levels of the ecological environment. He noted the fact that humans are not only the product of but also the producer of their own development. While highlighting development as being *nested* within contexts, Bronfenbrenner now placed greater emphasis on the processes that translate these contextual experiences into development. These processes include "not only the objective behaviours occurring in any given interaction but also the relevant subjective psychological states, such as beliefs and opinions of the interacting individuals" (Rosa and Tudge, 2013, p. 249). Bronfenbrenner's increasing interest in the complex processes enabling development evoked the sense of a network of influences that was dynamic by nature. Such a 'networked' model of development views ecological systems as "an overlapping arrangement of structures, each directly or indirectly connected to the others by the direct and indirect social interactions of their participants" (Neal and Neal, 2013, p. 722).

This further elaboration of the model addressed the concern that little explicit attention was paid to the role of the individual in Bronfenbrenner's earlier writings. Making the child more visible at the centre of her development sits well with the notion of 'agency', involving children's capacity to understand and act upon their world and foregrounding children's competence (James *et al.*, 1998). This approach seeks to understand the meanings children give to their own lives. Bronfenbrenner's revised perspective sees the child as actively participating in her own childhood, and this is in accordance with Malaguzzi's concept of the 'rich child' – the child who is "rich in potential, strong, powerful and competent" (1993, p. 10). This acknowledges that in addition to expressing their desires and wishes, children as agents can negotiate within their environment; critically, these interactions ultimately result in changing their environment.

Thus, Bronfenbrenner's bioecological theory goes beyond simply highlighting the active role that the child plays in her own development. It emphasises the fluid and relational nature of development through a focus on personal characteristics influencing present and future development. Bronfenbrenner criticised some of the shortcomings in his previous theorising:

> Existing developmental studies subscribing to an ecological model have provided far more knowledge about the nature of developmentally relevant

environments, near and far, than about the characteristics of developing individuals, then and now.

(1989a, p. 188)

Bronfenbrenner emphasised three kinds of characteristics of the developing child: (i) active behavioural characteristics/dispositions, (ii) resource characteristics and (iii) demand characteristics.

Active behavioural dispositions

The term 'active behavioural dispositions' refers to variations in the child's motivation, persistence and temperament. Even when children have equivalent access to resources, their developmental courses may differ as a function of individual personal characteristics.

> Lauren is 18 months old and sitting on the floor in her crèche. She is interested in the soft teddy sitting beyond her reach on the sofa. She crawls near the sofa and tries to pull herself up, hanging on to the sofa in order to try to reach the teddy. After several attempts, she falls back into a sitting position on the floor. Having looked around the room to see if anyone can come to her aid, she finally begins to tug cautiously on a rug hanging down from the sofa. As she pulls the rug, slowly teddy, which is sitting on the rug, moves forward. Lauren stops and looks around again, not sure about what she should do next. Eventually she pulls on the rug, and this time teddy comes tumbling down into her arms.
>
> Source: author observation in an early years setting

Lauren is demonstrating evidence of positive active behavioural dispositions such as the motivation to gain access to teddy and the perseverance to patiently experiment in different ways until she finally succeeds in achieving this. While her success in reaching teddy may not be a significant achievement regarding her developmental pathway, at the same time the positive dispositions she has shown are likely to be reinforced by the success of her attempts. Bronfenbrenner provides a rationale for how environments influence personal characteristics. However, a significant feature highlighted in this phase of his work was the potential for personal characteristics to change environments. The interaction between humans and their environments is one of reciprocity – the context in which a child is developing impacts on her development and, in turn, the child may shape her environment through these interactions. The particular characteristics of children, their ability to focus, to show interest in things, to become excited about events, contributes to shaping our responses to these children. In turn, we are affected by and through our interactions with the different children in our care.

Active behavioural dispositions may be positive or negative in impact. 'Generative' (positive) dispositions are characteristics likely to enhance interactions and elicit responses from the environment. These are associated with the ability to initiate or maintain reciprocal interactions with parents or other caregivers (Bronfenbrenner, 1993) and include curiosity, attentiveness and ability to defer gratification. Let's imagine how these might play out in the context of early years practice.

Markus is curious about dinosaurs and uses every opportunity to learn more about them. When the early years practitioner working in his daycare setting invites him to read with her, he responds enthusiastically by selecting one of his favourite books, which provides a comprehensive and colourful overview of the history and evolution of dinosaurs. Miniature figures of different types of dinosaurs are included with the book, and Markus actively demonstrates some interesting facts about dinosaurs. This in turn elicits a positive and interested response from the practitioner working alongside him.

Source: author observation in an early years setting

'Disruptive' (negative) dispositions are those characteristics which prevent or disrupt responses from the environment, including distractibility, aggressive tendencies, inability to defer gratification and tendency to withdraw from activity.

Lena wants to play at the sandbox. Julie, the practitioner, has explained that at the moment there are too many children playing at the sandbox. She encourages Lena to wait a short while until there is more space for her to play safely there. Julie invites Lena to join a different activity, and Lena insists on joining the other children at the sandbox. As there is not enough space for all children to play at once, some of the other children who were already playing with the sand become annoyed and refuse to allow Lena to play with them.

Source: author observation in an early years setting

Resource characteristics

Resource characteristics are not as immediately recognisable as dispositions. These include mental and emotional resources such as past experiences, intelligence and skills as well as material resources like access to housing, education and a responsive caregiver. According to Bronfenbrenner and Morris, these characteristics involve no selective disposition to action but, rather, are described as "biopsychological liabilities and assets" influencing the capacity of the child to initiate and sustain interactions (2006, p. 812). Developmental assets can take the form of ability, knowledge, skill and experience, which as they develop and evolve, expand the range of options and sources of growth available to the child.

> Jack loves music and enjoys the "music and movement" sessions that take place in his early years setting weekly. During these sessions, the children are introduced to musical instruments and invited to experiment with them. He particularly loves the percussion instruments, and his enthusiasm when playing with them motivates the children and adults in his room to explore further and enjoy these possibilities.
>
> Source: author observation in an early years setting

Other resource characteristics may operate to limit or disrupt the extent to which a child can thrive or even their ability to become involved in available interactions and activities. These characteristics include genetic inheritances like low birthweight, physical disability, and severe or persistent illness. Bronfenbrenner shows how the impact of these characteristics depends on a variety of factors. As Brewster (2004) notes in the context of a 'social model' of disability, the physical and attitudinal environment can disable a child far more than any impairment. Consider how a supportive early years setting limits the impact of a potentially disruptive resource characteristic in the following example.

> Elena is a bright, outgoing three-year-old, and today is her first day in preschool. Elena's mother has been anxious about her starting preschool because she has cerebral palsy and uses a wheelchair; her mother is worried about the ability of staff to meet Elena's needs. However, since the family and the preschool have spent time planning together, this morning Elena is met at the door by the preschool teacher, Sarah, who wheels her chair up the ramp, through the doors and into the preschool where she introduces Elena to another three-year-old, Hanna. "Hanna is feeling a bit shy this morning, Elena. I know that you really like chatting and playing, so can you spend a bit of time with Hanna and help her feel less worried?" As the girls play, Sarah shows Elena's mother the accessible bathrooms and the raised flower beds in the garden where Elena will take part in the planned gardening with the other children.
>
> Source: composite of author experiences working
> with children with disabilities

In Elena's case, her cerebral palsy could have represented a disruptive resource characteristic limiting her ability to benefit from early education. In some settings, she might not have been able to enter the building due to lack of wheelchair access, or it may be that staff fears would have left them unwilling to engage with Elena as a child with strengths as well as challenges. Here, the accessible environment and Sarah's recognition of Elena's social skills frames the latter's experiences and the perception of her resources very differently, to the benefit of Elena, her mother and Hanna, the little girl who may now have a supportive friend to help her through the transition from home to preschool.

Demand characteristics

Demand characteristics are those qualities of the developing person that can invite or discourage reactions from the social environment, influencing the way in which proximal processes are established. Demand characteristics include an agitated or calm temperament, attractive versus unattractive appearance, hyperactivity and passivity. Other characteristics that are more externally accessible, like age, gender and skin colour may also affect the establishment of effective interactions. The bioecological model of human development emphasises the importance of interaction between person and context; the personal characteristics and disposi- tions of the child elicit responses from the environment, and these responses influence the personal characteristics of the child and elicit further responses from the child. Thus, demand characteristics, as well as active behavioural dispositions and resource characteristics, are an influence on development and, at the same time, a developmental outcome, or a result of development (Bronfenbrenner and Morris, 2006). This process of interaction and influence can be understood as a spiral dynamic where the personal characteristics of the child interact with and influence the people and the environment around them in an ongoing cycle of transforma- tion. In understanding these influences, early years practitioners gain insight into children's behaviour, recognising the variety of factors that may influence behaviour. This allows early years practitioners to respond more sensitively to individual children.

Process–person–context–time: networked systems of influence

In the last phase of Bronfenbrenner's bioecological model, four key interacting elements of development are highlighted. This phase explored how individual characteristics of the child alongside features of their context, both spatial and temporal, influence proximal processes. Bronfenbrenner's model is often characterised as the individual developing within the nested systems. Although widely embraced, the model is not without its critics. For example, Downes (2014) argues that to contain the individual within the nested systems is to limit the impact of the systems on the individual and the individual on the systems. This can lead to a perception of static systems that are very difficult to change. Others argue on the contrary that the networked version of the model provides the possibility of considering the individual as an active agent within a dynamic context of interacting systems (O'Toole *et al.*, 2014; Neal and Neal, 2013). To reflect the dynamic nature

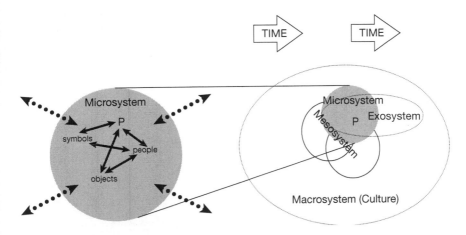

FIGURE 2.2 Urie Bronfenbrenner's PPCT (Process, the Person, Context, and Time) model. The active *Person* (P) engaging in *Proximal Processes* with people, symbols, and objects within a microsystem, in interaction with other *Contexts*, involving both continuity and change over *Time*

Source: Tudge (2008, p. 69)

of the PPCT model, Tudge (2008) has adapted the original model as shown in Figure 2.2.

Through a focus on this final phase of the evolution of the bioecological model of human development, we consider the four components of the PPCT model and look at how these can inform our interactions with children in early years practice.

Process

The distinguishing feature of Bronfenbrenner's later writings is his emphasis on processes in human development. Although he referred previously to proximal processes, it was only in the 1990s that they were defined as the "engines of development" (Bronfenbrenner and Ceci, 1994, p. 584; Bronfenbrenner and Morris, 1998, p. 996). Traditionally, the behaviour of others towards the developing person had been treated under the more inclusive category of the environment. However, in the bioecological model, a distinction is made between the concepts of environment and process, with the latter occupying a central position. Proximal processes relevant to early years practice include interactions like feeding or comforting a baby, playing with a younger child, activities between children of the same age, group or solitary play, reading and learning new skills.

Bronfenbrenner suggests that proximal processes are the primary mechanisms in development as it is through engaging in these activities and interactions that children make sense of their world. To be effective, interactions must occur on a regular basis and last for extended periods of time. The value of the adult role in respecting, supporting and extending children's learning is foregrounded in this conceptualisation. The nature and effect of proximal processes vary according to the characteristics of the individual, the features of the environment and the historical time in which development takes place:

> The form, power, content, and direction of the proximal processes effecting development vary systematically as a joint function of the characteristics of the developing person; of the environment—both immediate and more remote—in which the processes are taking place; the nature of the developmental outcomes under consideration and the social continuities and changes occurring over time through the life course and the historical period during which the person has lived.
>
> (Bronfenbrenner and Morris, 1998, p. 996)

Person

Earlier we reflected on the different personal characteristics that Bronfenbrenner identified – active behavioural dispositions (generative or disruptive), resource characteristics and demand characteristics – and how these operate to enhance or inhibit growth and development. We saw that although children may have equal access to resource characteristics such as intelligence and competence in a particular area, their developmental trajectories will be quite distinct depending on how these personal characteristics operate to interact with the environment.

Bronfenbrenner went on to provide a clearer view of children's active role in changing their context. Sometimes change is brought about in a relatively passive way. For example, a child's presence in an early years setting generates a change in the environment simply on the basis of how people respond to demand characteristics such as age, gender and skin colour. Let's focus on an important demand characteristic – gender – and how it might impact on the quality of child–practitioner relationships. Early years practitioners are sensitive to children's behaviours, and the quality of their relationships with children are likely to be influenced by their perceptions of the children's behaviours. However, early years practitioners' perceptions of a child's behaviour may be as much about what behaviours are *expected* as they are about the behaviours themselves, and gender stereotypes may be one source of these expectations. Practitioners may accept certain behaviours in boys, but hold girls to account for the same behaviours. A recent longitudinal study explored the extent to which children's gender influences the quality of the adult–child relationship in the early years (Runions, 2014). Findings suggest that practitioners' relationships with children are, in many cases, influenced by their perceptions of children's behavioural tendencies; however, in some cases, gender moderates the quality of these relationships. Specifically, boys who show greater emotional problems during the prekindergarten year and the kindergarten year were at risk for higher levels of conflict with adults than were girls who had emotional problems. The authors suggest this is possibly due to gender stereotyping, such as the expectation that boys do not cry or get upset. An interesting finding emerging in the follow-up study two years later was that emotional problems among girls tended to impact more negatively on the establishment of close relationships with the teacher in primary school. The negative impact that emotional problems had on teacher relationships with boys is in line with the risk evident in the previous two years. The authors suggest that the change in educators' responses to girls showing emotional problems may be explained by the fact that the environment is more structured and there is more pressure on educators to facilitate academic achievement. These findings support Bronfenbrenner's thesis that demand characteristics like gender can enhance or inhibit interactions and, subsequently, child growth and development. These findings also support the notion that educators' relationships with learners are differentially influenced by gender expectations, which inform and even direct their interpretation of children's behaviours (Runions, 2014).

REFLECTION

Identify the practical ways boys and girls are treated differently in your setting, either consciously or unconsciously. In light of increased attention to gender issues, what might the implications be for your practice?

The child's resource characteristics, like ability to communicate or skill in using technology, operate in a more active way to change the environment within the setting. A child who is a confident and competent communicator can motivate other children and adults to interact with greater ease. Practitioners can also provide an environment that motivates children to interact with each other and with the objects in the setting. The importance of providing appropriate materials that can facilitate children's positive interactions with their environment is foregrounded in Bronfenbrenner's focus on children's resource characteristics. A child who is curious about and skilled in information technologies will further develop these skills when provided with opportunities to engage and interact with such technologies. However, where no such opportunities are provided, the chances for developing these characteristics further will be restricted.

Context

Context is the component that is often most readily associated with Bronfenbrenner's theory. As we saw earlier in this chapter, Bronfenbrenner drew attention to the many contextual influences on children's lives, both proximal influences which are those immediate influences such as family, school and neighbourhood contexts and more distal influences such as sociocultural beliefs and values and the policies that are informed by these beliefs. Children's learning environments extend beyond the immediacy of the early years setting. While the child and her immediate environment are at the centre – the first level of influence – other levels too have a powerful influence on the child's wellbeing and capacity to learn. The second level contains the major settings experienced by the child: her home, the service or setting beyond her home and the relationships between these environments. The third level, which also influences the quality of children's experiences, encompasses the world of work, the neighbourhood, social media and informal social networks. This level includes the conditions that influence the wellbeing and support of the adults in children's lives: the demands, the stresses and the opportunities for development experienced by significant adults in each child's life. A particular cultural group may share a set of values, but for any particular value system to have an influence on a developing person, it has to be experienced within one or more of the microsystems in which that person is situated.

Time

The final component of the PPCT model is time, represented by the chronosystem. Bronfenbrenner identified three ways in which time could impact on proximal processes in children's development: 'microtime' – what is happening during the course of a particular interaction or activity; 'mesotime' – the extent to which activities and interactions occur with some consistency in the developing child's environment; and 'macrotime' – the historical context for a child's development and the timing of certain events in a child's life (Greene *et al.*, 2010). One illustration of the significance of microtime and mesotime for children's development is in free play. The time made available to children to engage in free experimental play, both the duration of periods of interaction and their frequency of occurrence over weeks and months, are relevant to the concepts of microtime and mesotime. Frequent availability of opportunities for free play facilitates play becoming more varied and complex over time (Santer *et al.*, 2007). An example of this is highlighted by Siraj-Blatchford *et al.* (2002) who note that in experimental play, children begin to categorise objects, an activity which comes before the development of more complex knowledge and understanding in mathematics and science. Bronfenbrenner suggests that developmental processes are also likely to vary according to the specific historical events that occur as the developing child reaches a particular age (macrotime). If we think of the children of refugee families in Europe, we understand that events closely linked to the historical time in which they are developing impact substantially on their development. Similarly, how these events may impact on a toddler is likely to be different from how they impact on an adolescent.

Implications for practice

In this chapter, we have explored how Bronfenbrenner's bioecological model of human development provided a focus on nested layers of influence that impact on a child's learning and development, including both proximal and distal contexts. We also outlined how the model evolved over time to provide a greater emphasis on proximal processes, interactions that take place on a regular basis and over extended periods of time. Looking at a late phase of the evolution of Bronfenbrenner's theory, we reflected on the PPCT structure and the implications of process–person–context–time factors for early years learning and development.

Key concepts for early years practice

1   *Children's development and learning is influenced by the changing contexts* surrounding the child, such as family, friends and communities, and by changes within the broader social and cultural context in which she is growing.
2   *The child as learner and the learning environment are closely connected.* A child develops language abilities in a setting where adults talk to children and to each other. Similarly, a child learns to explore in a setting where exploration is valued and possible and where the curriculum adopted reflects these values.
3   *Children's personal characteristics and dispositions interact with the personal characteristics and dispositions of other children and adults* in the early years setting.
4   *This process of interaction and influence can be understood as a spiral dynamic* wherein the personal characteristics of the child interact with and influence the people and the environment around her in an ongoing cycle of transformation.
5   *The child has a central role in how her development plays out.* As well as expressing their desires and wishes, children as agents can negotiate and interact within their environment, and these interactions ultimately result in changing their environment.

3
PROXIMAL PROCESSES AND RELATIONSHIPS

Introduction

One strength of the bioecological model, perhaps not developed fully during Bronfenbrenner's lifetime, lies in its potential to help us make sense of other theories within psychology, sociology and education. These disciplines are often experienced by those studying them for the first time as a collection of disparate theories with little obvious relation to each other or to real-world situations. Bronfenbrenner's focus on a network of development allows for many factors to be considered and enables us to consider the work of other theorists. Real children with real families in real early childhood settings do not exist in compartmentalised worlds for ease of study, and this is recognised by the bioecological approach. Bronfenbrenner's theory offers a powerful framework for understanding how different theories and approaches fit together.

In engaging with psychology, sociology and education, students often begin with a search for 'truth', or real solutions that apply in most, if not all, settings. They expect solid answers to their questions and to have the ability to be definitively 'right' or 'wrong'. This mirrors the development of the disciplines themselves over time. For example, we see in psychology the behaviourist emphasis on objective measurement of behaviour and developmental stage approaches, like those of Piaget, Kohlberg and Freud, which attempt to describe the development of all children regardless of circumstances. However, students quickly discover that the social sciences provide little in the way of 'hard facts', and many well-established theories may even seem to contradict each other. This leads students, following in the footsteps of the disciplines themselves, towards a sense that perhaps it is all relative and the only real answer that social science can give to questions on human experience is 'it depends . . . '. This can sometimes bring the student to an experience like that described by Gergen (1997, p. 4) as a "crisis in social psychology" – the questioning of whether psychology has anything to offer after all if there is no agreement on anything! However, the student that persists will notice commonalities across theories that may, when explored further, offer glimpses of a more coherent whole.

This chapter identifies one such recurring theme, the importance of relationships for child development. As Bronfenbrenner puts it, when it comes to supporting positive outcomes for children, "[i]n short, somebody has to be crazy about that kid" (1988/2005, p. 262). Using a bioecological lens, we explore the impact of relationships, focusing largely on the concept of proximal processes. This chapter aims to enhance understanding of the concept of 'process', drawing on other theories you may already have heard of: attachment theory, Baumrind's 'authoritative' parenting, Rogers' ideas on 'the relationship', insights from sociocultural theory and finally the cognitive theories of Jean Piaget.

Proximal processes

A reminder:

> Especially in its early phases, but also throughout the life course, human development takes place through processes of progressively more complex reciprocal interaction between an active, evolving biopsychological human organism and the persons, objects, and symbols in its immediate external environment. To be effective, the interaction must occur on a fairly regular basis over extended periods of time. Such enduring forms of interaction in the immediate environment are referred to as proximal processes.
>
> (Bronfenbrenner and Morris, 2006, p. 797)

Process is the defining component of the bioecological model (Rosa and Tudge, 2013), and it emphasises the importance of relationships. Bronfenbrenner considered relationships to be the main mode through which children develop. The bioecological model shows that lives are lived interdependently through a network of shared relationships, or 'linked lives'. According to Bronfenbrenner, the effect of process is more powerful than that of the context in which it occurs (Bronfenbrenner and Morris, 2006). More simply, strong, positive relationships may have the power to overcome the impacts of the most damaging environments, and even very positive environments may not be good enough without warm and loving relationships. Regarding early education, this means that we need to support the development of positive relationships between adults, between adults and children, and between children and their peers. When we think about 'quality', we should focus more on the relationships that happen in early years settings than on environmental factors since programmes that are characterised by stimulating and supportive teacher–child interactions are most effective for children (Sabol et al., 2013).

In early education in recent years, attention has increasingly moved away from methods of instruction for learning towards understanding the power of the interpersonal and the role of relationships in learning. However, Bronfenbrenner's concept of process goes beyond the interpersonal to incorporate "progressively more complex reciprocal interaction with objects and symbols" (Bronfenbrenner and Morris, 2006, p. 814); so in spite of the emphasis on interpersonal relationships, we cannot disregard the quality of the learning opportunities provided for children in early learning environments. It may be that good-quality early years services think about the quality of their contexts *and* the relationships within them.

Relationships in psychological theory

A number of key psychological theories may be incorporated within the framework provided by Bronfenbrenner's concept of process. One that was explicitly acknowledged by Bronfenbrenner as relevant to proximal processes was attachment theory (Ainsworth *et al.*, 1978; Bowlby, 1988), which offers one of the most well-known explanations of how babies and young children develop security within relationships.

Proximal processes and attachment theory

The central argument proposed by attachment theory is that the bond or attachment formed by an infant with the primary caregiver forms the basis of future relationships and psychological well-being. According to Bowlby (1988), the growing child needs to develop a sense of trust and, later, a growing independence; these are facilitated through affection, caring and the reasonably prompt satisfaction of infants' needs. When babies are hungry, in pain, fatigued or feeling anxiety, they cry. Bowlby thought that a parent's response in these circumstances forms the basis of attachment between infant and parent. If parents respond consistently and warmly, the baby learns to trust that his parent will always be there when he is in need, and secure attachment is formed. If parents fail to respond to the infant's need, in situations such as abuse or neglect, the baby learns that adults are at best unreliable and at worst scary and develops an insecure attachment to the parent.

Of particular interest to early years practitioners is the occurrence of 'separation anxiety' in babies when separated from their primary caregivers. Think about what happens when a parent first begins to drop a baby off to a crèche. Very often he cries when the parent is leaving although sometimes, as he gets to know the practitioner, the separations in the morning become less painful over time. Ainsworth would say this is because the baby has a secure attachment to his parent – he wants to be with the parent all the time because he feels safe when they are together (Ainsworth *et al.*, 1978). However, as the baby starts to develop a 'secondary attachment' to his early years practitioner, it becomes easier to say goodbye to his parent because he still feels safe in the relationship in the crèche (Bowlby, 2007). This shows the importance of strong relationships in early years settings, as predicted by Bronfenbrenner. These may be particularly important considerations for early years practitioners in centre-based services given that Ahnert *et al.* (2006) found secure child–adult attachments to be more likely in home-based care than centre-based care. This was linked to the requirement for practitioners in childcare centres to respond to the needs of a number of children at the same time. Nonetheless, these researchers found that once caregivers had attended to the needs of the group, it was then still possible for secure attachments to be formed in centre-based settings. For the individual child, the essential feature here is the extent to which the adult is engaged with either the group or the child himself.

REFLECTION

What can you do to help reduce 'separation anxiety' for babies and small children? How can you help them begin to trust that they are safe in the early years setting? What systems in crèches, preschools and other early years settings might inadvertently contribute to separation anxiety?

As children grow, their attachment becomes less reliant on being physically near their parent and more dependent on abstract qualities like affection and trust. Children become more confident in being without their parent for longer. From the perspective of attachment theory, it is often said that attachment provides 'a secure base from which to explore the world' – securely attached children can confidently explore the world because they know that their parent will be there for them when they return. The quality of attachment becomes 'internalised' as the child grows – a baby needs to be physically beside his parent to feel secure, but as he grows within loving relationships, he develops the understanding that he is loved and safe regardless of whether or not his parent is physically beside him. In attachment theory, this is known as the 'internal working model' of the relationship with the attachment figure. However, separation anxiety may be sparked in children when they are under stress, even when they are older – have you noticed how a child who falls while playing often runs back to his parent for comfort before going back to play? Bowlby would explain this by saying that a stressful situation (the fall) caused the child to seek his 'secure base' (the parent) for comfort and that once that comfort has been achieved, he can go and 'explore the world' again.

Importantly, the internal working model forms the basis of the child's concept of 'self' ('I am loved and lovable' or 'I am unloved and unlovable') and provides direction for future relationships, including those formed with adults and children in early years settings. When a child expects the world to be comforting and supportive, he approaches new relationships with this expectation; thus securely attached children tend to invite future supportive relationships. Equally, when a child expects the world to be dangerous and unsupportive, he approaches new relationships with this expectation; through defensiveness and fear, he may misbehave and reduce the chances of forming positive relationships in the future (Bowlby, 1973). This reflects Bronfenbrenner's description of the impact of demand characteristics on the response of others, with implications for future development.

This process of interaction between the child's traits and his experiences is known as 'internalisation' – personal characteristics both shape and are shaped by experiences in context. The concept of internalisation is important because it shows the power of relationships to influence the direction of future development. In the terminology of the bioecological model, early proximal processes produce proximal processes throughout development. In this way, proximal processes are the method by which internalisation happens. Indeed, Bronfenbrenner's statement that "through progressively more complex interaction with their parents, children increasingly become agents of their own development" (Bronfenbrenner and Morris, 2006, p. 797) could have been written by an attachment theorist.

Some aspects of attachment theory are contested. When early theorists like Bowlby and Ainsworth were writing about attachment, the phrase 'primary caregiver' was usually taken to refer only to the child's mother, but nowadays we recognise that this is inappropriate. First, ideas of mother–infant attachment formation are sometimes misused for political reasons to argue against women's right to work outside the home (Belsky, 1988). Also, families take many different forms, and fathers in particular may be equally important attachment figures for children (Berk, 2009). Nowadays, when most psychologists use the phrase 'primary caregiver', they mean the person who takes care of the child the most. Another problem with some early work on attachment was the assumption that security of attachment was 'set in stone' by three years of age and could not be changed after that. We now understand that while early attachment experiences are highly influential, attachment style can be fluid across the life course, depending on the availability of emotionally corrective experiences such as therapy (Taylor et al., 2015). Furthermore, recent work has emphasised the importance of considering contextual and cultural influences on attachment (Van Ijzendoorn and Sagi-Schwartz, 2008).[1]

Nevertheless, many central ideas surrounding attachment theory still hold true and are supported by research in neuroscience. Studies of the brains of infants have shown that when the stress hormone cortisol is released too often due to distressing experiences, it can change the structure of a baby's brain so that his future behaviour may be affected on the basis of those experiences (Balbernie, 2007). Equally, when the anti-stress hormones opioids and oxytocin are released during loving experiences, this can also change the structure of a baby's brain and so have an impact on his future behaviour (O'Connor, 2013). In early childhood, love matters because affection actually shapes a baby's brain (Gerhardt, 2004).

Children who are securely attached in infancy have been shown to be more curious and to have better problem-solving skills at age two, to have more social confidence at age three and to have more empathy and independence at age five, and they are less likely to have behaviour problems at age six (Berk, 2009). Therefore, security of attachment may predict the kinds of behaviours seen in crèches, preschools and primary school classrooms in the early years. Insecure attachment can lead to withdrawn behaviour when insecurity is directed inwards (psychologists call this 'internalising') or aggressive, violent behaviour when insecurity is directed outwards (psychologists call this 'externalising'). A neglectful or abusive parent may inhibit curiosity in the child – he is afraid to go and explore the world because he does not trust that the parent will still be there when he gets back – perhaps leading to withdrawn behaviour in the early years setting. Alternatively these negative early experiences may provoke feelings of 'hypervigilance' (always being on alert for danger, even when it does not really exist), leading to aggression, defensiveness and challenging behaviour in the early years setting. A calm atmosphere where practitioners are engaged and attuned to young children may mitigate the difficulties that could arise. This fits both with attachment theory and the bioecological model, whereby early experiences become incorporated into the person characteristics of the individual and, in turn, influence future experiences and processes.

Thus, future relationships may reflect the original attachment relationship that a baby forms with the primary caregiver, and Bronfenbrenner specifically identified teachers and early years practitioners as potential partners with children in the development of relationships whose prototype lies in the parent–child relationship. This is supported by the work of John Bowlby's son Richard who identifies the importance of a secondary attachment relationship when the child is in non-parental day care. The person characteristics of important adults in the child's life such as early years practitioners are, in bioecological theory, incorporated into the microsystem of the child, and the model predicts that person elements of those adults will impact on proximal processes just as much as the personal characteristics of the child (Bowlby, 2007). Put simply, the relationship between an adult and a child depends on the personal characteristics of both adult and child. This is supported by research on attachment between teachers and children: teachers' own attachment style impacts on the relationships he forms with the children in his class (Riley, 2011).

Think about and discuss how Bronfenbrenner's concept of proximal processes and theories about attachment would explain what is happening in the vignettes involving Luka and Jamie.

> Luka is usually an independent boy who likes to engage in self-directed play in his early years setting. However, today he has a cold and is not feeling well. He has spent the morning following his early years practitioner around the room and cries when the practitioner leaves to go to the bathroom.
>
> Source: author observation in an early years setting

> Jamie has recently been taken into care because his father was behaving violently at home. In school today, the class are learning a dance to go with the rhyme 'head, shoulders, knees and toes'. When his teacher takes his hands to show him how to place them on his head, Jamie kicks her and runs to hide under the table.
>
> Source: author observation in a primary school reception class

Proximal processes and parenting styles

The concept of proximal processes also allows for incorporation of the ideas of Diana Baumrind (1978, 1996). Bronfenbrenner indicates that a child's world must be stable, consistent and predictable. If their routine is chaotic, with no established rules, children find it hard to cope. However, if rules are too rigid with no room for flexibility, this is not beneficial either. This links with Baumrind's work showing that the parenting style of an individual mother or father can strongly influence the quality of processes between parent and child. Incorporating the work of others who have extended her original findings, Baumrind identified three features that consistently differentiate effective parenting styles from those that are less effective, including acceptance, involvement and emotional support, appropriate control to guide behaviour, and support for independence and autonomy, promoting self-reliance.

Baumrind identified three main parenting styles: authoritarian, permissive and authoritative. Authoritarian parents are low in acceptance, high in control and do not allow independence. They are often rejecting and expect the child to accept their judgment unquestioningly. Authoritarian parents suppress children's self-expression and independence, and they often criticise children and withdraw parental love when they are dissatisfied (Berk, 2009). Such psychological control can leave children unable to make decisions for themselves, leading to both withdrawn behaviours and defiant behaviours. Such parenting styles have also been linked with anxiety and unhappiness in children, low self-esteem, hostility and aggression, dependency and disinterest in the environment, being overwhelmed by challenging tasks, and poor academic performance; this is consistent with the prediction of the bioecological model that extreme rigidity of experience may have negative effects on children (Bronfenbrenner and Morris, 2006).

The other extreme identified by Baumrind is permissive parents. These parents exercise little control over children and allow them to make decisions for themselves even when they are not yet ready. In some cases, parents genuinely believe that this is the right way to raise children. They are warm, accepting and overindulgent, and they are permissive because they believe that children should be allowed to decide for themselves. Alternatively, some parents lack confidence in their ability to control their child and may not try to. Sometimes they are emotionally detached, and this is often linked to parental depression where parents are so overwhelmed by life stresses that they have little energy for interacting with their children. At its extreme, this style of parenting is child neglect, and this latter category is often treated in the literature as a fourth parenting style (Berk, 2009). Again, as predicted by the bioecological model, such extremes of disorganisation and lack of predictability within parent–child relationships have been linked with poor outcomes for children.

The most successful parenting style identified by Baumrind is the 'authoritative' style. This involves high acceptance and appropriate control while also allowing some freedom. Such parents are warm, attentive and emotionally fulfilling while maintaining firm and reasonable control. They focus on encouraging self-regulation but also on emotional expressiveness, communication and, where possible, joint decision-making, reminiscent of Bronfenbrenner's ideas on environments that are neither too fluid nor too rigid. A bioecological perspective indicates that these concepts only have value when viewed through the lens of cultural diversity. When we reduce 'good parenting' to checklists and simplistic formulas, we miss the point that there are many ways to be a good parent (Brooker, 2015). For example, the extent of 'autonomy granting' deemed appropriate varies across contexts and cultures. Equally, Belsky (1984) presents a model of parenting that shows the multiple determinants of parental functioning, illustrating that the behaviour of individual parents depends on many factors, such as the contextual supports and stress they experience. Viewing the work of Baumrind through a bioecological lens also highlights the importance of considering the multitude of influences on parenting styles.

Baumrind's work is sometimes simplified into two aspects of authoritative parenting that seem to contribute to its effectiveness (Gregory et al., 2010): 'support' (parental warmth, acceptance and involvement) and 'structure' (strictness and close supervision as reflected in parental monitoring and limit-setting). This conceptualisation is useful when thinking about parenting across contexts – it indicates that children need to know that they are loved (as shown in ways that are culturally and individually specific) and also what the (culturally specific) rules and boundaries are (Berk, 2009). Discipline and support for emotional expression are not seen as opposing each other but, rather, as coexisting, equally important aspects of good parenting.

The idea of 'styles' of interacting with children also makes sense within early years settings, helping us understand process between children and adults. An authoritarian early years practitioner would focus on strict discipline that may be perceived as unfair by children. He would use punishment and 'zero-tolerance' sanctions for even minor violations of rules, giving little consideration to the circumstances of behaviour or the child's intentions. Alternatively, a permissive practitioner would tolerate a wide range of behaviour, often with a level of disorder that inhibits children's learning. Like parents, permissive practitioners may be indulgent or neglectful. Authoritative early years practitioners aim for a 'middle ground' that allows for consistent, firm, but fair implementation of rules while also ensuring that children can express their creativity and direct the course of their own learning, and where their emotional needs are met. In the early years setting, children require both structure and support.

REFLECTION

What style do you display in your interactions with children? Do you need to develop more structure and guidance for children, having had perhaps too 'permissive' a style of interaction to date? Do you need to be more emotionally supportive to children? Are your expectations unreasonable, perhaps leading to too 'authoritarian' a style of interaction? Think about specific examples of interactions with children that did not go as you might have liked – what would an 'authoritative' adult have done in those circumstances?

Within a bioecological framework, we see that neither parenting nor early education happens in a vacuum. Baumrind shows how adults influence children, but Bronfenbrenner shows us that children also influence adults. The characteristics of children are also an element of Belsky's (1984) model of parenting. For example, if the parent is firm but warm, the child tends to comply with what they say; and when the child complies, the parent is likely to be firm but warm in the future. However, when parents discipline with harshness and impatience, children tend to rebel and resist; this is stressful for parents and they become harsher and more impatient, increasing their use of punishment. There are bidirectional influences between adults and children, each influencing the other – a key principle of the bioecological model. Equally, there are broader influences on family and school dynamics, such as socio-economic class and poverty, so parenting and teaching style may vary with context. Nevertheless, many psychologists believe that with appropriate support, most adults have the capacity to create positive contexts for children's learning and development. This idea is key to the work of other influential thinkers such as Carl Rogers.

Proximal processes and Rogers' humanism

Carl Rogers was a psychologist who originally worked as a therapist. Unlike other therapists who analysed people and told them what they should do, he relied on the capacity of the client to elaborate the issue. He focused on the ability of the person to direct the course of his own life, consistent with Bronfenbrenner's view of human beings as active agents in their development. Rogers believed that people are fundamentally good and would figure out the right course of action and behave well as long as they were given a supportive relationship within which to do so. This conscious rejection of a 'deficit model'[2] of human functioning in favour of a focus on growth has much in common with Bronfenbrenner (and also with Bowlby, Ainsworth and Baumrind). Rogers believed that children develop through the relationships they experience.

Rogers' techniques in therapy involved listening to the person and reflecting back to him what he said in an accepting and understanding way. For Rogers, this respect for self-direction (or, in Bronfenbrenner's terms, 'agency') applies even when the person seems to choose goals that do not make sense to the therapist; the function of therapy is to provide a supportive relationship within which the person can make decisions for himself. Rogers' concept of the relationship echoes Bronfenbrenner's concept of proximal processes in that both are impacted by the person characteristics of those involved. Unlike other therapeutic approaches that demand objectivity and separateness from the therapist, a Rogerian therapist makes up an important part of the human equation – "what he does, the attitude he holds, his basic concept of his role, all influence therapy to a marked degree" (Rogers, 1995, p. 19). Rogers requires therapists to exhibit three central characteristics: congruence (genuineness), unconditional positive regard (acceptance, trust) and empathy (understanding from the client's viewpoint – or their 'internal frame of reference').

Considering this approach in an early years setting rather than a therapeutic one, the role of a practitioner is to create a supportive, trusting relationship through what Rogers calls congruence, unconditional positive regard and empathy. This means respecting each child as an individual capable of positive growth. Rogers says that the greatest tool a therapist or an educator has in supporting the client or the child is acceptance. Acceptance of the child does not mean passivity or indifference – a lack of involvement is experienced by children as rejection. Both Bronfenbrenner and Baumrind show that for learning to happen, support needs to be provided alongside significant challenge. What is recommended by Rogerian approaches is active engagement or, in Bronfenbrenner's terms, bidirectional reciprocity of exchange (Bronfenbrenner and Morris, 2006). In Rogerian therapy, the counsellor must assume the client's internal frame of reference to see the world as he sees it (Rogers, 1995). An early years practitioner working with young children must also try to see the world through their eyes and be clear that this is what he is trying to do. This can be achieved in very simple ways. For example, rather than saying, "That's a lovely picture of a house", the Rogerian practitioner says, "Tell me about your picture" – it might turn out to be a giraffe! The early years practitioner should never assume he understands the child's perspective; rather, he should ask about it.

REFLECTION

How well do you listen to children? Do you try to see the world through their eyes? How can you make time in your busy day to enter the 'internal frame of reference' of children? What specifically can you do to achieve insight into how they think and feel?

Rogers' concept of person-centredness has been transferred to the educational arena through these ideas of self-direction and the importance of the relationship in an approach known as 'student-centred teaching'. The educator is seen as a 'facilitator', helping children to discover learning for themselves rather than giving direct instruction. Early years practitioners using this approach choose topics of interest to children rather than adults, and they provide interesting materials for children to make sense of themselves. Such practice is inclusive and welcoming to children from diverse backgrounds and of diverse ability. Of course, educators often guide learning towards short- and long-term learning goals that they are aware of although the child is not, and these may be goals that the child has limited interest in. Nevertheless, when educators actively focus on the development of relationships and on accessing the internal frame of reference of learners, student-centred approaches can be very powerful (O'Toole, 2015).

Rogers (1974) describes a list of "questions I would ask myself if I were a teacher", many of which are relevant to the concept of 'the relationship', or in Bronfenbrenner's terms, proximal processes. For example:

> Do I dare to let myself deal with this boy or girl as a person, as someone I respect? Do I dare reveal myself to him and let him reveal himself to me? Do I dare to recognize that he/she may know more than I do in certain areas—or may in general be more gifted than I?
>
> (Rogers, 1974, p. 2)

In asking such questions, Rogers emphasises respect for children and recognises that there is risk involved in the development of true and genuine human relationships. Understanding of proximal processes can incorporate Rogers' insights into the human emotions involved in the creation and maintenance of relationships. Thus, we can value both the 'thinking life and the feeling life', as Rogers refers to a holistic understanding of children's development in the context of their relationships.

Think about how the early years practitioner in this vignette is showing respect for children, accessing their internal frame of reference and supporting them to develop self-direction.

> It is coming up to Christmas and the setting where Jenny works usually puts on a Christmas play for parents. Last year, the children did a 'nativity' play, but Jenny feels uncomfortable with this because there are children from different religious and cultural backgrounds in the setting. She asks the children if they would like to write a play together. She suggests a theme – 'celebration' – and asks each child to think of the best way to celebrate a happy occasion. The children tell Jenny about different celebrations they have been involved in. "Now let's think of a story for our play about celebration", says Jenny. "What is the name of the person in our play? What do you think they might be celebrating?"
>
> Source: author experience in practice

The importance of sociocultural understandings within a bioecological framework

The vignette involving Jenny reminds us that relationships happen within the context of *culture*. In contrast to other developmental theorists like Piaget, Erikson and Kohlberg, Bronfenbrenner sought to challenge some of the idealised assumptions contributing to the notion that all children develop in similar ways regardless of their circumstances; he opposed the idea of 'the universal child'. Developmental psychology is generally recognised as having been the dominant and defining academic discourse in relation to children in the twentieth century (Woodhead, 2006). However, towards the latter half of the twentieth century, critical perspectives on developmental psychology strongly contested the focus on development in the absence of emphasis on the sociocultural contexts in which development occurred. Woodhead (2006) argues that many of the descriptions of children and childhood generated by what has been termed 'developmentally appropriate practice' (DAP; Bredekamp and Copple, 1997) have little or no relevance to the realities of the diverse nature of childhood, and they do not reflect the variance of the resources available to children and their families.

Many theorists in child development draw on socially, culturally and contextually specific assumptions about the nature and composition of children's relationships and home environments, the access to resources such as books and learning materials and the value placed on independence in childhood. Authors expressing concern about the value of such perspectives on child development are known as 'reconceptualists', and their approaches to framing childhood are largely informed by sociocultural theory.

According to Tzuo *et al.* (2011), the tendency in recent years to polarise developmental versus sociocultural or reconceptualist understandings of child-hood has been unhelpful. They identify the need for a synthesis of theory. If we are to fully understand the nature of childhood, we need to draw on a variety of theoretical perspectives. Bronfenbrenner's emphasis on development in context allows us to bridge the theoretical gaps between developmental psychology and reconceptualism, and the bioecological model provides a powerful framework through which to achieve such synthesis without losing coherence. A bioecological framework allows for a child-centred approach when considering individual children's development within various interacting microsystems whilst, at the same time, moving beyond this to incorporate aspects of reconceptualism at the mesosystem, exosystem, macrosystem and chronosystem levels. Bronfenbrenner's concept of process allows us to consider the reciprocal impact of these factors on relationships because the bioecological model helps us to think about the child in society. Vygotsky also highlighted the interaction between the social and cultural worlds of children. He proposed that it is through social interaction that ways of thinking begin to be appropriated by children and that development is shaped and supported by the social and cultural contexts in which it takes place (Smidt, 2013). This idea is the basis of a range of approaches to understanding child development that come under the banner of 'sociocultural theory'.

Proximal processes and sociocultural theory

The notion of process is also consistent with sociocultural theory, particularly Vygotsky's (1978) concept of the 'zone of proximal development' (ZPD). This is the idea that a child working alone rarely achieves to the level he could when interacting with a more expert other, usually an adult but often a peer. Children learn through problem-solving experiences shared with someone else (Schmidt, 2013). This concept is supported by extensive research on the benefits of cooperative learning, or learning in the context of relationships with others (O'Toole, 2014). ZPD underlies several key approaches to education in recent years, many drawing on the related notion of 'scaffolding' (Ellis, 2012). When scaffolding, the educator supports learning through social interaction and creates contexts for learning within the child's ZPD, gradually withdrawing support as the child becomes more able to manage by themselves. Through a bioecological lens, this reflects the use of process to support learning and development. The concept of scaffolding is illustrated by the vignette involving Lily.

At the beginning of the year, many of the children in Lily's class have not been potty-trained very long, and going to the bathroom independently is quite a challenge. In September, Lily reminds them when they haven't been to the bathroom for a while, brings them to the toilet area and reminds them to flush the toilet. She shows them how to wash their hands properly – "let's pull up our sleeves and turn on the water; now we'll get some soap; let's rub our fingers between each other; here's a song to remind us how to wash our hands". By December, Lily just reminds the children to go to the bathroom every so often, but they go by themselves. In May, Lily no longer has to remind the children about the bathroom; they just go by themselves when they need to.

Source: author experience in practice

Ellis (2012) indicates that the concept of scaffolding has to some extent fallen out of favour in recent years because it is seen as something that the adult *does* to the child. Contemporary sociocultural ideas about adult–child interaction during learning are more consistent with a bioecological interpretation of the bidirectionality of process. They emphasise 'intersubjectivity' (Bruner, 1996), which refers to interactions in which there is dynamic and engaged input from both adults and children. What is important with regard to both process and ZPD is the reciprocity (or two-way flow) between the learner and the early years practitioner.

REFLECTION

How do you 'scaffold' the learning and development of children you work with? Think of some concrete examples of how you initially gave a lot of support to a child but then gradually allowed him to do more for himself as his skills developed.

While consistencies between sociocultural approaches and a bioecological perspective are evident, it is important to note that Bronfenbrenner's description of process goes beyond interpersonal and social relationships to incorporate "progressively more complex reciprocal interaction with objects and symbols" (Bronfenbrenner and Morris, 2006, p. 814). This leads to consideration of the cognitivist psychology of Jean Piaget.

Interaction with objects and symbols

Piaget (1951, 2001) describes how a child comes to know his world by building cognitive structures, or mental maps, schemes, and networked concepts for understanding and responding to physical experiences within his environment. The application of Piaget's theory has presented a view of a structured, predetermined and universal course of development that has been extensively criticised (Burman, 2008; Morss, 2013; Woodhead, 1999) and does not fit well within a bioeco-logical model founded on recognition of individual differences and cultural influences on development. The timing of Piaget's developmental stages has been questioned (Aguiar and Baillargeon, 1999, 2002), and research in different cultural settings has shown that children in different cultures reach developmental stages at different ages based on their experiences (Rogoff, 2003). As Hayes puts it, young children develop "in a far messier and entangled way" than Piaget envisioned (2004, p. 2).

Nevertheless, consigning Piaget's work to "the dustbin of history" (James *et al.*, 1998, p. 9) may be to "throw out the baby with the developmental bathwater" (Woodhead, 2000, p. 31). Piaget maintained that over time a child's cognitive structures increase in sophistication, moving from a few innate reflexes such as crying and sucking to highly complex mental activities. Piaget projected the image of an active child, constantly trying to interpret and predict the world around him. He either predicts correctly or changes his ideas to survive. Bronfenbrenner and Morris (2006) describe proximal processes between the child and 'objects and symbols' in the environment whereby the opportunity to explore, manipulate and engage with new and sometimes challenging environments leads to progressively more complex engagement, thereby significantly changing the processes involved, their outcomes and the features of the environment that become most relevant. In Piaget's terminology (Piaget, 2001), Bronfenbrenner and Morris have described 'accom-modation', 'assimilation', '(dis)equilibration' and the process of child development.

Piaget's insights on how we make sense of the world around us through accommodation, assimilation and (dis)equilibration have largely been supported by up-to-date findings from neuropsychology on how information is encoded in the brain, albeit with two provisos: much neurological change happens on the *inside* before behavioural change is evident on the *outside*; and his idea of progressively more complex cognitive structures may be insufficient since up-to-date neuro-imaging techniques have shown the brain to be more complex and, to some degree, counter-intuitive in its pattern of development (Berk, 2009).

In educational terms, Piaget's emphasis on the 'teacher as facilitator' providing instructional materials that use demonstrations, illustrative examples and corrective feedback rather than direct instruction fits well with Bronfenbrenner's ideas on progressively more complex interaction between the child and the environment and is supported by the most up-to-date, constructivist understandings of how children learn (Berk, 2009). Considering the fact that Rogers (1974) also maintains that a good teacher should spend the majority of his time creating resources to support children's learning through discovery rather than directly transmitting knowledge, this may be one occasion where the fog of relativism clears to allow for some coherence across theories, coalesced through Bronfenbrenner's concept of proximal processes.

Implications for practice

In summary, when we use the concept of proximal processes to make sense of other important psychological theories, it becomes obvious that relationships are vital for children's development emotionally, socially and cognitively, and building good relationships should be a central area of concern for early childhood education. The analysis in this chapter has focused largely on 'process', but the bioecological model emphasises that such vital relationships are informed and shaped by the person characteristics of the children and adults involved, the context in which they take place and the time (both of the person's life and historically) in which those relationships are embedded. Bronfenbrenner says that we must understand process, person, context and time if we are to understand the child. Chapter 4 develops this idea that children's development through relationships must be understood in context.

Key concepts for early years practice

1   Many important psychological theories emphasise the vital nature of relationships for children's development. *All learning and development happens in the context of relationships.*
2   *Positive relationships between adults and children are reciprocal*: there is input from both adults and children (intersubjectivity).
3   *Relationships may be more important for development than environments and experiences.* Strong positive relationships may have the power to overcome the impacts of even the most damaging environments, and even positive environments may be insufficient to support positive development in the absence of warm and loving relationships.
4   *Notions of 'quality' in early childhood education should incorporate relationships.* Warm, caring relationships between adults and children may act as a preventative measure against systems that tolerate poor-quality provision and even abuse.

Notes

1   If you would like to read up-to-date work related to attachment theory, you may be interested in the Minnesota Longitudinal Study of Risk and Adaptation, which has followed the development of a group of children since 1975. You can access findings here: www.cehd.umn.edu/icd/research/parent-child/
2   A deficit model emphasises what a child cannot do rather than what he can.

4

UNDERSTANDING DEVELOPMENT IN CONTEXT

Introduction

The bioecological model acknowledges that children do not develop in isolation; rather, development is embedded within and across many contexts such as family and home, school, community, society and culture. Young children learn and develop in the midst of society, and the ordinary spaces, places and people they come in contact with have a profound influence on them (Hayes, 2013). Each of these ever-changing and multilevel settings influences, either directly or indirectly, the pattern of child development and learning. Such contexts extend beyond the child's immediate environment (e.g. home and early childhood setting) to encompass the broader sociocultural contexts in which development is embedded.

Building on the concepts outlined and discussed in the previous chapters, we now explore the contexts that inform and guide children's learning and development. Ultimately, all the contextual factors influencing a child operate through the child's immediate environment – the people, places and things with which the child has direct contact. However, the values of a particular culture are also reflected in the structure of the settings in which children spend their time. This chapter explores how the bioecological model can offer a framework to incorporate many sociocultural insights on understanding development in context. In particular, we further interrogate the idea of 'internalisation', or the incorporation of contexts for development into the personal characteristics of the developing child.

Bronfenbrenner's theory highlights the importance of actively linking early years settings to other important environments in the lives of young children as well as understanding the rich "funds of knowledge" (Hedges, 2014; Wood, 2013) children bring with them from the various contexts in which they are developing. Increasingly, the number and range of contexts young children traverse on a day-to-day basis are expanding, creating a potential for 'culture shock' where these are very different. When the culture of the home and that of the early years setting are different, it may be difficult for children to adjust (Brooker, 2015). Resolving such shocks can be addressed through the concept of the mesosystem.

Bioecological theory and sociocultural theory: learning and development in context

There is consistency between Bronfenbrenner's concept of proximal processes and sociocultural ideas such as Vygotsky's ZPD and the related notion of scaffolding. In his book on learning a second language, Ellis (2012) outlines key components of sociocultural theory, and a reading of this through a bioecological lens highlights several consistencies between the two approaches. These key ideas include ZPD and scaffolding, but also 'mediated learning', 'internalisation' and 'self-regulation'.

Zone of proximal development

Vygotsky's concept of ZPD is relevant not only to the process element of Bronfenbrenner's PPCT model, but also to the person and context elements. Chapter 3 illustrated that a child working alone rarely achieves to the level that she can when interacting with a more expert other. Indeed, like the bioecological model, "ZPD is premised on the view that development has both a social and a psychological dimension" (Ellis, 2012, p. 532). Sociocultural theory and the bioecological model are two of the few accounts of human development that go beyond traditional ideas of 'nature versus nurture' to investigate how the social and the psychological interact to direct outcomes. Both recognise that nature and nurture are intertwined and that development is fundamentally linked to the context in which it takes place. Thus, the bioecological model offers a potential framework through which to bring together the traditionally polarised perspectives of developmental psychology and reconceptualist approaches rooted in sociocultural theory (O'Toole, 2016). Children are not all the same. As Frønes puts it: "There is not one childhood, but many, formed at the intersection of different cultural, social and economic systems, natural and man-made physical environments. Different positions in society produce different experiences" (1993, p. 1).

Mediated learning

As in the bioecological model, sociocultural theory indicates that development begins with the traits and dispositions of the child – the things they have inherited biologically from their parents – but recognises that children continue to develop through the "interweaving of cultural and biological inheritances" (Lantolf and Thorne, 2006, p. 59). The child's own personality and abilities are impacted by her experiences, her contexts and her culture to influence how she will turn out. In sociocultural terms, this is known as 'mediated learning'; in Bronfenbrenner's terms, such interweaving between person and context happens through proximal processes. Sociocultural theorists believe that "mediated minds are developed out of the social activity that is embedded in the cultural values of particular communities" (Ellis, 2012, p. 524). This means that children's and adults' thinking and development is directed by their relationships and the culture and contexts in which they find themselves. Thus, hypothetically, if we were to take identical twins (genetically exactly the same) and split them up at birth, raising one in one culture or context and the other in another, the course of their development may be quite different. This is in harmony with a bioecological perspective on the child in context which, rejecting the idea of the 'universal' child, emphasises diversity and individual differences even within cultures through the concept of a web of development with interacting and multidirectional contextual influences. Recognition of this fact is important in ethical terms because when early years practitioners insist on viewing all children and parents as the same or similar and educational interventions are designed based on this flawed perception, we run the risk of inadvertently reproducing the very inequalities we aim to address.

Self-regulation and internalisation: the interaction between 'person' and 'context'

According to sociocultural theory, as the child develops and becomes more proficient, she begins to depend less on adults for direction and more on internal 'self-regulation'. These sociocultural concepts of internalisation and self-regulation can be readily accommodated and explained within a bioecological framework. Internalisation arises when experience in context becomes incorporated into the person characteristics of the child and so influences the direction of future development.

The bioecological model envisions the child as an active agent in her world, both influenced by and influencing the environment, or context, in which she is living. As we have seen, a child's dispositions may be generative, inviting positive interactions with other people, or disruptive, potentially leading to negative interactions with others. These positive or negative interactions then impact, through the power of proximal processes, on the direction that the child's development will take. This is significant since most research on child development treats personal characteristics as developmental outcomes rather than recognising that they are both outcomes and producers of development. More simply, Bronfenbrenner shows how a child's characteristics prompt certain reactions from others and those reactions then impact on the future development of the child's characteristics, which in turn prompt further reactions, and so on. This transformative dynamic process is illustrated in the vignette involving Tania.

Tania is three years old and attends Aileen's community-based preschool three mornings a week. Tania is bright and full of energy, and she loves to take control of her own activities. She dislikes being told what to do by adults, and when she feels her autonomy being challenged, she reacts badly, sometimes shouting and becoming quite stubborn. Aileen knows Tania well, and the two have developed a warm way of working together that meets both of their needs. When it is time for free play to end and for children to get ready for lunch, Aileen gives Tania the job of setting out the plates for everyone because she responds well to the responsibility. As a result, she usually agrees to end her play at the appropriate time, even when she is enjoying herself.

On Monday, Aileen is out sick and Christine is working with Tania. When the time comes for free play to end, Christine asks Tania to put away the doll she is playing with. Tania is enjoying herself and refuses. Christine tells Tania that she must do what she is told as it is time for lunch. Tania sits on the floor holding the doll tightly and refuses to move. Christine raises her voice slightly, warning Tania to comply. Tania throws the doll on the floor and marches over to where the plates are kept. Christine, unaware of Tania's usual job, tells her to come immediately to the lunch corner and sit down. Tania picks up the plates and in temper throws them on the ground, shouting that it's not fair. Christine removes Tania to a corner to calm down.

Source: author experience in practice

In this example, we see how an active child with her own dispositions (in this case a *disruptive* tendency towards stubbornness and temper) provokes two very different reactions from two different practitioners, leading to two different outcomes. Bronfenbrenner shows how such interactions over time can influence the dispositions developed by children. The bioecological model predicts that if Tania regularly experiences calm, supportive interactions, like those with Aileen, she will learn to manage her emotions more appropriately over time. In sociocultural terms, she will learn self-regulation. Alternatively, if Tania regularly experiences interactions based on conflict, such as those with Christine, she is likely to become more prone to temper and stubborn responses. This is a good illustration of the concept of internalisation: how personal characteristics both shape and are shaped by experiences in context. These personal characteristics are described by Bronfenbrenner and Morris (1998, 2006) as 'dispositions', 'resources' and 'demand characteristics'.

Dispositions, resources and demand characteristics

As we have learned, Bronfenbrenner identified three key characteristics of the developing child, which contribute to her engagement with others and her environment. Dispositions can be either positive (generative) or negative (disruptive) (Bronfenbrenner, 1995). Generative dispositions involve curiosity, tendency to initiate and engage in activity and readiness to defer gratification in pursuit of long-term goals. Disruptive dispositions, on the other hand, include: impulsiveness, explosiveness or distractibility; or apathy, inattentiveness, unresponsiveness or a general tendency to withdraw from activity (Bronfenbrenner and Morris, 1998, p. 1009). Positive resources relate to skills, knowledge and experience and enhance the trajectory of development. Alternatively, a child may have limited resources through their genetic endowment, low birthweight or severe illness, and this can compromise their development. Demand characteristics are reflected in the difference between people in, for instance, the way they attract attention, and they relate to characteristics that might elicit a particular response such as gender, age or skin colour.

The important thing about these characteristics is that they "first appear as one of the components of the (bioecological) model and therefore as an influence on development" (Rosa and Tudge, 2013, p. 253) while, at the same time, they can be seen to be a developmental outcome as a consequence of interactive experiences. These concepts have been interrogated by authors including Bourdieu and Passeron (1977), Brooker (2015), Carr and Claxton (2002) and Katz (1988, 1993). Next, we incorporate these insights into a bioecological framework in order to elucidate the concepts.

Dispositions

Early writing on the meaning of 'dispositions' fell within the traditional nature–nurture debate. Katz (1993) highlights the definition of dispositions in *A Comprehensive Dictionary of Psychological and Psychoanalytical Terms* as "the sum of all innate tendencies or propensities" (English and English, 1958, p. 158) with the implication that dispositions are solely internal to the person, little influenced by external contexts. Conversely, Carr and Claxton (2002) note the work of Lave and Wenger (1991) who argue that learning and behaviour are so situation specific that there is no such thing as dispositions, or traits and inclinations that are stable across contexts. However, through the lens of a bioecological perspective, neither position on dispositions seems quite right. While theories of 'personality', represented by the English and English (1958) definition, overlook the effects of internalisation of experience, it seems that such polarised sociocultural thinking as that of Lave and Wenger (1991) neglects the power of the mesosystem and how individuals 'drag' their experiences with them from setting to setting (Slesnick *et al.*, 2007).

Instead, a bioecological perspective views the development of dispositions dynamically through the power of *process*. A child's dispositions influence the way she experiences the world and so acts in it, in turn influencing the way the world responds, in turn influencing the development of further dispositions, and so on. Dispositions are seen as being operative from early infancy onward, evolving over the life course and being manifest even in old age. Experiences in early childhood are considered particularly powerful, and this has relevance for the *time* element of the model also. Dispositions are not just seen as a result of biological inheritance but, rather, reflect the interaction between innate traits and the contexts in which development occurs. The individual acts upon the environment and in turn 'embodies' the micro and macro environment around them so that experiences and *context* become part of the *person*. This can happen at individual level and at the level of a broader culture as sociocultural theory has shown us. Specific cultures develop individual ways "of standing, speaking, walking, and thereby of feeling and thinking" (Bourdieu, 1990, p. 70). Thus, the child develops knowledge and skills required for effective proximal processes at a given stage of development, which may dictate how well a child functions in certain settings. Bronfenbrenner refers to such knowledge and skills as 'resource characteristics'.

Resources

Some writers using a bioecological approach tend to see resource characteristics as applicable across contexts, but in keeping with the emphasis in this chapter (and this book) on the importance of context and culture, it is important to note that the knowledge and skills needed to function well in one society may differ from those required in another. Remembering the importance of a sociocultural understanding of childhood experiences, we must recognise that the resources required for particular contexts may vary and are often based on what Bourdieu calls a 'cultural arbitrary' (Bourdieu and Passeron, 1977). As Brooker explains, "[c]ulture is itself arbitrary: there is no objectively right or wrong way to bring up children" (2015, p. 43). Sensitivity to cultural values and beliefs can be incorporated in early years practice, in curriculum frameworks and in national standards.

Language is a good example of how the resources required to function well may differ across contexts. A child attending an early years setting in Ireland, for instance, would benefit from possessing the resource of speaking English, but this would not be an important resource for a child attending a setting in China. Even within specific languages (like English or Chinese), there are many differences based on context, and this is particularly relevant to social class. Children with middle-class accents and linguistic constructions may 'fit in' more easily in middle-class educational settings. However, Pinker (1994) found more internal grammatical consistency in Black English Vernacular in the US than in the language patterns of academics presenting at conferences. This shows that the style of language used by particular groups can be seen in error as somehow inferior because outsiders do not always understand its complexities, and this illustrates the importance of understanding experiences in context. In other words, rather than possessing any inherent value of itself, the resource characteristic of speaking 'proper' English only becomes more useful based on what is valued in certain contexts.

Demand characteristics

It is important for early years practitioners wishing to ensure fair treatment of all young children and their families to be mindful of factors such as cultural and socio-economic background. Tudge *et al.* (2009) list 'demand characteristics' (those which invite or discourage reactions from the social environment of a kind that can foster or disrupt the operation of proximal processes) including age, gender, skin colour and physical appearance – all characteristics that are subject to application of prejudiced beliefs in particular circumstances. The dispositions of a working-class child might be inappropriately seen as a 'disruptive demand characteristic' in the largely middle-class educational system. Tudge *et al.* (2009) describe 'resource characteristics' as those not immediately apparent but sometimes induced, not always accurately, from demand characteristics; for example, educators may assume inaccurately that the level of 'intelligence' or 'motivation' possessed by working-class children is lower than that of middle-class children. The occurrence of such unfounded assumptions by educators, based on social class, is well established. As Bronfenbrenner and Morris explain, personal characteristics:

> Place that person in a particular environmental niche that defines his or her position and role in society. Recognition of that ambiguity moves us to change in focus from developmentally relevant characteristics of the person to their counterparts in the structure and substance of environmental contexts as they affect developmental processes and outcomes.
>
> (2006, p. 814)

Temperament

Also relevant is Thomas and Chess' (1977) concept of 'temperament'. Tempera-ment refers to the child's tendency to respond to the environment in characteristic ways, regarding energy levels, persistence and the extent to which she gets upset if she cannot reach her objectives. They distinguish between 'easy', 'difficult' and 'slow-to-warm-up' babies (Thomas and Chess, 1956), similar to Bronfenbrenner's notion of generative or disruptive dispositions. Temperament may be seen as an innate part of the *person*, but its expression and its impact are portrayed as intricately bound up with the *context* in which that person is developing:

> Temperament is always expressed as a response to an external stimulus, opportunity, expectation, or demand. It can be considered a dynamic factor that mediates and shapes the influence of the environment on the individual's psychological structure. Therefore, a similar stimulus may evoke different behaviour in different individuals, and different environmental stimuli may evoke similar behavior. It follows that temperament should be primarily rated in terms of the social context within which it occurs.
>
> (Coldsmith *et al.*, 1987, p. 509)

The view of person characteristics impacting on and impacted by environmental factors (context) is particularly congruent with the concept of 'goodness of fit' (Chess and Thomas, 1991). This indicates that a child born with a 'difficult' temperament can have this aspect of their personality exacerbated through inconsistent, harsh or neglectful interactions with adults or, alternatively, minimised through supportive, calm and responsive contexts, as in the example of Tania in the vignette above.

Learning dispositions

The concept of 'dispositions' has also evolved in the Early Childhood Education literature. Carr and Claxton (2002) focus largely on 'learning dispositions', as opposed to the wider range of dispositions explored by Bronfenbrenner, but their work is interesting and relevant, not least because they devote considerable analysis to the question of whether dispositions are innate or context specific. Carr and Claxton (2002), in line with bioecological theory, indicate that dispositions can be transferred across domains but, at the same time, are not 'fixed'. They maintain that it is possible to support the development of positive learning dispositions within early years settings, particularly through the use of innovative methods of reflection and assessment, and that this is more important than teaching children specific knowledge or skills. They state that "[t]he manifestation of learning dispositions will be very closely linked to the learning opportunities, affordances and constraints available in each new setting" (Carr and Claxton, 2002, p. 12), highlighting the idea that learning and development happens in context.

In defining dispositions, therefore, and deciding which traits qualify for the title, the literature provides a number of alternatives, and Table 4.1 shows a small number of illustrative examples of specific dispositions identified by various authors. Katz (1993) notes the definition provided by Resnick: "The term disposition should not be taken to imply a biological or inherited trait. As used here, it is more akin to a *habit* of thought, one that can be learned and, therefore, taught" (1987, p. 41; emphasis in original). Katz herself maintains that dispositions "can be thought of as habits of mind, tendencies to respond to situations in certain ways" (1988, p. 30). Carr (1999) indicates that dispositions allow us to edit and interpret experience. Carr and Claxton develop this theme, "defining a disposition as a tendency to edit, select, adapt and respond to the environment in a recurrent characteristic

TABLE 4.1 Examples of 'dispositions' that are important for optimal functioning

Disposition	Author
'Educational competence' – dispositions to think, persist in tasks, give opinions, contribute ideas and work collaboratively	Bronfenbrenner (1979)
Courage, curiosity, playfulness, perseverance, confidence and responsibility	Carr (1999)
Resilience, playfulness and reciprocity	Carr and Claxton (2002)
Confidence, curiosity, intentionality, self-control, relatedness, communication and cooperation	Goleman (1996)

kind of way" (2002, p. 13). This echoes Bronfenbrenner's ideas that dispositions determine how the child experiences and so interacts with the world and that this impacts on the quality of dispositions as either generative or disruptive.

REFLECTION

Think of an interaction you have had with a child that you would characterise as negative. What 'dispositions' in the child provoked a reaction from you? How might you have responded differently so as to create 'goodness of fit' in the environment and promote the development of 'generative dispositions' while minimising the development of 'disruptive dispositions' in the child?

Active agents within a limited range of choices

The bioecological model foregrounds the influence of diversity and the futility of expecting all children, parents and teachers to behave in the same way regardless of the individual characteristics they bring to a situation. The definition of dispositions provided by Perkins leads to intriguing questions about how much or how little we humans are in control of the way we behave and the decisions we make in life – "[d]ispositions are the proclivities that lead us in one direction rather than another, within the freedom of action that we have" (1995, p. 275). Bronfenbrenner shows that the way a child's experiences become a part of her *person* characteristics may dictate the future choices made. However, this is not to support determinism as is often charged. Rather, his theories stem from a joint freedom–determinism base, seeing the child as simultaneously in control of her behaviour but also constrained by the circumstances in which she finds herself.

REFLECTION

How 'free' are we as human beings? Do we make our own decisions and behave the way we do through free will? Or do the traits we inherit and the experiences we have combine to lead us in certain directions that are largely out of our control? This is known as a debate between 'freedom' and 'determinism'. Discuss with colleagues where you stand in this debate.

Even very talented children (and adults) find it difficult to achieve if they are not given the opportunity to do so through access to resources such as supportive relationships and positive learning environments. In bioecological terms, while the child is an active agent in her world, options are filtered and narrowed by particular contextual influences. This resonates with Vygotsky's (1978) ideas of the social formation of the mind and modes of thought through the mechanism of culture. In fact, it is consistent with sociocultural theory generally, particularly activity theory and the idea of 'motives': "[s]ubjects are constrained by the components of an activity system but they also possess agency and thus are able to reconstitute it to suit their own motives" (Ellis, 2012, p. 536).

This also applies to processes of educational change because individuals make choices in educational settings within the institutional norms of these settings and in the context of their own personal and cultural experiences (Downes, 2014). Therefore, while later versions of the bioecological model have somewhat moved away from sole emphasis on *context* towards a stronger emphasis on *process* (Bronfenbrenner and Morris, 2006), there is no denying the importance and influence of context in a 'systems' approach to understanding human development. Contexts for development are still key – even in more up-to-date iterations of the bioecological paradigm – to how development happens within a relational process. Particularly, it must be remembered that young children may traverse many different contexts at any point in time, and their developmental trajectory may in part depend on the 'linkages' created between these different microsystems. This is a central consideration in Bronfenbrenner's concept of the mesosystem'.

REFLECTION

In order to illustrate the concept of the 'mesosystem', try to identify all of the different settings in your own mesosystem (e.g. home, work, social settings, etc.). How well linked are they? Have you ever experienced a sense of 'culture shock' in moving between settings?

Promoting 'linkages' in the mesosystem: context and culture

Adjustment to early education can be particularly difficult for children from backgrounds outside the dominant culture and who have limited experiences beyond the family. Speaking a language at home that is different from that spoken in the educational setting may predict adjustment difficulties through an increased sense of dislocation (Margetts, 2003). Margetts also found that difficulties attributed to other factors, such as socio-economic status and gender, were ameliorated when children spoke the language of instruction as their first language. Parents as well as children can sometimes experience this 'clash of cultures'. Tobin *et al.* (2013) report how parents of immigrants tended to have quite different expectations of preschool than preschool teachers in the US context, and they indicate that policymakers and educators are still very much struggling with how best to serve a diverse population of children and parents. It can be difficult for parents to maintain their own sense of linguistic and cultural identity while, at the same time, supporting their children to make a life for themselves and succeed at school in their new country. It may be that language and identity are inseparable:

> The connection between language and identity is a fundamental element of our experience of being human. Language not only reflects who we are but in some sense it *is* who we are, and its use defines us directly and indirectly.
>
> (Llamas and Watt, 2010, p. 1)

What are the implications when a child experiences an early years setting where the language spoken is not the same as that spoken at home? Kraftsoff and Quinn (2009) note that on entering the context of formal education, children of minority groups often acculturate to the dominant culture at a faster rate than their parents, and Machowska-Kosciak (2013) indicates that they can initially reject the home language and culture in favour of the dominant language and culture. This can be very distressing for parents given the importance placed by many, with regard to cultural identity, on their children speaking their language (O'Toole, 2016). Educators need to work with the cultural and linguistic goals of parents because they are central to the identities of children, families and communities, and loss of first language can lead to loss of self-worth, breakdown of family relationships and inability to become socialised into the family's culture (Siraj-Blatchford and Clarke, 2000). There is some evidence, however, that educational settings often fail to do so (Hornby and Lafaele, 2011), and research indicates that parents from minority cultures tend to be less involved in their children's education (Robinson and Harris, 2014). The early years practitioner has an important role in easing children's transitions across linguistically and culturally diverse contexts.

Similar difficulties in engaging with educational settings have been identified for children and parents based on socio-economic status. Challenges experienced by working-class children within early education can be seen as stemming from a 'mismatch' between the contexts and cultures of school and home:

> Cultural resources, such as values, attitudes, language skills and styles of interaction, are acquired in school more quickly by children already familiar with them. School success is predicated on such cultural capital so that middle-class [children] who are more familiar with the dominant culture will fare better.
>
> (Byrne and Smyth, 2010, p. 27)

This mismatch is important for early years practitioners to explore because issues related to socio-economics may impact on the behaviours of educators. Expectations of children from working-class backgrounds have been consistently low (Robinson and Harris, 2014), and there is extensive research to show that such expectations can often become 'self-fulfilling prophecies'. For various reasons such as cultural bias in testing and poorer educational and social opportunities, certain groups, including those from lower socio-economic backgrounds, tend to score lower on IQ tests (MacRuairc, 2009). It is important to emphasise here that it is often these external reasons, rather than the individual's ability, that impact on outcomes of standardised assessment such as IQ tests. This is crucial with regard to expectations because Good (1987, 1993) found that once educators were given a child's IQ score (not always accurately), they adjusted their teaching. With those of lower IQ, educators waited a shorter time for answers, more frequently gave the answers rather than giving clues or chances to respond, praised less frequently, smiled less often and demanded less work. Such behaviours had a negative effect on educational outcomes for children. Expectations may also extend to interactions with parents (Dockett *et al.*, 2012), and there is extensive evidence of negative stereotyping of working-class parents (Robinson and Harris, 2014). As Reay puts it, "[w]here children's class and cultural background bears little resemblance to that of their teachers, connections between home and school may be minimal and tenuous" (2005, p. 26).

Context and family

Another key issue of diversity for consideration within a bioecological framework is family structure. According to Berk, "the family is the child's first and longest-lasting context for development" (2009, p. 563). The family has a strong influence on children, and most educators recognise parents as the child's primary and most important educator. Families represent the primary setting in which most children's lives are shaped and influenced. Within family contexts, children gradually internalise social standards and expectations, which facilitates, in turn, better self-regulation skills and responsibility. Central to this process are the parental behaviours and discipline responses that children experience within family settings. However, the concept of 'family' is open to a diversity of interpretations, and different parenting arrangements bring different challenges and benefits for the social and emotional development of children. Increasing pluralisation and diversity in family contexts is likely to exert influences on parenting styles and practices, which, in turn, impacts on children's psychological well-being (Halpenny *et al.*, 2010).

While an extensive body of research has shown the benefits of traditional family structures involving two parents (Bronfenbrenner and Morris, 2006), it is the relationships or process within these family contexts that actually matter rather than who is a part of the family *per se*. The presence of another adult who gives support and love to the primary caregiver is key to positive functioning within families, so that 'other adult' could be a same-sex partner, a grandparent or some other close individual, not exclusively the other biological parent of the child. As Bronfenbrenner and Morris put it, "it would seem that, in the family dance, it takes three to tango" (2006, p. 824). This prediction of the bioecological model has to some extent been supported by recent research showing that children of same-sex couples are, in many cases, happier and healthier than population samples (Crouch *et al.*, 2014). Previously, much of what we knew about the effects of family transition (such as divorce) on children focused solely on child outcomes regarding family type or structure and emphasising parental absence. However, some research has focused on the profound importance of the quality of family processes or interactions prior to, during and following family transitions (Halpenny *et al.*, 2008). Consistent with bioecological thought, this approach draws our attention to the importance of family interactions and how these interactions may evolve and progress over time. Proximal processes and positivity of relationships within families may be more influential on outcomes for children than whether families are structured in traditional ways.

This is important to remember with regard to the increasing culture of testing for 'school readiness' using checklists that impose a cultural arbitrary on what constitutes 'good' parents and home learning environments, disregarding diversity in families (Brooker, 2015). Early years practitioners must be cognisant of and sensitive to the needs of different types of families and different family contexts.

REFLECTION

Consider this quote from Adrienne Rich:

> When those who have the power to name and socially construct reality choose not to see or hear you, whether you are dark-skinned, old, disabled, female, or speak with a different accent or dialect than theirs, when someone with the authority of a teacher, say, describes the world and you are not in it, there is a moment of disequilibrium, as if you looked into a mirror and saw nothing.
>
> (1986, p. 199)

Would all children in your early childhood setting see themselves in the 'mirror' you provide? And their parents? What assumptions do you bring to your interactions with them that are based on your own cultural, linguistic, social, class-based and gendered 'normality'? Could these assumptions create challenges for the children and parents? What practical measures could you take to minimise such challenges and instead create 'linkages' between the contexts of home and early childhood setting?

Differences based on factors such as socio-economic status, language, culture and religion can contribute to disjuncture in the mesosystem and can be implicated in difficulties for children, parents and early years practitioners alike. However, contextual factors can worsen or ameliorate these potential difficulties; thus the importance of early years practitioners contemplating practice through a bio-ecological lens. This understanding highlights the fact that 'children' and 'parents' are not homogeneous groupings and that processes in early years settings may be extensively impacted by both person-based and context-based factors.

Understanding development in context

Bronfenbrenner identifies some features of an optimally structured environment, or context, for child development. One important aspect is the provision of "objects and environments that invite manipulation and exploration" (Bronfenbrenner and Morris, 2006, p. 815), reminiscent of Piaget's ideas about the child learning through exploration and discovery. Another recommendation is the creation of stability and consistency within settings, avoiding chaotic contexts but, at the same time, maintaining a measure of flexibility to respond to individual needs (Bronfen-brenner and Morris, 2006), as also identified in our discussion of Baumrind's work.

Bronfenbrenner supports strong contact and mutual support between microsystems (e.g. home and school or different educational levels) through the concept of the mesosystem. Many early education settings attempt to create these 'linkages' by holding events like Intercultural Days, and schools often develop educational classes for parents to encourage their involvement. Smyth *et al.* (2009) found that English-language classes were particularly useful in attracting immigrant parents to become involved with Irish schools, but some authors argue that there is little evidence internationally of more than lip service to the ideals of 'partnership' with parents from diverse cultural and linguistic backgrounds. Support structures are sometimes based on 'socialisation' (Hornby and Lafaele, 2011). This means that rather than attempting to shape education to ensure the creation of a context where everyone 'fits in', schools and preschools attempt to shape parental attitudes and practices so that they facilitate and meet the needs of the educational setting or of the broader society.

This is central to the work of sociolinguists (such as Cummins, 2000, 2001, 2005; Cummins *et al.*, 2005; Ntelioglou *et al.*, 2014) who emphasise the need to draw on children's home culture and language as both a learning resource and an important repository for children's pre-existing knowledge. Approaches like Intercultural Days can be merely tokenistic, a sort of 'tourist' interculturalism (Murray and O'Doherty, 2001). Initiatives like language classes for parents may take a somewhat deficit approach with parents seen as not having the skills to participate in their children's education as opposed to drawing on the skills they do have (Kavanagh and Hickey, 2013). Asking parents to speak the language of the dominant culture in the home should be treated with caution since maintenance of the primary language in their children may be essential to cultural identity and ethnic pride (Kraftsoff and Quinn, 2009), and the potential for language loss is great when parents choose to, or are required to, speak the dominant language (Burck, 2005).

Implications for practice

In creating nurturing contexts in early childhood education, most important in Bronfenbrenner's eyes are the proximal processes that take place within them:

> In order to develop—intellectually, emotionally, socially, and morally—a child requires, for all of them, the same thing: participation in progressively more complex reciprocal activity, on a regular basis over extended periods of time with one or more other persons with whom the child develops a strong, mutual, irrational attachment, and who are committed to that child's development, preferably for life.
>
> (Bronfenbrenner, 1989b, p. 5)

Bronfenbrenner and Morris (2006) stress the importance of strong proximal processes in terms of providing a buffer in less ideal contexts. Bronfenbrenner draws on the work of Rutter (Rutter *et al.*, 1998) to show that the impact of protective forces, such as strong, supportive proximal processes with an important adult, on the development of resilience in children is even greater in 'at-risk' contexts. Therefore, while the latest version of the bioecological model does still acknowledge the importance of the micro-, meso-, exo- and macrosystems within which a child develops, such context factors are emphasised less than in earlier models, and now the relationship (process) is foregrounded. This is consistent with the maturation of developmental psychology generally and the move away from simple linear models of causality towards understanding of the interaction of risk and protective factors (Downes, 2014).

Key concepts for early years practice

1   *Children's development is inextricably linked with the context in which it occurs.*
2   *Children's dispositions (person) and their experiences (contexts) are reciprocal.* Children's dispositions influence how they experience the world, but children's experiences can be 'internalised', in turn influencing the development of those traits. This influences how children act in future contexts, impacting in turn on developmental outcomes, and so on. In this way, children develop through their relationships.
3   *Diversity is a key feature of what it means to be human.* It is senseless to expect standardisation of outcomes for children or families, socially, emotionally, behaviourally or educationally. It is important for early years practitioners to create respectful 'linkages' between the various contexts experienced by children to avoid a sense of 'culture shock' in the mesosystem.
4   *The course of human development is neither completely free nor completely predetermined.* Children are active agents within a narrow range of choices that are defined by complex interactions between personal characteristics and the contexts and relationships in which they find themselves.

5 Less than optimal contexts may be overcome through the power of positive relationships, and contexts that on the surface appear to be supportive of development in fact lose their power in the absence of supportive relationships. *Resilience is best understood as being reliant on a complex interaction of protective and risk factors with the personal characteristics of the child.*

5

A BIOECOLOGICAL PERSPECTIVE ON EDUCATIONAL TRANSITION

Introduction

In his lifetime, Bronfenbrenner called for the bioecological model to be confronted with real-world data to test its predictions and key principles (Bronfenbrenner and Morris, 2006); he wanted to know whether events in the real world could be predicted and explained by the bioecological model. This chapter draws on practice-based research to identify and animate key elements of the model impacting on early educational pedagogy and practice while enhancing understanding of why the model is so powerful and how it can be realised in practice. Specifically, the chapter applies a bioecological lens to research on educational transition in early childhood. There is increasing recognition of the importance of educational transitions for children and their families (O'Toole et al., 2014). Much work on educational transition is framed within a bioecological approach, and in fact Brooker refers to Bronfenbrenner as "the 'father' of transitions studies" (2008, p. 5). The concept of the mesosystem in particular is very powerful in helping to explain children's experiences as they move across settings.

Young children make many transitions on a daily basis – for example, going from home to crèche, transitioning from playing with friends to eating a meal, moving from engaging in family life to going to bed – but the move from preschool to primary school may be the "big one" (Brooker, 2008, p. 2). Children may be particularly vulnerable at these times, and even the most secure and confident children can experience challenges during transition to primary school. Early educational systems vary widely internationally and even within countries, and it is beyond the scope of this chapter to explore all of them. The research analysed here refers to systems whereby children enter preschool at approximately three years of age and transfer to a separate primary school at some point between the ages of four and six. In keeping with the theoretical framework provided by bioecological theory, the exploration of transitions in this chapter uses the PPCT structure and identifies important *process* factors (such as relationships between home and school), *person* factors (such as language, gender, cultural background and socioeconomic background) and *context* factors (such as support structures) that can be vital at this crucial *time*. Key principles and predictions of the bioecological model are in turn elucidated and confirmed by the findings of research on educational transition.

A key concept of the bioecological model is that development is not linear and passive. On the contrary, factors influencing both developmental outcomes and experience of the educational journey are complex, intertwined and mutually influential. It is important to remember that "the principal main effects are likely to be interactions" (Bronfenbrenner, 1979, p. 38). Many of the factors explored here regarding educational transition are indeed interactive and work together in nonlinear and unpredictable ways. Attempting to stay true to a process–person–context–time framework leaves us with the near impossible task of separating out key factors in order to study them while, at the same time, analysing and presenting them in all their complex interdependence. In an attempt to structure the literature, this chapter draws on Bronfenbrenner's more recent emphasis on process as central to understanding events across all levels of systems. Research on transitions has supported a bioecological interpretation, identifying the central role of relationships in positive educational transitions as well as opportunities for those involved to build and maintain these relationships (O'Toole, 2016).

Educational transition – a crucial 'time' in early childhood

Educational transition can be crucial to outcomes socially, emotionally and educationally. Transition can bring discontinuity and may cause social and emotional turmoil as well as discontinuities in learning. Equally, transition can bring many academic and social opportunities for children, and positive experiences of transition tend to position children well for ongoing positivity of educational outcomes (O'Toole *et al.*, 2014). Therefore, the extent to which children experience smooth educational transitions may have long-term implications for their future educational experiences and for later functioning, emphasising the importance of events in the chronosystem. When children have positive experiences in transitioning from early years settings to primary school, they are likely to regard school as an important place and to have positive expectations of their ability to learn and succeed. Such positive early experiences can be influential in interrupting cycles of social and economic disadvantage and can contribute to resilience among young people. Negative or traumatic experiences of transition can have significant impacts on future self-efficacy beliefs, motivation and academic achievement (Educational Transitions and Change Research Group, 2011).

Educational transition is a time of rapid change in a child's life, and this can be stressful for young children. Think about how you felt starting a new job or on your first day in college. You may have been excited about the opportunities ahead of you, but also somewhat nervous about how well you would cope with challenges and whether you would make friends. Research highlights the turbulent feelings associated with educational transition, with children often feeling both nervous and excited, a mix of optimism and anxiety, perceptions of a challenge and a threat (O'Toole, 2016). Dockett and Perry (2007) describe how children starting primary school both celebrate 'getting big' and worry about what that might mean. These feelings are illustrated in the vignette involving Joshua.

> Joshua is starting 'big school' next week. Two weeks ago he went to a shop and tried on a new uniform. His mother keeps saying that this means he is now 'big', and even though that is exciting, she sometimes looks like she is crying when she says it! Joshua wonders if there is something sad about being big. It makes him feel a bit worried. The uniform is scratchy and he prefers his tracksuit. His dad says that he will learn lots of new things and make lots of new friends in big school. Joshua is happy about that. On the other hand, he has a lot of friends in preschool. Maybe he will just stay there instead.
>
> Source: adapted from O'Toole (2016)

Experiences of transition can be very positive, and children value the new educational experiences on offer as well as the extended opportunities to make new friends. However, a significant minority of children experience difficulties in transitioning from preschool to primary school, and some children may therefore become disengaged from education from the very beginning (O'Kane and Hayes, 2006). International research (Margetts and Kienig, 2013) identifies the stress of adjusting to a new setting that tends to be physically much larger, with strange buildings and classrooms, as well as the challenge of a new teacher, new academic and behavioural expectations and a new, more diverse group of classmates (Ring et al., 2015). To use bioecological terminology, educational transition may lead to disjuncture in the mesosystem of the child as he moves from one familiar microsystem (preschool) to a new, unknown microsystem (primary school).

Proximal processes: the importance of relationships for educational transition

Bronfenbrenner identifies the potential power of *process* to overcome difficulties caused by *context*, and the literature on educational transition shows that relationships within the mesosystem may be key to smooth moves between microsystems.

Children's friendships

Children's friendships are important in transition from preschool to primary school; if children go to school with others that they know from preschool, linkages in this mesosystem are strengthened through maintenance of common elements across settings (Ledger *et al.*, 2000). Unfortunately, Ledger *et al.* (2000) found that the majority of friendships formed in preschool did not survive the transition to primary school. When preschool friends transition to the same primary school, teachers often separate them, aiming to encourage independence and the development of new friendships. Early years practitioners informed by a bioecological perspective are empowered to advocate for young children through their awareness of the importance of context and of maintaining key relationships across transitions. Transition to school is a social process, and young children must engage in complex social interactions at school. Relationships with their peers may provide protection to children during transition, and it is often through friendships, particularly with older children and siblings, that children develop their understanding of school culture and norms. Peer mentoring is often presented as an effective intervention to ease the process of educational transition (Dockett and Perry, 2013), showing how context can support process.

REFLECTION

In your experience, what other practical measures can early educators take to support the development of positive friendships during the transition from preschool to primary school? What approaches and systems might serve to disrupt friendships?

Children's relationships with adults

Positive child–parent relationships are also considered a protective factor in educational transition. Children who report that their parents spend time interacting with them and listening to them tend to also report liking school and liking their teachers, and they tend to have higher academic self-concepts at times of educational transition. Equally, children with characteristically positive patterns of interaction with their parents are more likely to seek their parents' involvement in education (e.g. through help with homework) than those children whose patterns of interaction are characteristically antagonistic (Ames, 1993).

Attachment theory is identified by Bronfenbrenner and Morris (2006) as providing key insights into proximal processes between children and parents, and it may have particular relevance for children at times of educational transition. When children experience stress, as is perhaps inherent in any move between microsystems, separation anxiety may be reignited, even in older children. Separation anxiety has been noted in children starting primary school and in their parents. Children who have attended some form of preschool prior to entering primary school may be less likely to suffer debilitating separation anxiety on the first day of school as they are more used to being with other adults and other children and making friends, highlighting the interactive nature of personal factors and experience as predicted by the bioecological model.

Children with insecure or disorganised attachments may be significantly impaired in their ability to form relationships in the school setting, either with other children or with adults, and their behaviour may be influenced by defensive reactions such as hypervigilance, internalising and externalising reactions to stressful experiences (Riley, 2011), such as those potentially experienced when starting school. Therefore, attachment style and its effects on children's ability to cope with new situations may be vital in determining the extent to which an individual child can cope with educational transition.

REFLECTION

Think back to your exploration of separation anxiety in Chapter 3 and the strategies you thought of to help reduce separation anxiety in babies and small children transitioning to an early childhood setting. Develop those thoughts further. How could early childhood educators at preschool and primary levels work together to help minimise attachment-related difficulties for children transitioning between their settings?

Think about how Bronfenbrenner's concept of proximal processes and Bowlby and Ainsworth's theories about attachment would explain what is happening in the vignette involving Shira.

Shira has been attending a crèche since she was 18 months old, and when she was three, she transitioned to the Montessori group within that setting. When younger, she would cry every morning when her mother dropped her off, but as she got older, she no longer cried each morning. She is now five years old and it is her first day at primary school. When her mother tries to leave, Shira holds on to her, cries and begs her not to leave, just like she did when she was a baby.

Source: author observation

Baumrind's (1971) ideas on 'styles' of interactions between adults and children are relevant to children's transition to primary school. Permissive parenting, or permissive approaches by early years practitioners, can impact on experiences of educational transition. They may lead to impulsivity, disobedience and demanding children who are dependent on adults, less persistent on tasks, poor in academic achievement, with antisocial behaviour. Such behaviour may affect children's experiences of educational transition because teachers often identify those with behavioural difficulties as being at risk of a problematic transition from preschool to primary school (O'Kane and Hayes, 2006). Chapter 4 explored the dynamic process of interaction between a child's personal characteristics (dispositions, resource characteristics and demand characteristics) and the environment through the power of relationships. This is important to remember when thinking about children's behaviour because it illustrates how traits like 'naughtiness' or an inability to sit still and follow direction are not solely internal to a child. Instead, they are the product of complex processes of interaction between the child and his environment.

The bioecological perspective moves beyond deficit models in identifying how individual person characteristics interact with environmental contexts in a process of 'interinfluence' so that individual children are not simply viewed as 'bad' or 'naughty'. The behaviour of individual children may be linked to parenting style since an authoritative approach has been correlated with upbeat mood, self-control, task persistence, cooperativeness, high self-esteem, responsiveness to parental views, social and moral maturity, favourable school performance and more prosocial behaviour (e.g. Berk, 2009; Gregory *et al.*, 2010). Of course, the parenting style of a particular mother or father is in turn developed through a complex interaction of factors including culture, personal experiences of parenting and life stresses; it is also important to avoid deficit models in thinking about how parents interact with their children. The skills and dispositions fostered in children by authoritative parents may be vital to the success of children in education generally and in times of educational transition specifically. In fact, INTO (2009) maintain that children who come from a family environment defined as 'democratic' are more likely to experience successful educational transitions due in large measure to higher self-esteem and greater ability to adjust to new settings, a finding supportive of Baumrind's conceptualisation.

The literature indicates that relationships between children and parents may influence experiences of educational transition through their effects on children's behaviour, socio-emotional adjustment and academic competence, as predicted by the bioecological model. To use bioecological terminology, this means that strong proximal processes between parents and children support positive transition within the mesosystem. However, parents are not the only important adults influencing children's experiences of educational transition, and the bioecological model also notes teachers and other early years practitioners as key components of a child's microsystem. A central aspect of the relationship between children and educators is the practice of discipline, and changing disciplinary structures and behavioural expectations of children during educational transition may lead to difficulties. There are varying disciplinary structures and styles in different educational settings, and disciplinary approaches and behavioural expectations often vary within settings. The approaches that educators take in terms of discipline can significantly impact on children's experiences of educational transition. If a child encounters very different disciplinary styles from early years practitioners and primary school teachers, it can be challenging for the child to adapt.

Mirroring the application of Baumrind's ideas to parenting styles at times of educational transition, approaches to discipline in educational settings can be related to concepts of 'authoritarian', 'authoritative' and 'permissive' styles (Gregory *et al.*, 2010). Authoritarian practices may be highly ineffective for children at times of educational transition, and excessive strictness can elicit antagonistic responses from them. Such styles are also linked to decreased academic performance (Gregory *et al.*, 2010). This makes sense when we consider the influence of brain structure on learning and emotion: the same structure in the brain (the limbic system) controls both emotion and the transfer of information from short-term to long-term memory. If children are frightened by the adults educating them, the 'fight–flight' instinct may be engaged, and the processing power of the limbic system is engaged with that, shutting down higher-level cognition and limiting the child's ability to learn.

Permissive or neglectful styles may also be damaging for children, and it may be that authoritative educational climates are most conducive to positive outcomes for them, particularly in times of potential stress and vulnerability such as transition. Unfortunately, however, there seems to be a move in many countries towards more authoritarian methods as children progress through the educational system. There may be massive shifts in behavioural expectations for children once they enter primary school; indeed, INTO characterise these expectations as "overwhelming demands" (2009, p. 45) on small children. They maintain that "the most experienced stakeholders in the transition process (the adults) [expect] the least experienced stakeholders (the children) to make all the changes" (2009, p. 45).

It is particularly unfortunate that relationships between children and educators seem to become less supportive as children move up through the educational system since it may be that the quality of these relationships is the defining factor in children's perceptions of positive educational experiences. Having a trusted adult to talk to outside of the family has been shown to be supportive to children's development and resilience (Masten and Reed, 2002). Equally, positive interactions with teachers have been shown to raise self-esteem and motivation (Downes *et al.*, 2007), supporting the bioecological ideas that relationships are vital and that traits such as 'self-esteem' and 'motivation' are not solely a function of individual person factors, but rely also on internalisation of experiences and relationships. These effects may be particularly powerful in times of transition; positive teacher–child relationships are particularly crucial to positive experiences of transition where children experience factors exposing them to risks of difficulty at this time – those who are vulnerable in transition tend to benefit most from supportive relationships with educators (Burchinal *et al.*, 2002).

A review of the literature on educational transition supports the bioecological emphasis on the power of process to support children through potentially vulnerable times. A key component of the bioecological lens taken to educational transition is the understanding of transition within the mesosystem. Bronfenbrenner proposes that a child's development will be enhanced if two settings in which he is involved are strongly linked, emphasising the importance of including families, particularly parents, in children's educational transitions.

'Processes' between home and school

When children are transitioning from preschool to primary school, parents are usually the stable factor for them at such potentially unstable times, and it is they who provide the social, cultural and emotional supports children need during transition. A bioecological perspective conceptualises transition as "embedded within social contexts and enacted through relationships and interactions" (Dockett et al., 2012, p. 58), acknowledging that one of the major aspects of continuity for children at times of educational transition is their family experience. Therefore, one of the most important features of a child's mesosystem may be the relationships with and between their parent(s) and their early educators – "[s]trong relationships form the basis of a successful transition to school" (Dockett et al., 2012, p. 65).

Educational research indicates that parents are a vital factor in educational success for children and particularly for the successful transition from preschool to primary school. Transition can be quite demanding for the whole family, and transition into primary school is recognised as a significant milestone that may be traumatic in some cases for the child, the parent or both (O'Toole et al., 2014). Even when children have attended preschool, parents experience significant changes with the move to primary school, such as altered schedules and changing expectations of them. Becoming the parent of a school-going child can be anxiety-inducing for parents because of the potential for other adults, specifically teachers, to make judgments about their parental skills (Dockett et al., 2012). This emphasises afresh the importance of positive relationships between parents and teachers. Where such positive relationships are not forthcoming, educational transition can be challenging for parents. In findings similar to the mixed emotions described by children, parents have reported feeling both a sense of achievement as they reach the milestone of sending their children to school and a sense of loss as they begin to separate from their child (Dockett et al., 2012; O'Toole, 2016; O'Toole et al., 2014). Therefore, supports for families at times of transition may be vital.

Transition offers an opportunity for parents to collaborate with schools to strengthen and support each child's learning and development, and parents' knowledge of children may have much to contribute to their successful transition and the school's understanding of how to facilitate this (Mhic Mhathúna, 2011). According to Dockett et al. (2012), 'family readiness' or the ability to support children at school is crucial to the development of 'school readiness' in children. Recent research into perspectives on school readiness (Ring et al., 2015) expands this idea and indicates that not only do the child and family need to be 'ready' in order to promote positive experiences of transition, but the school also needs to be ready, and this research even refers to 'community readiness'. This interpretation of school readiness in children has a strong bioecological flavour to it, emphasising child development in context. It also offers confirmation of the idea that children's characteristics such as resilience at stressful times are to be conceived not solely as internal characteristics, but also as dependent on the supports and relationships available to the child.

REFLECTION

In your experience, do early years settings involve parents in their children's educational transitions? Discuss examples of how parental involvement can be facilitated and supported.

Family support is linked to achievement after transition and the influence of encouraging parents is cumulative, supporting the bioecological emphasis on the developmental impact of early experiences. The specific parental behaviours and inputs that may be helpful in support of children's transition into primary school include promotion of children's independence, talking positively to children about their own school experiences and asking about the child's day in school, having good communication with the teacher and the school, and ensuring that belongings are child-friendly (INTO, 2009).[1] Overall, it may be that educational transition is an opportunity for relationship-building between teachers and parents. It gives families the chance to build links for their children between prior-to-school and at-school experiences; it also allows educators to build relationships with children, families and communities through sharing their own expertise while also recognising the expertise of others. Of course, while parents may represent a key 'bridge' for children and early educators within the mesosystem, relationships between educators at the levels of preschool and primary school may be equally important.

The 'process' of schools and early years settings

The cultures of early years settings and primary schools can be very different, with the two educational sectors often developing largely independently of each other. They can vary widely in their objectives and approaches to education. Educational transition represents an opportunity for educators at different levels to work together and draw support from each other. Good communication between staff at preschool and primary school may support a satisfactory start at school for children through the common aims, educational approaches and understanding of the two staff groups. However, communication between the two educational levels can be limited; there may be differences in language use and cultural expectations as well as distinctions in meanings between early years practitioners and primary school teachers (O'Kane and Hayes, 2006). In many countries, educators at the two levels attend different training programmes and work with different pedagogical approaches and methods, and early years practitioners and primary school teachers also often have very different expectations of each other.

Cultural differences between the two levels are often exacerbated by systemic structures, preschools and primary schools often falling under different administrative auspices and adhering to different regulations and inspection processes. The knowledge of early years practitioners about primary school procedures may be vague, just as the understanding of primary schools of what happens in early years settings may be unclear. Clearly the quality of communication, as well as the quantity, needs exploration. This is important because it may be that discontinuities in the mesosystem at times of transition are emphasised for children when professionals do not hold mutual views on what is appropriate, making poor communication and weak processes between educational levels a barrier to children's successful transition. A bioecological perspective shows how events at exosystem, macrosystem and chronosystem levels can impact on such issues, and certainly mechanisms to ease transition, such as the ideas of 'key persons', 'passports' or 'snapshots', have high profile in educational policy internationally at present (Fitzpatrick, 2015; Ofsted, 2014; O'Kane and Hayes, 2013). A number of measures to overcome barriers to communication across educational levels have been identified in transitions research. These include establishment of common policies for transition across both settings, meetings between preschool and primary school teachers and the development of 'profile forms' to explore the specific needs and interests of children, visits to the preschool by primary school staff and vice versa, and communication between the two levels regarding curriculum and teaching methods (Mhic Mhathúna, 2011).

REFLECTION

If you are currently working in the preschool sector, how much do you know about the early years of primary school, the curriculum and approaches to teaching and learning? How much contact do you have with your local primary schools?

If you are a primary teacher in the early years, how much do you know about what happens in preschool? How much contact do you have with the early years settings that feed in to your school? What practical measures could early educators at both levels take to support children and families during the transition from preschool to primary school?

Viewing the move from preschool to primary school as a transition within the mesosystem underlines the importance of providing 'bridges' for children between their microsystems. Relationships with other children and important adults like parents and educators can potentially provide such bridges, and it is important for early years practitioners to nurture them. Equally, adults' relationships with one other can be crucial in supporting smooth transitions for children, so early years practitioners should be proactive in working towards positive relationships with colleagues at the other level of early education; preschool and primary school educators must work together for the benefit of children transitioning across their sectors. Of course, this emphasis on process and relationships does not entirely negate the need to explore and understand the influences of person and context on experiences at this time of educational transition.

Person factors impacting on experiences of educational transition

The bioecological model emphasises diversity and the inappropriateness of expecting all children or adults to behave in the same way. The vignette involving Ava and Orla may help us to explore these ideas.

Ava and Orla have attended preschool together for the past two years. Now they are five and starting 'big school'. Orla's parents both grew up in the area, and her mother attended the primary school she will be going to. Her family speak English and a little Irish, and both her parents have experienced the Irish educational system to degree level. Ava's family are from Poland and have lived in Ireland for three years. Her parents' English is improving rapidly, but they still struggle sometimes to understand what Irish people are saying. In Poland, early education is quite different, and Ava's parents are not quite sure what to expect of primary school. They are quite anxious, and Ava is beginning to think that maybe 'big school' is something to be afraid of.

Source: adapted from O'Toole (2016)

Ava and Orla are both five years old, both are girls, and both have benefitted from the same preschool provision. However, their experiences of starting school may be quite different. Orla's parents understand what is expected since they have been through the Irish educational system themselves. Their communication with the school is facilitated by the fact that English is their first language. Therefore, they are less nervous than Ava's parents and are able to transmit positive messages about starting school to Orla. They both grew up in the neighbourhood and so are likely to have a network of support, friendships and family available to them. Ava's parents have no experience of the Irish educational system and only an emerging knowledge of supports available in the area. Their communication with the school is hampered by a language barrier, and while Ava herself is used to communicating in English in preschool, Polish is still her first language and she is more comfortable in that medium. Ava is becoming aware of how anxious her parents feel, and she is beginning to feel quite anxious herself. Clearly there are risk factors that make Ava somewhat more vulnerable during transition than Orla, and while of course Ava may have a wonderful experience of starting school, her early educators need to be aware of her needs. These are complex issues and should not be thought of in simple terms. However, as predicted within a bioecological framework depicting the child as an active agent, the literature shows that personal dispositions, skills and characteristics possessed by individual children can have a profound influence on their experiences of educational transition.

REFLECTION

What 'person' factors can you think of that might impact on the experiences that children and families have at times of educational transition? Write down as many as come to mind and compare your answers with the bullet points that follow.

Children's experiences of educational transition may be influenced by:

- *Specific skills and abilities*: Social skills, independence, language and communication skills, and the ability to sit, listen and concentrate are important for success at primary school. The ability to follow direction, take responsibility for their belongings, wait and take turns, seek help when needed and cope with frustration are also noted.
- *'Self-esteem', 'self-concept' and 'self-efficacy'*: Children with low self-esteem and self-efficacy beliefs and poor self-concept are vulnerable during transition.
- *Behavioural difficulties or special educational needs*: Children with behavioural difficulties or special educational needs sometimes struggle during transition in the absence of appropriate supports.
- *Gender*: The literature generally indicates that boys are more vulnerable than girls during educational transition.
- *Preschool*: Children may be more 'school ready' when they have attended a *good-quality preschool* as they may have developed social skills such as sharing and taking turns.
- *Language, culture and religion*: Educational settings sometimes seem to represent the dominant culture, and depending on supports available, where the language, culture or religion of the home differs substantially from that of the school or preschool, children may be vulnerable.

- *Socio-economics*: Educational systems usually represent middle-class values and culture, and low socio-economic status is associated with less positive transitions for children.
- *Family structure*: Children with older *siblings* often find the transition easier as they may have already visited the school, and siblings can also provide informal information about the school as well as a sense of protection from older children.

In considering the impact of diversity on educational transition, early years practitioners must also consider how person factors might impact on parents' capacity to support their children at these times.

REFLECTION

Consider the families whose children attend your early years setting. Do all parents have the skills and knowledge and the cultural and economic capital required to support their children in transitioning from preschool to primary school? What factors might impact on parents' ability to engage with the transition? What can you do to support families? Are there any structural aspects of your early years setting that potentially empower or limit parents' capacities at these times?

In many cases, parents do not perceive schools to be as open and accessible as the schools and teachers perceive themselves to be, and parental evaluations of transition arrangements are often considerably poorer than those of professionals (Hall *et al.*, 2008). Dockett *et al.* indicate that "the responsiveness of teachers is a key element in promoting family engagement at school" (2012, p. 58). This is important to note because parents' proactivity may be limited by feelings of intimidation, especially when the culture, language, religion or socio-economic status of the home differs from that of the educational setting. Early years practitioners may have a particularly important role to play in these processes because anxious parents often seek support from them during transition if their relationships are already well established.

A responsibility rests with both educational settings to facilitate parental understanding of what to expect and what is expected. Policies and practices must be well explained. They should also be aware of and work towards a balance in power relations, and this may be particularly true for parents whose backgrounds differ from the dominant social, linguistic and cultural group. Hornby and Lafaele (2011) maintain that schools often view parents as tools for increasing children's achievements, as cost-effective resources or as methods of addressing cultural inequality and disadvantage, but parents' goals are more likely to be focused, naturally, on their particular child. Transition is an adaptive process for children and families so it is necessary to involve all stakeholders about communication in the process. Brooker recommends "a serious and respectful listening, and not . . . a home school dialogue that assumes the school is always right" (2005, p. 128).

Think about the dynamics at play in the vignette involving Jane and Lydia. How might the teacher involved interpret the situation differently, potentially resulting in more positive outcomes? Is there a role for the early years practitioners in Lydia's preschool in supporting the family through the process of transition?

When Jane was a little girl, she hated school. Her mother often forgot to give her lunch, and her memories of school largely involve feeling hungry, finding it hard to pay attention and being shouted at by teachers for not knowing the right answers. Jane's daughter Lydia has just transitioned from preschool into the primary school where Jane went as a child. She has received a note from Lydia's teacher asking her to call to the school to discuss a matter related to Lydia's learning, but each time she is in the schoolyard, Jane feels sick and frightened and can't bring herself to go in. After a week, the teacher phones Jane. Jane shouts at the teacher, tells her that she's just picking on Lydia, that she won't come up to the school to listen to them bad-mouth her daughter, and hangs up the phone. The teacher chats to her colleagues in the staffroom about how parents from Jane's estate just don't care about their children's education and there's nothing she can do to help Lydia if the mother won't fulfill her responsibilities.

Source: adapted from O'Toole (2016)

Bronfenbrenner's bioecological model provides us with a theoretical framework to look beyond the individual person to the context in which they are developing and the relationships (processes) through which they do so. This may help to avoid a problem-focused deficit narrative whereby children and their families are 'blamed' for any potential educational difficulties or certain groups of parents are seen as 'not interested' in their children's education. It allows us to see a comprehensive picture of how individual characteristics interact with, are influenced by and impact on the context in which they find themselves.

REFLECTION

'Person' factors may lead some parents to feel excluded from the educational system and nervous when interacting with it. Write down as many as you can, then compare your answers with the bullet points below.

Parents' experiences of and engagement with their children's educational transition may be influenced by:

- *Socio-economics*: Working-class parents sometimes feel excluded by the middle-class educational system.
- *Language and culture*: Parents from other countries may not understand the norms of an educational system, and teachers may not understand cultural practices that vary from the dominant culture. Linguistic differences may also lead to challenges in home–school communication.
- *Gender*: Early education is largely dominated by women, posing challenges to the engagement of some fathers.
- *Family structure*: Parents who have had a child attend primary school already may find transition easier since they know what to expect; single parents or those with poor support networks may find it difficult to engage with their children's school; same-sex couples sometimes meet with limited under-standings of what 'parenthood' means, which can lead to challenges with accessing information about their children.
- *Support networks*: Parents sometimes leave behind many of their formal and informal support networks when their children leave preschool, and it can be challenging to develop new supports at primary level.
- *Employment status*: Parents who work long hours may have little time to engage with their children's education. Parents who are unemployed may have little money to support it.

We need to deconstruct these statements a little; a bioecological perspective shows us that children's development is akin to a web, not a straight line. No one factor – preschool attendance, for example – will automatically predict the behaviour and development of a child. Not all preschools are of sufficient quality to support the development of relevant skills in children. It should also be noted that it is not always easy to define 'quality' with regards to preschool provision, and systems intended to rate the quality of early education programmes may not actually reflect impacts on learning (Sabol *et al.*, 2013). We must also consider how various factors interact.

Equally, no one factor alone will determine a parent's involvement with a child's transition. One of the key messages for early years practitioners that emerges from consideration of the literature on parental involvement in educational transition through a bioecological lens is that it is not enough to find out how to best mould parents to support the aims and agendas of schools, but they must in turn be supported at times of transition.

When we think about the impact of the dispositions, skills and characteristics of individual children, parents and teachers, we must acknowledge that person factors do not operate in isolation of contextual circumstances. Person, context and time factors mutually interact to influence process for children, parents and schools at times of educational transition. Much research on educational transition focuses on and acknowledges the key impact of the contexts in which such transitions take place (Margetts and Kienig, 2013).

The impact of context on educational transition

Bronfenbrenner and Morris (2006) note this focus on the contexts in which children develop as a key achievement of their work, and certainly research on educational transition appears to have been strongly influenced by the bioecological emphasis on context. The literature identifies the vital nature of formal structural and contextual supports within schools and preschools for children and families during transition and highlights a number of contextual considerations that may help or hinder individual children (Dockett and Perry, 2013). Approaches worth considering within early years settings to support children in their transition from preschool to primary school include:

- extensive *contact with primary schools* by preschool children before enrolment;
- encouraging *independence in preschool*;
- *discussion* about starting primary school;
- sending letters to and having meetings with *parents* before term starts;
- ensuring strong *communication between the preschool and the primary school* regarding both curriculum and educational approaches as well as the needs of individual children;
- *mentoring systems* whereby older, more experienced children support younger children through transition;
- efforts to ensure *continuity of curriculum*, recognising that curricula move from more child-oriented, play-based approaches to more subject-oriented pedagogy on transition to primary school.

Of course, we must engage with these ideas critically. For example, the concept of 'independence' is contested. Brooker (2008) notes that at preschool, independence tends to mean the child choosing his own activities, whereas at primary level, independence tends to mean the ability to follow instruction and stay on task (a task chosen by adults) without intervention. In some ways, these skills are actually the complete opposite of each other, despite being given the same label of independence, and so it is little wonder that parents, preschool teachers and primary school teachers sometimes disagree on the skills required (Brooker, 2008; O'Kane, 2015). We must emphasise 'ready schools' as well as 'ready children' or 'ready families' (Brooker, 2008; Ring et al., 2015). The quality of parents' interaction with schools at times of educational transition can be impacted by structural and contextual supports provided to them.

According to O'Toole (2016), considerations include:

- whether a *whole-school approach* is taken, both to encouraging parental involvement in their children's education generally and to supporting children and families to manage the process of transition;

- *facilities* such as a parents' room to support communication;
- *proactive invitations* to parents to become involved in the life of the school;
- *cultural awareness* including awareness of language and socio-economics – supporting children and families to express their cultural identity rather than expecting them to conform to the cultural identity of the school;
- *formal and informal* measures to support *communication between home and school.*

Implications for practice

In summarising the research evidence explored in this chapter, we can see that positive proximal processes for children during educational transition can be supported through promoting friendships; developing a structured series of peer interactions with older students; supporting students to manage the logistical demands of the new setting; involving families and communities, particularly parents; avoiding jarring cultural shifts in educational approaches and behavioural expectations; and ensuring availability of supports for children with specific vulnerabilities such as special educational needs or behavioural difficulties.

Key concepts for early years practice

1 *Educational transitions* can represent *crucial times* for children and families, socially, emotionally and educationally.
2 *Individual 'person' factors can leave some children and families more vulnerable during educational transition.*
3 A bioecological perspective on educational transition identifies a *responsibility for early years practitioners to be proactive* in developing relationships to support children during these potentially crucial times.
4 *Contextual supports* can be vital in achieving this.

Note

1 It should be noted that not all research on 'parental involvement' is as clear on what that means, and the literature has been extensively critiqued by writers such as O'Toole (2016), Robinson and Harris (2014) and Hornby and Lafaele (2011) for failing to clarify what is meant by 'partnership' between home and school.

6

LOCATING THE CHILD AT THE CENTRE OF PRACTICE

Bronfenbrenner's model places the child at the centre of a complex network of family, social and cultural influences and emphasises that she actively participates in and influences the interactions within and between these settings. The young child directs her own learning through ongoing interactions with the environment – both the children and adults she shares her time and space with and the objects located in that space (Halpenny and Pettersen, 2014). Children are seen as competent social actors within a complex network of social and cultural influences, thus placing children and significant adults at the heart of contemporary educational processes (Wood, 2007):

> Our image of children no longer considers them as isolated and egocentric . . . does not belittle feelings or what is not logical. . . . Instead our image of the child is rich in potential, strong, powerful, competent and most of all, connected to adults and other children.
>
> (Malaguzzi, 1993, p. 10)

In this chapter, the concept of the child as an active, interested and influential agent in shaping her learning in early years settings is further explored. Drawing on key principles of Bronfenbrenner's theory, the importance of building a pedagogy promoting and respecting children in practice in early childhood is reinforced.

We begin by reflecting broadly on the term 'agency' with regard to early childhood and on the different ways in which it can be expressed. We then think about how, in practice, agency translates into different aspects of children's development and learning, focusing on the importance of independence and interdependence. We reflect further on how we can develop effective strategies to deepen our understanding of children's ideas and opinions in early years settings.

Finally, we highlight some of the tensions and discussions around the viability and feasibility of locating the child at the centre of practice in early years learning.

Pedagogical approaches to young children's learning have been influenced by the values and beliefs predominating at different times and across different cultures throughout the last two centuries. From the beginning of the twentieth century up until the middle of the twentieth century, principles of young children's learning tended to conceptualise a universal child, passive and open to being moulded or shaped by the environment and the individuals within that environment. Some of the key principles underpinning learning included a focus on reinforcing learning through external reward. Such approaches to pedagogy placed a lot of emphasis on 'extrinsic' motivation in order to promote learning. This refers to learning that is driven by external incentives or rewards. Children typically feel encouraged to repeat actions when those actions meet with praise and approval from adults. Such motivation can be very positive and effective, but if relied upon exclusively or excessively, children may not engage in these actions when the rewards are no longer present. In contrast, "intrinsic motivation has been defined variously as a tendency to engage in activities for their own sake, just for the pleasure derived in performing them or for the satisfaction of curiosity" (Covington and Müeller, 2001, p. 163). A child who is curious and encouraged to explore activities in which they have a personal interest is likely to develop these abilities further and, in this way, expand her abilities.

REFLECTION

What do you understand by the terms intrinsic and extrinsic motivation? Can you think of how these terms might be applied to children's learning in the early years? How might strategies based on extrinsic motivation operate to facilitate children's learning? What are some of the limitations of facilitating children's learning through extrinsic motivation? How can educators best support and promote intrinsic motivation in children's learning in the early years?

In the middle of the twentieth century, the translation of Vygotsky's work into English (Vygotsky, 1978) influenced an increased focus on the child as a component in her own learning. Later theorists drew on both a social and a constructivist approach to learning based on the principle that children construct their own knowledge through observing and interacting with their environments. In contrast to previous approaches, the role of the child in constructing her experience of the world is characterised as active in that children are considered "agents of experiences rather than simply undergoers of experiences" (Bandura, 2001, p. 4).

The agentic child in early years

In contrast to the 'universal child' typically portrayed by some of the earlier developmental theorists such as Piaget, Bronfenbrenner characterised each child as having a unique and very particular set of experiences which, in turn, generates a very particular life story. Each child is an active learner growing up as a member of a family and community with particular traditions and ways of life. In recent years, the promotion of young children's agency has been identified as foundational to learning, development and well-being (Mashford-Scott and Church, 2011). Agency in childhood is understood as a quality allowing the child to engage in 'intentional action' to achieve the particular goals valued by her. It is widely acknowledged that children learn and develop through active interaction with others and participation in their environments, and these principles have been increasingly foregrounded in early years practice.

The concept of agency in early childhood provides a good illustration of Bronfenbrenner's depiction of the child at the centre of her development. The characteristics of each individual child are important to consider in the expression of agency as highlighted in the bioecological model of development. Much literature has drawn attention to the importance of children's agency, especially children's competence and knowledge (Corsaro, 2005). Children's agency must be carefully conceptualised to accommodate the specificity of different children's lives, what is shared between children and, finally, what is universal to children and adults (Valentine, 2009). Early years practitioners can facilitate and support children's agency through their emphasis on each child as a unique person with a unique constellation of abilities, interests, needs and experiences. It is also important to facilitate children's agency in their interactions within a group setting. Supporting children's agency in early years practice also requires that practitioners are aware of the family background and particular communities and cultures in which children are growing up and negotiating their agency.

Greene and Hill (2005) point out that this conception of the role and status of children has ethical implications because, quite simply, it recognises their 'personhood'. According to Christensen and Prout (2005), this necessitates new conceptual understandings, viewing children as autonomous, social actors who influence their circumstances as well as being influenced by them. The idea of children as persons with agency who can act with intention is consistent with a bioecological model of the child as an active agent in her world. Greene and Hill (2005), however, identify schools as one area where children often have little or no voice and recommend giving children input into school systems. Similar points have been made by Clark *et al.* (2005) with regard to children's agency and voice in preschool settings.

REFLECTION

What practical measures can early years practitioners take to support the development of children's agency? How can we support children to become confident learners, allowing them to make decisions about what they learn and when? Think about the children you work with in early years settings and note down some of the ways in which children express their agency. What are some of the strategies they use to achieve this?

Consistent with bioecological theory, many writings on agency in childhood emphasise competence in individual children and draw attention to the importance of interaction between individuals and the societies in which they live. Some of the questions generated by such an approach focus on how children act to achieve their goals and what strategies and resources they use to gain control. Locating the child at the centre of her learning involves a focus on the particular knowledge, dispositions, actions and behaviours children bring to negotiate their learning experiences.

Markstrom and Hallden (2009) carried out an ethnographic study on children's strategies for agency in the context of a Swedish preschool. An interesting dilemma they highlight is the potential conflict between individual interests and collective interests embedded within institutions such as preschools. Within the preschool, the days are scheduled and the practitioner's role is to organise the group of children. Equally, the importance of giving children a free space and time to develop individual interests is of central importance. In this interesting study, children's strategies for navigating these tensions were explored. Children's experiences of and approach to the institution, the collective, the other individuals and the daily routines were negotiated among the children themselves and between the children and the preschool teachers. The study shows that children bring certain issues into question and use different strategies when doing so. One strategy, illustrated in the vignette below involving Peter and John, is for children to negotiate with adults and other children to stay out of collective activities and to be in control and realise individual ideas about activities and everyday life. In this vignette, all the children are asked to come together and play in the play hall during free playtime.

Two four-year-old boys, Peter and John, express a preference for listening to a CD Peter brought with him to preschool that day. Peter asks the preschool teacher if he and John can listen to Michael Jackson on the CD player. The preschool teacher is quiet for a long while.

Preschool teacher: Hmm, you ask such difficult questions. Everybody is
                         going to the play hall now.
[Pause] Could you do it in this room?
Peter: We can be in the other room so we don't disturb you.
Preschool teacher: You won't disturb anyone. What do you say about this
                         room?

The boys look happy. The preschool teacher brings the CD player, starts it up
and leaves the room.

Source: adapted from Markstrom and Hallden (2009)

In the example, although the two boys are part of a collective and *all* children are supposed to play in the play hall, Peter and his friend succeed in negotiating with their preschool teacher to be allowed to follow their own ideas rather than what the schedule or routines prescribe. Markstrom and Hallden (2009) note the fact that in the interaction with the preschool teacher, they use their knowledge of the collective norms and routines to get access to time and space. In this case, Peter says that the boys can be in another room so that they do not disturb the others – the collective and the activities in the play hall. The children view themselves as competent in negotiating activities but also negotiating having some time and space of their own. The authors reflect on this further as follows:

> The children are actors in making time for children by navigating among the scheduled and 'predefined' activities. The actors use their knowledge about the teacher's social order in the preschool where the preschool teacher makes a suggestion and the children know that they have the choice of either accepting the decision or negotiating other options. This knowledge is used as a resource in realising their own strivings and purposes.
>
> (Markstrom and Hallden, 2009, p. 117)

Children in the study often help each other to get what they want. Consistent with bioecological theory, this study provides us with an opportunity to focus on how children shape their own experiences through reciprocal interactions with their environment rather than seeing children as passive products of social structures. From these examples, we can see that children's agency can be expressed in many different ways including exercising power with or over others through strategies that suggest elements of self-interest, such as refusal to play, inclusion or exclusion of peers, and drawing and maintaining boundaries. Agency can thus be expressed in multiple ways.

Negotiating the tensions around children's agency in the early years

Along with recognition of the relationships between agency and development, the promotion of children's right to agency has received a steady increase in attention internationally. The United Nations *Convention on the Rights of the Child* (UNCRC; United Nations, 1989) positions children as being entitled to fully participate in and influence matters that concern them. However, tensions exist around the extent to which young children possess agency. A key consideration reflected in these tensions is balancing the desire to facilitate children's agency and right to autonomy with their right to be protected from harmful and damaging experiences. Respecting children's competencies is not an alternative to protecting their vulnerabilities (Woodhead, 2006). Neither is children's right to participation and agency in opposition to their right to protection (Smith, 2013). As stated in the UNCRC, "[t]he child's right to be consulted in matters that affect them should be implemented from the earliest stage in ways appropriate to the child's capacities, best interests, and rights to protection from harmful experiences" (United Nations, 1989, General Comment 7, Paragraph 14).

Beliefs and uncertainties around young children's capacity for self-regulation and self-reflection also underpin these tensions (Mullin, 2007). Such perspectives are informed by traditional discourses, typically portraying children as incompetent and immature. Contemporary, sociocultural perspectives argue that young children are highly skilled co-constructors of their own development (Ahn, 2011). However, challenges to supporting children's agency in early years practice are located in the constraints around the implementation of a particular curriculum and the associated organisational demands (Mashford-Scott and Church, 2011). Transition from early years settings to primary school provides a good illustration of this tension. As explored in Chapter 5, in primary school settings, meeting the needs of the individual agentic child may present a greater challenge than in the early years setting as educators are working with greater numbers of children within a collective context and striving to cover a more structured and demanding curriculum.

Consistent with Bronfenbrenner's focus on the significance of macrosystems for development, perceptions of children's competency and agency are also strongly influenced by the cultural context in which they arise (Chen and French, 2008). In Australian indigenous communities, young children are seen as holding the same rights and responsibilities as adults and, for example, may sleep and eat whenever they choose (Townsend-Cross, 2004). Activities like climbing, sliding, balancing, jumping from heights and hanging upside down can be considered risky in some cultures and yet be part of everyday activities in others (Tovey, 2010). Despite these differences in perception of young children's competence, there is increasing consensus across a wide range of cultural contexts that it is important to facilitate choice in young children's decisions and actions. The belief that one of the main purposes of early childhood education is to develop children's independence and self-confidence resonates across many differing cultural contexts.

Supporting children to be active participators in learning

Bronfenbrenner's positioning of children at the centre of their development highlights increased participation for young children in matters affecting their lives. Participation in early years practice can be broadly understood as children having the right to be supported in expressing themselves, becoming visible and having an impact in a social context. Bae (2009) notes that the overall goals of children's participation and the desired outcomes are relatively indistinct. The emphasis is on process, not outcomes.

Increasing policy support for early years practice is focused on preparing children for school and reducing the likelihood of later school failure. Early childhood is expected to enhance society in terms of preparing future citizens to become productive members of society. One danger of such a focus is that the lived experiences of the 'present' child in early years settings may be disregarded. While the outcomes discourse emphasises the importance of the product of early education, it distances and obscures the contribution of the day-to-day practices within early years settings (Hayes, 2015). The processes involved in such practices play an important role in developing capabilities in children that allow them to be competent, strong and active participators in their learning and development. It is therefore important for early years practitioners to recognise the value of education that is present-focused for development and learning through enhancing the well-being and mastery of children (Hayes, 2013).

Listening to children in early years practice

Respectful listening to young children by adults is essential for engagement with children as competent individuals. To facilitate children's active participation in their early learning, we need to find ways to access and give expression to their own experiences, world views and actions. This requires a child-oriented paradigm. Sommer *et al.* posit that:

> In being involved in caring and learning activities with infants and young children, adults are barred from directly entering the child's experience. But being 'child-oriented,' that is, in practice carefully observing a child's patterned actions, responses and utterances and interpreting these through empathetic imagination, can be a head start in a professional journey enhancing the understanding of the child's specific perceptions of their world.
>
> (2013, p. 462)

When early years practitioners take a child perspective, they seek to understand the child's perceptions, experiences, communication and actions in the world; in this sense, the child's perspective is mediated by the adult. Sommer *et al.* (2013) draw attention to five principles that need to be in place if we are to implement a child perspective approach in practice:

- *Seeing the child as a person*: A child-oriented perspective sees the child as a person with the same needs as other human beings – to be seen, respected, included, loved and influenced by others. This principle highlights the significance of respecting each child as a person in her own right and responding to each child's ideas, thoughts and desires, relating to children as independent and thoughtful human beings. This requires early years practitioners to recognise that each child has her own set of experiences and a unique life story and is an active learner growing up as a member of a family and community with particular traditions and ways of life.

- *Empathic participation with the child*: Working with young children, practitioners must be able to grasp the intended meaning in a child's initiatives and respond accordingly; they must be emotionally available. Efforts to understand young children's desires and intentions include participating in conversations with babies, toddlers or young children. Skilful use of questioning during these conversations can elicit children's theories and understandings, enabling them to share feelings and engaging them in speculation and imaginative thinking (Dunphy, 2008). An important aspect of empathic participation with young children is the use of gestures such as imitating actions, gaze, touching and pointing. Practitioners and children co-construct meaning through words but also supplement children's linguistic resources and abilities through the use of gestures and non-verbal expression.

- *An interpretative attitude of respecting the child's utterances and world of meaning*: This involves seeing utterances as meaningful extensions of a child's way of understanding and experiencing and exploring the child's world of meaning as an object of study in its own right instead of reducing it by comparing it with adult ways of understanding. This principle emphasises the importance of practitioners developing strategies for deepening their knowledge and understanding of the child's world, ideas, perspectives and wisdom. Practitioners should develop sensitivity towards children and aim to improve their ability to conduct conversations with them and engage them in multiple activities assisting them in expressing their ideas (e.g. drawing and looking at photographs).

- *Guiding the child in a sensitive way by adjusting and expanding her initiatives and ways of understanding in the direction of the educational goal or object*: This involves supporting and encouraging interests, emotional involvement and exploration in activities that are important for development. The importance of developing learning environments that allow children to learn at their own pace and extend their learning over time is foregrounded in this principle. Children need time and space to produce work of quality and depth. Imagination, creativity and symbolic behaviour (reading, writing, drawing, dancing, music, mathematics, role playing and talking) develop and emerge when conditions are favourable. The most effective learning comes from simple but versatile materials and environments that extend the child's imagination and can be adapted by children to suit their own learning needs and level of understanding (French, 2007).

- *Early care and education is a dialogical process between the child and the practitioner:* Both contribute to the learning objective – sometimes the adult is dominant, sometimes the child. Through expressive signals and appeals, a child invites the adult to respond in a particular way. Thus, both the child and the practitioner are jointly responsible for the outcome – they are co-producers of the care and education that the child receives. This final principle emphasises setting up opportunities for children to participate in creating meaning about content or learning objects. The child as agent and learner constructs her knowledge through interactions with the practitioner and other children. These experiences are integrated and interpreted in each child's personal meaning-making. Practitioners, parents and other adults must develop sensitivity to the child's perspective in order to get into a dialogue with the child – a dialogue that is necessary for young children's creation of meaning.

REFLECTION

With a colleague, review and discuss the five principles of a child perspective approach set out by Sommer *et al.* (2013).

What aspects of your practice facilitate engagement with children as unique persons in their own right? What strategies do you use to facilitate 'empathic participation' with children in early years practice? Identify some of the potential challenges involved in accessing and interpreting young children's world of meaning. How can practitioners deepen their knowledge and understanding of the child's world? Think of some of the ways in which you can support children in adjusting and expanding their initiatives to encourage interest and exploration and extend imagination and creativity. Identify some ways in which early years practice is a dialogical process between children and practitioners.

Interdependence, intersubjectivity and the agentic child

In our efforts to capture some key aspects of the central role that children play in their learning and development, we see that the concepts of sharing, negotiating and constructing meaning and knowledge are evident. It is wise to be wary of creating unnecessary conflict between the concepts of independence and inter-dependence (Mashford-Scott and Church, 2011). Much research on the early years shows that agency and autonomy in children is associated with more coopera-tive, sharing behaviours (Bandura, 2001; Mosier and Rogoff, 2003). Similarly, engagement within a group can promote individual agency and autonomy (Rogoff, 2003). In keeping with bioecological theory, children's learning and sense of agency and autonomy develops in a complex web of interdependencies. Learning and development involve establishing shared understanding or intersubjectivity, and this, in turn, is the basis for the joint construction of new and more advanced conceptual structures. Children also value interdependent relationships that reinforce their sense of identity and belonging and help them to realise their desire to enjoy each other's company and to support and learn from each other (Kernan, 2010).

As previously discussed, Bronfenbrenner drew our attention to the importance of proximal processes – reciprocal interactions which are repeated and endure for substantial periods of time. Now we consider the importance of play as a vehicle for the expression of children's agency and child-centred learning. Play also provides us with an excellent opportunity to see proximal processes at work.

Play as a vehicle for agency and proximal processes in early childhood

Models of learning in the early years provided by thinkers such as Froebel, Montessori, Steiner and Malaguzzi focused on the active playing and learning child. Unlike teacher-based curricula aimed at instruction and the transmission of knowledge, 'play curricula' were (and are) seen as being more holistic, inclusive and participatory.

Internationally and in the UNCRC, play policies propose that choice is characteristic of play, and research on children's perspectives consistently shows that they value freedom from structure, making choices and having time to themselves (Wood, 2014). The inclusion of play is a key component of the unique nature of early years practice. Children are viewed as active, inquisitive and playful, and therefore it seems natural to have play-based learning as central to early years practice. The underlying assumption is that play forms the basis of childhood development. Research also indicates that children learn best in an environment that allows them to explore, discover and play (Daoust, 2007). Therefore, many early years curriculum frameworks have incorporated play as a means of learning for children.

Play typically involves an intense relation with the immediate social and physical environment (Singer, 2013). A child actively chooses to play with a friend or an adult, and she plays with objects from her environment. The child is active also in the creation of a play-world, distinct from the 'normal world', in which rhythms, rules and structure play an essential role. Even the youngest babies participate and share in the creation of this play-world. Observations of caregiver–baby interactions show that both partners create a play-world together by imitating each other, through eye contact, and in taking turns repeating, varying and improvising sounds (Trevarthen, 2011). There is also a structure of repetition in play with the physical environment, and this is emphasised in Bronfenbrenner's theory. Children can influence these repetitive series of actions so that they grow into a more comprehensive ritual. For instance, Corsaro (2010) introduces us to a lunch that is concluded with singing, clapping of hands and, finally, letting the heels drum. A shared play-world often has the character of a 'magic circle' (Huizinga, 1950) where children create their own images and narratives while listening to a story being read aloud. Children easily become totally absorbed in their play with cars or dolls, or in their role as a tiger or a dog. Consider how the adult in the vignette involving Isabelle and Sophie has misinterpreted the shared play-world of these children. The adult is outside the magic circle.

> Sisters Isabelle and Sophie have constructed a tent out of blankets in their bedroom. Their mother enters the room, and noticing that the side of the 'tent' has fallen down and one blanket is caught behind the bed, she tries to help by fixing it. The children are annoyed because that side of the tent has been torn by a giant, and he hid their door, turning it into a magic portal to his world. It took them a long time to get the tent just right and now their mother has ruined it.
>
> Source: author observation

In this case, the adult has transgressed the 'rules' of the play-world. Young children also love to play with the rules of their caregivers by transgressing them for fun (Corsaro, 2010). One example from Corsaro's ethnographic research involves children slapping loudly and screaming and all the while looking to see whether the practitioner has seen what is going on, and laughing even louder if it has not been noticed. What he illustrates so colourfully in the studies he has carried out (see Corsaro, 2010) is that children, even very young children, direct their play activities to explore the boundaries of their world – boundaries typically drawn by adults. Thus, play allows children a very effective means of bridging the great difference in power that exists between them and the adults in their world. Through play, agency can be expressed in different ways by children through their knowledge, dispositions, actions and behaviours. As Wood (2014, p. 15) puts it, "agency can thus be expressed in multiple ways within the many paradoxes of play such as seeking order and disorder, creating and subverting rules, being inclusive and exclusive and being sociable and unsociable".

In our exploration of how children are located at the centre of their learning and development in early years practice, and consistent with Bronfenbrenner's theory, it is also important for us to consider the tension in practice between supporting and promoting children's agency and the need to provide appropriate boundaries to support the development of self-regulation and positive social and emotional development within early years settings. A child's ability to learn and to function as a contributing member of society rests heavily on the development of social competency and emotional health, which begins at birth and is greatly influenced during the preschool years (Boyd *et al.*, 2005). Preschool programmes that pursue the highest standards of quality will contribute substantially to this development.

Corsaro (2010) describes how rituals help children reconcile themselves to the inevitable. Rituals include such daily occurrences as, for example, children taking leave of their parents, sitting at table for lunch or the activities that take place at the beginning and end of the day. An example of practitioners using play and humour to soothe and influence children's behaviour is provided in the vignette involving Nicola.

> Nicola is roaming around the room although she has been asked by Donna (teacher) twice to remain seated until she has finished her lunch. Nicola ignores both requests and heads in the direction of the kitchen. Donna asks her once again to sit down but this time with smiles, saying: "Nicola you have a carrot, a big juicy carrot. You will be the envy of all the rabbits in the world". Nicola grins and sits down at the table.
>
> Source: adapted from Brennan (2005, p. 116)

In this way, the practitioner draws on the magic of pretend play to create a shared reality in which both adult and child can share in freedom. Children are not simply influenced by their environments but act in ways that change and even transform those environments. What better illustration of this acting on and transforming environments than pretend play. By creating imaginary roles and events, children choose to write the script for endless situations, challenge the logic of adult rules and develop their own internal logic. These opportunities to direct and control scenarios in pretend play allow children to exercise and affirm their agency. Wood captures the power of proximal processes in pretend play when she writes:

> Through such meditational means and activities, children exercise individual and collective agency because they are learning about the internal rules that govern play, the self-control and self-regulation that are needed to sustain play, and ways of resisting adults' rules or boundaries. These processes therefore have particular significance as forms of affirmation for children as agents in their ability to change their circumstances, and in their learning and development.
>
> (2014, p. 14)

Locating the child in early years assessment

We conclude this chapter with a brief focus on the role children can play in assessing their own learning and skills in collaboration with practitioners in early years settings. Assessment of children's learning typically involves using a range of tools at different times to generate a comprehensive picture of the learning and development that is emerging (Dunphy, 2008). Assessment must also take account of the multimodal dimension of children's learning, as we have seen in the sections above. Documenting children's use of imitation, gesture, facial expression and other features to supplement their linguistic resources demands sensitivity by the practitioner to recognise these skills and competencies. Regarding children's role in the assessment of their learning strategies, the Mosaic Approach developed by Clark and Moss (2001) provides a very effective illustration of how we can use a variety of tools to facilitate children in conveying their ideas and feelings to early years practitioners. Children can communicate their ideas and opinions on their learning in a range of symbolic ways, including verbally and through photographs and drawings. Relevant here also is the work of Carr and her colleagues where, working *with* children, they develop 'learning stories' to document children's learning. These learning stories are used in many ways, both as assessment *of* and assessment *for* learning (Carr and Lee, 2012). Discussions with children about their drawings or listening to children explain their drawings to others can give the practitioner rich insights into children's understandings, preoccupations, sense of identity and interests.

Another creative way of drawing children into the assessment process is the use of portfolios. Portfolios involve gathering together evidence of early learning and development and of children's progress in relation to learning goals. When compiling portfolios on younger infants and toddlers, the educator in collaboration with parents selects materials from which they draw a range of information on the children's learning. It is beneficial to encourage children as early as possible to play a role in assessing their learning.

> As soon as they can, children should be encouraged to participate in the selection process with adults. The processes of compiling, talking about and sharing portfolio work will also contribute to children's ability to think and talk about their own learning and that of others – helping them to become meta-cognitively aware. It also involves children in the process of self-assessment wherein they begin to be aware of goals for learning and of the possibility of setting their own goals, and reflecting on and making judgements about their own progress towards those goals.
>
> (Dunphy, 2008, p. 32)

Implications for practice

Bronfenbrenner's bioecological model positions the child at the centre of her learning and development in early years practice. The unique constellation of dispositions and characteristics that individual children bring to their early years settings influences and shapes the experiences they have within these settings. Early years practitioners play an important role in facilitating and supporting children's agency and participation in their learning and development. Children's agency must be carefully conceptualised to accommodate the uniqueness of different children's lives, what is shared between children, and finally what is universal to children and adults.

Key concepts for early years practice

1 *Locating the child at the centre of her learning involves a focus on the particular knowledge, dispositions, actions and behaviours that children bring to navigate and negotiate their learning experiences.* Early years practitioners facilitate and support children's agency through their emphasis on each child as a unique person with a unique constellation of abilities, interests, needs and experiences.

2 *It is important to facilitate children's agency in the context of their interactions within a group setting.* Children learn to negotiate with adults and other children in order to have some control over their actions and realise individual ideas about activities and everyday life. In keeping with bioecological theory, children's learning and sense of agency and autonomy develops in a complex web of interdependencies.

3 *Tensions exist around the extent to which young children can be considered to possess agency.* It is of paramount importance that we balance children's right to agency with children's right to be protected from harm. Beliefs and uncertainties around young children's capacity for self-regulation and self-reflection also underpin these tensions. Practitioners can provide appropriate boundaries to support the development of self-regulation and positive social and emotional development within early years settings.

4 *Through play, agency can be expressed differently by children through their knowledge, dispositions, actions and behaviours.* Such expression can include exercising power with or over others through strategies that suggest elements of self-interest, such as refusal to play, inclusion or exclusion of peers, and drawing and maintaining boundaries.

5 *Practitioners working with young children must be able to grasp the intended meaning in a child's initiatives and respond accordingly, being emotionally available.* Efforts to understand young children's desires and intentions include participating in conversations with babies, toddlers or young children and being able to enter into a dialogical process with children.

7

CREATING RICH LEARNING ENVIRONMENTS

One key component of children's microsystems in the early years is the learning environment, which plays a central role in supporting children's development and learning. Context is extensively elaborated in the bioecological model and is identified as central to understanding development and informing good-quality practice. The importance of the environment as the 'third educator' in the early years setting is highlighted by, among others, those who follow the Reggio Emilia model of early education. The early years practitioner can be a creative architect of learning and development, with careful environmental planning creating points of interest, exploration, quiet, creativity, safe risk and aesthetic pleasure for the child. This chapter considers how to provide a learning environment that contributes to children's development and wellbeing. However, in keeping with bioecological theory, the early years setting must also be understood in terms of the other contexts in children's lives. Therefore, it is necessary for early years practitioners to take account of the contexts from which children come, working at building strong bridges between these contexts. This is particularly relevant in situations where children of diverse cultural backgrounds attend the setting. From a bioecological perspective, the early learning environment can be understood as a complex, interrelated set of elements and relationships. Throughout this chapter, we apply a bioecological lens to identify some of the features that may create a rich learning environment for young children.

Creating an invitation to learn

Perhaps the most important feature of any learning environment is that it is welcoming – not only a space where children feel a sense of security and belonging, but also a dynamic and stimulating space that offers the child an invitation to explore and discover. Curtis highlights the importance of creating responsive environments allowing for "co-operative play, large muscle activities, high drama, messy play, the sounds of childhood, working through conflict and the importance of family engagement . . . offering children rich childhood experiences where children can build their passions and attention over time" (2001, p. 42). Spaces carefully designed and drawing on children's perspectives are welcoming and encourage children's natural responses of curiosity, exploration and communication. Inviting surroundings also enhance children's positive learning dispositions and sense of belonging. Children love to create their own worlds at their own pace and to their own scale in any environment they can manipulate or modify (Strong-Wilson and Ellis, 2007). Spaces allowing for experimentation and transformation of the environment are also likely to be rich in learning experiences.

Young children thrive in calm and predictable early learning environments that give them opportunities, encouragement and time to develop and learn, where the pedagogical process is relational, responsive and reciprocal. Key features of rich learning environments include:

> Spatiality; placeness; materiality; affordances of the environment; everyday life and design concepts such as aesthetics; orientation for solar gain and natural light; introverted spaces; indoor circulation; flexibility, transparency, indoor-outdoor connectedness; compatibility of building with natural terrain and the architecture of the surrounding neighbourhood and meeting places, which enhance our knowledge of children's wellbeing and experiences of learning.
> (Kernan, 2015, p. 6)

Our exploration of rich learning environments is guided by Bronfenbrenner's PPCT structure, highlighting important process factors (e.g. affordances for reciprocal interactions with people, objects and symbols in the environment), person factors (e.g. age, language, gender, cultural background and socio-economic background) and context factors (with an emphasis on the mesosystem and 'softening boundaries' between early childhood settings and home and community contexts). The implications of historical time (macrotime) are also considered with particular reference to children's interactions with technology in early years settings and the implications of potential future changes in features of early learning environments. The significance of informing learning environments through a focus on mesotime and microtime is also explored.

Proximal processes and learning environments in the early years

As we have explored in previous chapters, the bioecological model sees development as a process of interaction between an individual and the environment. These interactions occurring regularly and over extended periods of time are termed proximal processes. Implicit in rich learning environments in the early years is provision of opportunities for children to engage in progressively more complex reciprocal interactions with the people, objects and symbols in those environments. One concept which helps to bring together Bronfenbrenner's proximal processes with the notion of a rich learning environment in the early years is that of 'affordances' – features of the environment that contribute to the positive interactions which occur within these environments (Greeno, 1994). The concept of affordances is used increasingly in research on early years practice to gain insight into the relationship between children and their environment (Kernan, 2007). Heft (1988) developed a functional taxonomy of children's outdoor environments that subsequently became influential amongst some play environment designers and researchers. This highlighted the quality of surfaces available to children – objects which could be grasped, attached and non-attached objects, climbable objects, etc. – and each category was further defined in terms of its affordances. The value of this approach is that it offered a way of thinking about environments that was fundamentally active and goal directed and which supported children's activity, curiosity, exploration and creativity (Kernan, 2007).

A recent study by Lynch and Hayes (2015) explored how very young children learn to negotiate objects and spaces of everyday life in the home. One aim of this study was to identify some of the affordances of the physical environment that influenced the child's learning. The physical environment was identified as a learning environment when it provided affordances for interactions meeting the needs of children's play interests and choices. Consistent with Bronfenbrenner's concept of proximal processes, as these young children's play interactions developed over time, the function of the play spaces became more complex, affording opportunities for climbing and sliding. A range of physical features are, therefore, required to afford multiple play opportunities. The significance of proximal processes for guiding learning opportunities is underscored by the study's identification of a "just-right environment" including transactions between the infant, the physical environment and the social environment. This requires the ability of an adult "to orchestrate the environment for available affordances . . . in a way that maximises successful interactions" (Lynch and Hayes, 2015, p. 22).

Guerrettaz and Johnston (2013) further conceptualise affordances as the potential starting point of the meaning-making process, involving active engagement between the child and the environment. Affordances that enhance children's experiences in early years settings can perhaps best be understood as those features of the environment that children value and which allow them greater possibilities for furthering skills of exploration and imagination. A key feature of designing and shaping a rich learning environment for children in the early years is the ability to tune in to and perceive the environment from the perspective of the children inhabiting their space, thereby generating shared moments of discovery (Kernan, 2015). Significantly, drawing deeply on how young children perceive and use space to create meaning, in keeping with a bioecological approach, positions the child at the centre of his learning environment.

REFLECTION

Discuss with a colleague/fellow student your understanding of the concept of 'affordances' in learning environments in early years practice. To what extent are you aware of the affordances that may enhance learning opportunities for children in their early years setting? How can we learn to better perceive affordances from children's perspectives?

Early years learning environments inviting complex reciprocal interactions are designed to capture children's interest and curiosity and to challenge them to explore and to share their adventures and discoveries with others. Such environments can stimulate thinking, imagination and creativity, thereby enriching communication. Kernan (2015) identifies features that contribute to rich learning experiences and support positive proximal processes within a learning environment. Specifically, she highlights designated interest areas providing opportunities for choice of activity and manipulative materials; these should be plentiful and freely accessible to children, and there should be a high level of child–material interaction. Children benefit from rich and stimulating play choices both outdoors and indoors.

Finding the balance between indoor activities and outdoor explorations is also part of a purposeful planning process. Access to outdoor play opportunities can be influenced by practitioners' views on their benefits and challenges. Kernan and Devine (2010) explored outdoor experiences in early years settings in Ireland, identifying three key discourses: a discourse of freedom and spontaneity in childhood; a discourse of 'naturalness' and rich sensory experiences in childhood; and a discourse of safety in childhood. Interviews with parents, practitioners and policy officers generated a construction of the outdoors as simultaneously a space of freedom and of risk for children. The former was spoken of in terms of spontaneity and freedom to explore; the latter reflected concerns around traffic, 'stranger danger' and fear of litigation in the event of personal injury. The authors conclude that in an increasingly risk averse society, especially regarding children, this construction of the outdoors means it has become marginal in the experiences of many children in early years services, leading to invisibility of children in outdoor spaces.

The extent to which outdoor learning environments offer affordances for risk-taking and physical activities was also explored in Australian early years settings (Little and Sweller, 2015). In this study, despite practitioners' firm beliefs that the environment in their settings supported children's engagement in moderate to vigorous physical activity, insufficient space and regulatory restrictions relating to recommended height limits on climbing apparatus were identified as factors limiting opportunities for challenging, physically active play. Outdoor space and adult support were also identified as important factors in early learning environments to promote physical activity and risk-taking. Affordances for risky play create invitations for children to challenge themselves and extend boundaries within a setting where the safety and wellbeing of the child are paramount.

Risky play has been defined as thrilling and exciting forms of play that involve a risk of physical injury (Sandseter, 2007). In keeping with bioecological theory, affordances for risky play involve interactions between the environment and the child. These affordances are unique for each individual and correspond with the child's size, strength, skills, courage and fear. Armitage (2011) suggests that children should have access to four types of risky play experiences: experience of height and depth; experience of movement and speed; experience of den buildings using tools; and experience of fire. To provide access to experiences of height and depth, equipment like climbing frames and slides provide opportunities for children to climb up, jump down, slide and generally explore the sensation of height and depth. Climbing frames designed with multiple platforms and levels allow children to experience different levels of height, which provides multiple opportunities for challenge. Affordances for experiencing movement and speed can be provided through spaces that allow children to run around freely without constraints. The experience of moving through the air is also facilitated through the provision of swings. Providing children with access to the natural environment and constructing tree swings is an exciting alternative (Armitage, 2011). Experiences of building dens and using tools create invitations for children to change and transform their physical environment, and many early years settings provide access to this form of play by providing materials such as old sheets, netting, rope and poles.

Generating affordances for experiencing fire could involve constructing a well-sited firepit and allowing children to experience fire in a controlled way. Activities such as cooking around the fire pit and storytelling by the light of a fire are activities that provide children with unique and pleasurable learning experiences. The question as to whether there are greater affordances for risky play activities in natural settings rather than in preschool play spaces was explored by Sandseter (2007) in one traditional and one nature preschool in Norway. Findings suggest that the nature playground does not afford a higher frequency of risk-taking play among children but, rather, a higher level of risk in children's play. Children seek out risky experiences in most play environments. However, experiences of risky play in natural settings are likely to provide greater opportunities for more intense, exhilarating and thrilling play situations than the ordinary playground.

REFLECTION

Taking Armitage's four types of risky play (experience of height and depth, experience of movement and speed, experience of building dens using tools and experience of fire), reflect on how your learning environments might provide affordances for such play. List any changes you might make to enhance the opportunities.

A rich learning environment also optimises opportunities for generating interactions with the people who share these spaces. The design of learning environments in the early years should encompass spaces and resources encouraging children to cooperate with each other, thereby stimulating and fostering connection and communication. An example of such spaces are 'experiential centres' in which children can choose to gather together to explore their interests and discuss and plan their play explorations (Saskatchewan Ministry of Education, 2009). Rich early learning environments support engagement with the people and objects within them. Providing invitations to experiment together, share curiosities, stimulate and support cooperative ventures, and negotiate roles and routines can deepen children's sense of self-worth and belonging. Belonging is about having a secure relationship with or a connection to a particular group of people (NCCA, 2009). This can be nurtured within a learning climate which allows children to feel the security of their connections with other children and adults. Research has shown that rich learning environments in early childhood can help children to become emotionally strong, self-assured, and able to deal with challenges and difficulties, creating an important foundation for learning and development (NCCA, 2009). Spaces that invite children to interact with each other also provide invaluable opportunities for them to manage and regulate their emotions in situations of conflict and disagreement.

Flexibility in learning environment designs is also an important consideration. As children's interests change, possibilities for transforming their surroundings contribute significantly to extending learning experiences. Simple illustrations of such flexibility include providing a variety of objects on tabletops and transforming tabletops with mirrors, seasonal flowers or herbs with appealing aromas to provide children with greater sensory learning opportunities (Saskatchewan Ministry of Education, 2009).

REFLECTION

How does your early years setting help to generate a sense of belonging and self-worth for children? To what extent is the learning environment flexible enough to allow children to transform surfaces and materials?

The role of the educator in rich learning environments

Early years practitioners play a central role in building and developing an environment that motivates children to interact with each other, with the participating adults and with the objects within their space. These early experiences support children in becoming confident and competent communicators. Well-designed early learning environments can promote positive learning dispositions in children. As outlined in previous chapters, learning dispositions are characteristics, innate or acquired, that facilitate rich learning experiences for children. Such dispositions include curiosity, playfulness, perseverance, confidence, resourcefulness, risk-taking, social competence and the ability to work with others (Mitchell *et al.*, 2008). By capturing children's interest and curiosity and reflecting these in both indoor and outdoor environments, practitioners play an important role in fostering positive learning dispositions in young children. Through their interactions with other children, with adults, with materials and with concepts, children learn about the world and their place in it. As adults, we have a powerful role in facilitating this development through providing good-quality early learning environments that encourage children to develop positive, generative dispositions of curiosity, persistence, responsiveness, the tendency to initiate and engage in activity, alone or with others, and to inhibit the more disruptive dispositions of impulsiveness, explosiveness, distractibility or, at the opposite pole, apathy, inattentiveness, un-responsiveness, lack of interest in one's surroundings, feelings of insecurity or shyness (Hayes, 2013). Observing, listening to and creatively documenting children's activities in their daily routines provides unique insights into their collective interests and pursuits and also their individual curiosities and learning dispositions. Significantly, documenting children's ideas and activities generates new information about additional props and resources for extending learning.

Some key messages in this chapter so far centre on the value of welcoming and stimulating learning environments to generate and sustain rich interactions and learning processes for children in early years settings. This involves designing open spaces for movement and connecting with others, making available a variety of materials and flexible furnishings, facilitating spaces for lively interactions and communication and dramatic play scenes as well as spaces for quiet and calm reflection. The importance of an attentive and responsive practitioner in creating and sustaining rich learning environments is also highlighted.

Transforming the environment through interactions

As noted in previous chapters, bioecological theory emphasises the dynamic nature of development. Children are not simply influenced by their environments; they also act in ways that change and even transform those environments. With progressive, reciprocal interactions with objects, symbols and people in their learning environment, children have possibilities for transforming their environments and this, in turn, impacts on how they respond to and develop through the changing nature of the milieu in which their learning occurs. Through their interaction with the environment, children change it (as a result of actions and interactions) and the environment influences what they can accomplish. Rogoff (1998, p. 691) describes development as "transformation of participation", and Dunphy explores this further:

> Transformation occurs at a number of levels: for instance, the learner changes
> at the level of their involvement, in the role they play in the learning situation,
> in the ability they demonstrate in moving flexibly from one learning context
> to another, and in the amount of responsibility taken in the situation.
>
> (2008, p. 14)

Transformation can occur to a greater extent if we can develop learning environments rich in opportunities for children to become involved in their learning, to be active and directive in their learning experiences, to have access to different contexts for their learning and to have the potential for increased responsibility. Implicit in this is an understanding of early learning as an active, social, dynamic and transforming process and the role of the adult as responsive and flexible (Hayes, 2007).

A key feature of children's play is spontaneity, and it is this that allows children the freedom to explore and make connections between familiar and novel information. Pretend play requires the ability to transform objects and actions symbolically; it is furthered by interactive social dialogue and negotiation; and it involves role-taking, script knowledge and improvisation (Bergen, 2002). One of the earliest sources of creative imagination is the ability of the child to substitute one object for another in pretend play. Research has highlighted many aspects of play that feature in spontaneity, including enhanced social and emotional skills, language and communication skills, imaginative and divergent thinking skills and problem-solving (French, 2007). However, while acknowledging the importance of spontaneity in children's play, the value of providing a rich environment in which children can become confident players and learners is equally emphasised. Early years practitioners manage the learning environment to optimise the quality of pedagogical learning through play for children. Practitioners can facilitate learning through play by planning an environment that provides a wide range of play possibilities, structuring both the indoor and outdoor environments to reflect children's individual strengths, interests, abilities and needs (NCCA, 2009). Through careful documentation of children's activities, we can identify the types and quality of children's play and reflect these in the learning environment by providing relevant props, toys and objects. Play can be quiet or noisy, messy or orderly, funny or serious, strenuous or effortless. It can take place inside or outside, and it develops as children grow and change.

Person factors and rich learning environments

Child characteristics considered most significant for their potential to influence future development are called 'active behavioural dispositions'. These dispositions can be classified as 'developmentally generative' (such as curiosity, a tendency to engage in activity, responsiveness to initiatives, etc.) or 'developmentally disruptive' (such as distractibility or readiness to resort to aggression). Dispositions are very closely linked to the learning opportunities, affordances and constraints available within a learning environment. Reflecting Bronfenbrenner's emphasis on the ongoing interaction between the child's characteristics and those of the people and objects within the learning environment, Carr highlights that "learning dispositions tend to notice, take up, modify, and are modified by affordances and constraints across learning environments and activities" (2004, p. 6).

Children's dispositions are environmentally sensitive. They are acquired, supported or weakened by interactive experiences in an environment with significant adults and peers (Bertram and Pascal, 2002). Significant adults obviously include practitioners in early years settings. For example, in Reggio Emilia-inspired schools, practitioners purposely integrate materials from nature into activities. An ordinary tree branch can become the core for cooperative ribbon weaving, and this sort of activity is an invitation to children's dispositions, such as cooperation, creativity, problem-solving and inventiveness.

An interesting study of learning dispositions and the role of mutual engagement in early years settings examined relationships between learning dispositions and what is termed 'learning architecture' (Duncan *et al.*, 2008). This research explored how children's dispositions 'travel' between the various settings and activities the children participate in, such as home, their early years setting and then later in school. The authors argue that dispositions can be described as "attunement to [the] constraints and affordances" (2008, p. 108) in any given setting. Furthermore, dispositions can be seen to "reside in the reciprocal and responsive relationships between children and other people, places and things, or in participation in activities of various kinds" (Carr, 2004, p. 6). Reflecting bioecological theory, Carr emphasises that dispositions are both shaped by and shape the interactions that children have with others – people, places and things. An extract from Duncan *et al.*'s study (the vignette involving David) provides a good illustration of Bronfenbrenner's construction of development as an interactive process between the child and the learning environment.

David attended his early childhood centre one day a week. He had been going to the early childhood centre for two to three years on a part-time basis. The centre was licensed for 25 children aged two and a half and over.

[. . .] A house was being built a few doors down from the centre and, on this particular morning, a concrete mixer had arrived to pour the floor. The building process had been watched very closely by the children at the centre over a number of weeks and so very quickly the decision was made to all go down and have a closer look – but not too close – at what was happening. David was very interested in the concrete mixing. . . . He described to the teacher the use of 'cement' and water in the making of concrete and demonstrated prior knowledge of the whole process.

Back at the centre, David says to his friend, "I'm going to start making concrete. Do you want to help me start making concrete?" His friend agrees and they run off to the sandpit. David obviously has a very clear objective in mind as he starts to dig a hole and then look around for some water. He says:

> You go and get the normal buckets and I'll pour it in then I'll come back over. I'm making concrete. Could you get me water . . .?

The teacher helps them organize the water and then move things around in the sandpit to give them more room. Over the next few minutes more children start to join in the activity and soon concrete making takes over the whole sandpit.

During all the digging and mixing with water, another child makes a suggestion which David responds to immediately and which is followed up on by the teacher . . .:

Child 1:	You need some flour, but not real flour. [*Imitates, offers expertise*]
David:	Just pretend flour. [*Agrees*]
Teacher:	Pretend flour, what do you think the pretend flour would do? [*Extends*]
David:	Just make different colour. [*Responds*]
Teacher:	Oh, we could add some flour and see what happens to your texture, couldn't we? Should I get some? [*Offers to help*]
David:	Then get some, get some flour. Look out, I've got a mixture [*as another child blunders into his hole*]. [*Instructs, protects the task/agenda*]
Child 1:	We're going right down to the bottom, eh? [*Seeks clarification*]
David:	No, I'm not. We need just concrete mixture and don't put sand in the concrete mixture. [*Adds expertise, clarifies the task – not digging a hole – and protects the task/agenda*]
Child 1:	Na. [*Agrees*]
David:	She's going to get some concrete flour, I think. It's going to be fine, we don't need to dig. We don't need to dig. [*Reminds, reassures, instructs*]

At this stage the field observation notes read: "David is putting everything into mixing his concrete, he is using his whole body to mix it. His technique looks like he has watched/done this before."

Source: Duncan *et al.* (2008, p. 113)

Duncan *et al.* identify how the learning architecture in this situation supported David's interactions by drawing attention to the following features within the environment:

- *Time for interaction – mutual access by participants*: . . . children were invited to decide for themselves if they wanted to stay or do other things. Thus, David was not kept from his desired objective – mixing concrete – for a long period of time. . . .
- *Joint tasks and activities – negotiable enterprises with common meaning*: Throughout the concrete-mixing episode, David interacted closely with the other children and adults. The teacher supported the children in their negotiations with each other in sharing the resources and ideas. Ideas expressed by other children were listened to and taken up. . . .
- *Opportunities for peripheral participation and multiple entry points*. Children came and went throughout the whole sandpit activity. Some [worked] on the edge of the activity; others were attracted by the action but then played their own games in the water trough that was being used. If others wanted to join in but were unsure of what to do, they were invited to ask David to help, and he did so very willingly. . . .
- *Tools and artefacts that support communicative competence*. . . . there was a big sandpit with a multitude of containers, shovels, tubing, pipes and water troughs – enough for everyone to have a turn. Again, negotiations with turn taking were necessary, and the [practitioner] modelled and suggested strategies for the children to use in order to achieve this.

(Duncan *et al.*, 2008, p. 115)

Drawing together some of the key messages from this observation and analysis of David's interactions and how they were supported by the learning environment, Duncan *et al.* (2008) suggest that through the success of his engagement in episodes such as this, David strengthened his dispositions of reciprocity, expecting tasks to be mutually meaningful to participants, and moving from the periphery to the centre of deep engagement. Earlier in this chapter, we explored the importance of a learning environment that creates an invitation to learn. This resonates with Wenger's (1998) notion of a 'community of practice' or perhaps in this case a community of learners:

> Children enter a community of practice, such as the early childhood centre or the new entrant classroom, and through their engagement in the various activities, with the people in the setting, and using the tools and resources available to them, they come to belong to that community of learners. The learning architecture of the educational setting can work either to support or inhibit this.
>
> (Duncan *et al.*, 2008, p. 115)

Consistent with bioecological theory, 'dispositions' evolve in a dynamic pattern through the power of process. A child's dispositions influence how he experiences the world and so influence the way in which the world responds, which affects the development of further dispositions, and so on.

Children have diverse needs and belong to different cultures and social groups, resulting in their participating differently in early years settings. Providing access to a wide range of learning opportunities and activities is a defining feature of rich learning environments, but it is also important that environments are open to all the person characteristics children bring with them. A welcoming learning environment invites and accommodates individual differences in abilities, skills and competencies. Rich learning environments reflect diversity in family types and differences in socio-economic class and culture. Early years settings allow children to actively construct images of themselves through interactions with people and materials in their immediate environments. There are many ways of reflecting the diversity of young children's lives – displaying children's artwork and reflecting the diversity of the world through a variety of toys, books, magazines, pictures and musical instruments. Drawing on what they see around them, children access essential information about who and what is important. Therefore, every effort should be made to create a setting that is rich in possibilities for exploring diversity (Robinson and Jones-Diaz, 2006). Creating a learning environment that respects diversity sets the scene for fostering children's positive self-concept and attitudes. Assisting children in developing positive ideas about themselves and others allows them to initiate conversations about differences and generates possibilities for them to compare, explore and become familiar with diverse beliefs, lifestyles and cultural contexts.

REFLECTION

In what ways can the planning and resourcing of early learning environments contribute to ensuring diversity and equality of opportunity in children's activities? What materials can be used to promote positive identities and attitudes to diversity? How can we empower children and foster feelings of confidence through careful design of early learning environments?

Rich learning environments also encompass features relevant to person characteristics, such as a child's age. Such environments support the abilities of children and include features to invite learning for very young babies and toddlers as well as children of preschool age. Some affordances within the learning environment for younger children include opportunities for gross and fine motor development; hand–eye coordination; language and communication development; emotional expression and social competence; imagination and creative skills (Bradford, 2012). During the first three years of life, children's brains are highly active, and brain development needs "affection, stimulation, and meaningful interaction – language, touch, eye contact, exploration, play" (Early Childhood Matters, 2013, p. 5). The profound importance of young babies' interactions with adults for developing language acquisition has been demonstrated in fascinating research in the field of developmental neuroscience, providing substantial evidence for the complex interaction of nature/nurture influences on human development (Kuhl, 2010).

Person characteristics also include gender, and children sometimes show different kinds of behaviour and make different choices in their play based on their gendered experiences. Being attentive to the different play areas and how they might be used differently by girls and boys can help to challenge some of the limitations caused by provision of gender-specific resources. For example, traditionally, the home play area is often characterised as being dominated by girls, while boys choose more risky outdoor play (Nutbrown and Clough, 2009). Girls may need support to extend their play activities beyond the home corner and to take risks outdoors, and boys may need help in negotiating their way to engage with and enjoy domestic play. Representing each child in the early years environment involves more than simply adding a range of diverse resources. Resources need to be discussed and explored with children, and practitioners should tune in to, listen to and observe how children are interacting with them.

An inclusive learning environment should, wherever possible, make the usual range of play and learning opportunities offered indoors and outdoors accessible to children with additional needs (Kernan, 2010), ensuring that they have freedom to explore, create, take risks, make choices, accept challenge and develop friendships (Sayeed and Guerin, 2000). Learning environments must be inviting for children with additional needs, providing a space where they are relaxed and valued, enhancing their opportunities to engage in, initiate and sustain play.

Context factors and rich learning environments

Bronfenbrenner is probably best known for highlighting the many and multilayered levels of influence on development associated with the different contexts in which children develop and learn. In this section, we reflect on some of these contextual influences with emphasis on the mesosystem (links across microsystems), the exosystem (more indirect environmental influences that have a profound influence on a child's development, even though that child is not directly involved with them) and the macrosystem (broader social and cultural influences). The final sphere of influence within bioecological theory is the chronosystem, which focuses on the influence of time.

In the second level of contextual influence on development, the mesosystem, Bronfenbrenner draws attention to interactions and interdependencies between the elements within the child's microsystems. There are many ways in which interactions within and across different microsystems operate to impact on the early learning environment. A particular focus in this chapter is on the possibilities for designing learning environments to maximise opportunities for bridging communication between children's home and early childhood education settings. A number of studies have identified the profound influence of children's home environment on their wellbeing in early years settings and more broadly. The Effective Provision of Pre-School Education (EPPE) study (Melhuish *et al.*, 2008; Sylva *et al.*, 2004) found that a home learning environment where parents were actively engaged in activities with children promoted intellectual and social development in children. Although parents' social class and levels of education were related to child outcomes, the quality of the home learning environment was more important. The importance of enhancing continuity and alignment between learning environments offered by the home and early years settings is emphasised in these research findings. Drawing attention to the notion of the malleability or fluidity between home and early years settings, Kernan talks of "softening the boundaries" (2015, p. 6) between these environments and reinforcing the connections between children's families and communities and the learning environments they inhabit.

Increasingly, the early care and education of babies, toddlers and young children is shared among parents, families and practitioners. By working together and sharing information, adults can help to facilitate access to valuable information contributing to more meaningful experiences for children in both home and early years settings. Another aspect of softening the boundaries between these settings is the practice, where possible, of home visits. Home visits are part of the mesosystem, promoting interaction between home and early years settings. They allow practitioners to learn more about the child's exosystem and macrosystem, especially regarding parents' occupations, family culture and parental attitudes and beliefs. This can provide important contextual information for enhancing children's learning and development.

REFLECTION

How can early years practitioners gather and exchange information with children's parents and families to improve the early learning environment? How can early years practitioners help parents to support their children's learning and development?

Bronfenbrenner also highlights the many contexts in which children are not directly involved but which significantly impact on their wellbeing and development. He called this level of influence the exosystem. A number of factors play a very significant role in shaping the design, layout and intention of early years settings and practice, though some of those involved in the design of the physical environment have little connection with the needs of the children they are designing spaces for. Lippman describes a "responsive approach" (2010, p. 1) to designing environments that asks: how does the environment shape the learner and, in turn, how does the learner influence the environment?

The designer can then create a learning environment that is more responsive to the needs of children and that is more aligned to the needs of twenty-first-century education. Policymakers, who play a significant role in influencing the quality of provision of early years practice, could also be considered as part of the exosystems that influence the development of rich learning environments. Policy design and decisions around early years practice do not happen in a vacuum but, rather, are ideologically and culturally specific, reflecting the social, political, cultural, economic and historical context in which they are derived (O'Donoghue Hynes and Hayes, 2011).

Learning environments are also culturally shaped and moulded. Attitudes to the design and development of learning environments are typically affected by the sociocultural values and beliefs that inform them. One example of this is how we perceive and construct indoor and outdoor learning environments. Early years settings are an important context for children's engagement in physically active play. The emphasis on outdoor play in Nordic countries has prompted early years practitioners in different cultural contexts to establish greater fluidity between indoor and outdoor learning environments. Fjortoft (2001) explored the relation-ship between environmental affordances and children's play and development, particularly outdoors; findings suggest that environmental complexity and diversity in nature are highly associated with increased play opportunities and activities.

Time factors and rich learning environments

We saw in Chapter 2 that within the bioecological model, time is conceptualised at three levels: microtime, mesotime, and macrotime (Bronfenbrenner and Morris, 2006). Microtime refers to what is happening during specific episodes of proximal processes. Mesotime refers to the extent to which processes occur in the person's environment, such as over the course of days, weeks or years. Macrotime refers to historical time and how proximal processess may be affected by the changing times in which development takes place.

One key feature of rich learning environments referred to throughout previous chapters is a calm, unhurried environment where children have space to interact with objects and people in their surroundings. The term microtime evokes this sense of attending to what is happening in the moment – the child's 'now' activities – rather than focusing on what might be the outcome of these activities. Rich learning environments informed by the concept of microtime emphasise opportunities for children to respond to the affordances present in their surroundings without limiting those opportunities by excessive structuring of the time available for exploration. The term microtime also evokes the *being* child rather than the *becoming* child – the child who is actively engaged in the present moment in the construction of their learning and experience of childhood. The term mesotime refers to broader intervals of time, over days and weeks, in which proximal processes can develop and become more complex, consistent with bioecological theory. A focus on the relevance of mesotime to early years learning prompts us to think about the central role of the practitioner in facilitating meaningful learning experiences through planning and the provision of rich learning opportunities over time. Time must be made available for planning rich learning experiences:

> Practising a nurturing pedagogy both challenges and permits practitioners to give time to planning for the 'soft' and messy aspects of early learning and to encourage playful interaction, exploration, dialogue and collaborative learning to encourage and support babies', toddlers' and young children's learning. The learning environment, and children's interaction with it, should be challenging and rich in both language and content. This can be either directly, in terms of the content of social interactions with an adult or advanced peer, or indirectly, through the carefully considered provision of materials, objects, activities and opportunities.
>
> (Hayes, 2007, p. 16)

REFLECTION

Work with a colleague to identify what you understand by the terms microtime and mesotime. Think about the ways in which you provide opportunities for children's learning and development to take place in an unhurried way. Identify some barriers to providing these opportunities for children in early years settings. How can early years practitioners play a central role in providing meaningful learning experiences through a focus on mesotime? Identify some barriers to providing these experiences in early years settings. How might we begin to overcome these barriers?

Macrotime refers to historical time and some of the changes in lifestyles, values and beliefs that accompany the passing of time from one generation to another. Many aspects of macrotime are relevant to early learning environments. However, one of the most significant fields of change, and one that impacts on all our lives, is the field of information technology. Developments in this field prompt examination of the roles of practitioners and children as they constitute wider societal influences that inform and shape learning environments. Changes in IT impact on children's learning and their lives, and they are often quick to embrace the possibilities for how we live and learn in the twenty-first century. Creating rich learning environments in the early years necessitates focusing on the potential impact of technology on methods of teaching, modes of learning and connections to societal and global contexts (Warger and Dobbin, 2009). The rate of change in this area and the extent of reach of this change requires early years practitioners to be alert, informed and ready to adapt.

Technology and its role in early years practice tends to generate tensions and fears around the risks and dangers that children may be exposed to through access to the internet and to technology more broadly. Some educators fear that technology in early years settings may threaten children's desire for active, physical exploration of their environments. Alternatively, technology has been welcomed in the early years as empowering children, and the use of new technologies is facilitated in positive and meaningful ways. Buckingham (2008) suggests that these two competing perspectives of concern and celebration are symptomatic of viewing children in a sentimental way, especially in Western society. He emphasises that new technologies in fact rely upon many of the forms and conventions of old technologies. However, he also notes that while much research refutes the idea that computer games, for example, are antisocial, very little is known about how children perceive, interpret and use new media.

The importance of connecting macro and micro perspectives, locating children's relationships with media within the texture of their daily lives while also understanding economic and political forces at stake, is foregrounded in these arguments. Current tensions between proponents of established forms of literacy like reading, writing and numeracy and proponents of new forms of literacy are very real (Drotner, 2008), and it is interesting to explore how these tensions may be resolved in future early learning environments. For the early years practitioner, it will be important to strike a balance between incorporating technological advances into settings while also ensuring high-quality social and interactive learning environments.

Implications for practice

In this chapter, we focused on the importance of creating a welcoming learning environment where children encounter invitations to learn in a space that not only provides them with a sense of security and belonging but also offers dynamic and stimulating opportunities for them to explore and discover new experiences and concepts. Guided by the PPCT structure, we explored the concept of rich learning environments through a focus on the process, person, context and time factors that may influence the development of such environments.

Key concepts for early years practice

1   *Rich early learning environments provide affordances for children's learning that invite and support complex reciprocal interactions* designed to capture children's interest and curiosity and to challenge them to explore and share their discoveries with others. Such environments can stimulate thinking, imagination and creativity, thereby enriching communication.

2   *A number of features contribute to rich learning experiences and support positive proximal processes within a learning environment.* These include designated interest areas providing opportunities for choice of activity and manipulative materials that are plentiful and accessible, and where there is a high level of child–material interaction. Children benefit from rich and stimulating play choices both outdoors and indoors.

3   *Flexibility in the designs of learning environments is an important consideration.* As children's interests change, possibilities for transforming their surroundings contribute significantly to extending learning experiences.

4   *By capturing children's interest and curiosity and reflecting these interests in both indoor and outdoor environments, practitioners play an important role in fostering and promoting positive learning dispositions in young children.* Through their interactions with other children, with adults, with materials and with concepts, children learn about the world and their place in it.

5   *Transforming the environment through interactions can occur to a greater extent where learning environments are rich in opportunities for children to become involved in their learning,* to be directive in their learning experiences, to have access to different contexts for learning and to have potential for increased responsibility.

6   *Through careful attention to and documentation of children's activities, we can identify the types and quality of children's play* and reflect these qualities in the learning environment through provision of props, toys and objects aligned to the differing interests of children.

7   *A rich learning environment is one that invites and accommodates individual differences in abilities, skills and competencies.* Rich learning environments reflect diversity in family types and differences across socio-economic class and culture.

8   *Creating rich learning environments focuses on the impact of time on learning experiences.* This influences micro and meso levels, where it is important to plan and provide for calm and extended periods for play and learning in early years settings. Influences may also be at the macro level where changing values, developing technology and societal expectations impact on educator and learner roles and modes of learning and discovery.

8

EARLY EDUCATION AS A DYNAMIC PROCESS

Introduction

Different theories of development illuminate different aspects of development with varying challenges for educational principles and practices. System models like Bronfenbrenner's have been criticised as being either too focused on context (Downes, 2014) or exhibiting a preoccupation with individualism and ignoring the power of interactions (Penn, 1997). However, Bronfenbrenner's model provides a comprehensive framework, allowing visualisation of the complex dynamics of development in different contexts incorporating social, cultural and temporal elements.

Although most well known for his nested systems model of human development, Bronfenbrenner's contribution to our understanding of the role of interactions and relationships in children's development is of particular significance. A feature of the final iteration of his model (Bronfenbrenner and Morris, 2006) is its focus on the role of the interactional, relational process. He defined the model as "an evolving theoretical system for the scientific study of human development over time" (Bronfenbrenner and Morris, 2006, p. 793). His theoretical system conceptualises the dynamics of development as the interplay between the four key elements of development: process, person, context and time (PPCT). Bronfenbrenner emphasises the importance of interactions between the individual and the social, spatial and temporal contexts. This construct of a dynamic and reciprocal relationship between individuals and their contexts is central to the pedagogy of early education. It foregrounds learning as a complex, dynamic and interactive process in which knowledge is created through transformation of experience (Hayes, 2013).

The construct of proximal processes and their role as engines of development is important. The quality of proximal processes is mediated by social interactions, and this provides a link between the structure and the processes of development, with implications for practice in the early years. This harmonises the view of the child as a biological reality – a 'structure' – and the view of the child as a participant in the environment – an 'agent'. Neither is sufficient in itself. The bioecological framework provides a model within which different educational approaches can be considered, drawing on a multi-theoretical perspective. Proximal processes have certain distinctive properties and depend on the activity of the developing person as well as the context. You will recall from Chapters 3 and 4 that proximal processes are more likely to lead to positive outcomes for children when they occur in sensitive, responsive and stable environments. Bronfenbrenner proposes that if early learning environments are chaotic or seriously disadvantaged, the presence and impact of high-quality proximal processes, parental and/or educational, might act as a protective feature. To be effective, proximal processes must occur on a regular basis over an extended period of time. Activities must continue long enough to become increasingly more complex; mere repetition does not work. Equally, developmentally effective proximal processes are not unidirectional; they are bidirectional, interchanging between the givers and receivers. In interpersonal interactions, this means that initiatives do not come from one side only; there must be reciprocity of exchange between, for instance, the adult and the child. The child or adult can initiate the interaction and should be allowed time and space to do so. Finally, proximal processes are not limited to interactions with people, but can involve interactions with objects and symbols. Children respond to and act upon the environments surrounding them, and so they alter these environments. For effective reciprocal interactions to occur, the objects and symbols in the immediate environment must be of a kind that invite attention, exploration, manipulation, elaboration and imagination.

Adults have a profound impact on the learning experiences of children. Research tells us that effective practitioners reflect on their practice and quality of provision for young children in order to create experiences in early years settings that are affirming for all involved. The contemporary view of children as active agents in learning and development requires practitioners to understand that even very young children contribute to their own development. This is not to underestimate the vulnerability of the child or the very powerful protective role of the adult. It does, however, challenge adults to reconsider the child as competent, to reflect on practice and to recognise the diverse nature of each child when planning early care and education, designing learning environments and providing learning opportunities. It also provides a context within which children can be valued for their own sake in the present, the here and now. Focusing on the present moment allows development of meaningful engagement and extended learning. The present moment, microtime within Bronfenbrenner's chronosystem, is that moment-to-moment connection where sustained shared thinking (Siraj-Blatchford, 2009) can occur – where the adult sets the scene for children's engagement with the world.

In this chapter, Bronfenbrenner's emphasis on development as a dynamic process is explored with reference to a pedagogy of early years practice that values the present moment for its immediate developmental contribution while also acknowledging its potential in respect of later development.

Considering development and learning

Katz and Chard (1994) introduce the reader to two aspects of development: the normative and the dynamic. They note that, traditionally, early years practice has drawn heavily on psychological research, studying the child in isolation from everyday life. Such studies focus on normative development, providing us with a general descriptive guide of what children at particular ages can be expected to achieve and how they can be expected to behave; such descriptions are often called milestones. While useful as general points of reference, developmental milestones can become problematic if we depend on them to guide early years practice with groups of young children. Features of normative development fail to take account of the diversity of individual children and the importance of context. Each child presents with different capabilities, interests and experiences. Katz and Chard (1994) identify three interrelated dimensions of dynamic development:

1 developmental change over time with experience;
2 delayed impact of earlier experiences affecting later functioning;
3 long-term cumulative effects of repeated or frequent experiences.

This reminds us that children's early experiences have potential long-term consequences.

The idea of normative development has been particularly influential for curriculum development and practice in early education. In early years practice, for instance, we see the focus on normative development when we observe practitioners offering the same activity (e.g. making a snowman mobile using materials prepared by the adult) to all children for a particular length of time. While this might keep children busy, it shows limited understanding of the capabilities and interests of each individual child in the group and limits opportunities for them to imagine and create their own response to the idea of a snowman mobile.

The normative dimension of development addresses the question of what most children can and cannot do at a given age and draws on the work of Gesell in child study and Piaget in studies of cognitive development. The influence of consideration of development from a normative perspective alone is evident in the publication *Developmentally Appropriate Practice in Early Childhood Programmes* (Bredekamp and Copple, 1997). This presents a variety of early education materials and activities and identifies them as either 'appropriate' or 'inappropriate' for children at different ages and stages of their lives. The description (or prescription) of 'appropriate' here is closely tied to the contribution these materials and activities make to the development of the child towards operational thinking and conceptualises development as continuous progress toward adulthood.

The DAP approach to early years practice has been criticised (Dahlberg and Moss, 2005) because it suggests that all children develop in a predictable way. While this may appear to be the case over time, at an individual level, on a daily basis, things are far messier and more entangled. An overemphasis on milestones in early childhood results in less attention being given to the dynamic dimension and the opportunities for development that arise in children's day-to-day lives.

Research indicates that dynamic development matters most when considering young children's learning and the early years environment that is provided. 'Childish' behaviours should be regarded as adaptive to the period or situation and not presumed problematic or imperfect; rather, they are important responses to the particular 'niche' of childhood:

> The idea that a behaviour, such as play, has immediate rather than deferred benefits is consistent with the view that development is an adaptation to the specific demands of a niche, such as childhood. The important point to stress here is that behaviour may serve different functions at different periods of development.
>
> (Pellegrini and Bjorklund, 1998, p. 17)

Sometimes, there is continuity of behaviours over time; for instance, a physically active infant is likely to be active during her preschool and school years. However, there can also be a developmental link across time between two apparently dissimilar behaviours, and this is more difficult to track. For example, the ability to engage in make-believe play at age three is closely related to word reading at age five; thus, make-believe play can be seen as evidence of developing literacy skills (Pellegrini and Bjorklund, 1998). Make-believe play and word reading involve different response modes, but they are theoretically related in that they both involve manipulation of symbolic representation. The essence of 'being developmental' in practice challenges early years practitioners to value the moment for its immediate developmental contribution to the individual whilst acknowledging (but not over-emphasising) its potential for later developmental outcomes. Viewing development as a dynamic and discontinuous process allows one to view behaviour in early childhood as being adaptive to the demands of childhood.

Sensitivity to both the normative and dynamic dimensions of development is critical in early years practice. The distinction between what young children can do and what they should do is especially serious in the early years because most children appear willing, if not eager, to do what is asked of them. They are often willing to attempt to meet even the most unrealistic expectations when encouraged by important adults in their lives. Therefore, many authors (Pramling-Samuelsson and Asblond-Carlsson, 2008; Singer, 2015) caution against adult-led, prescriptive models of early years practice. Such approaches are geared towards the achievement of specific learning outcomes in, for instance, literacy or numeracy rather than attending to the process of how children become literate and numerate. Evidence suggests that it is more important to attend to the process of the present and the dynamics of individual development in everyday practice. During the early years, it seems that *how* children learn rather than *what* children learn matters most. Where early years practitioners are too concerned with what a child should be learning at a particular stage, not only may they miss the learning/teaching moments of everyday, but they may also act to inhibit the child's learning. Researchers have found that toddlers often blur the boundaries between play and not-play activities even though adults see a clear distinction. This can result in children experiencing confrontations and commands from adults with many comments like 'no, don't do that' and 'put that down' (Singer, 2015) where adults misinterpret adaptive processes of learning as misbehaviour.

Consider the behaviour of the children in the vignettes involving Ilinka, Eyad, and Annelise and Ruby. How does the environment facilitate interactions? Are the materials available to them contributing to their play? What role has the adult?

> Nine-month-old Ilinka is in a high chair being fed by early years practitioner Ella. Ilinka repeatedly puts her hands into the bowl of food, squashes it with her fists and throws it onto her tray, squealing each time it makes a noise – 'splat!' Ella is irritated because she needs to get Ilinka fed and the eating area cleaned up before it is time for 'messy play'.
>
> Source: author observation in an early childhood setting

> Ten-month-old Eyad is playing on the floor while his father cleans the house. He is very interested in a plant in the corner of the sitting room because it has a leaf that hangs down; Eyad likes hitting it to see it going back and forth. Every time he crawls over to it, his father lifts him away and says 'ah-ah, dirty, you'll spill the dirt all over yourself'. Eyad has lots of toys on the floor to play with, but he really wants that plant.
>
> Source: author observation

> Three-year-olds Annelise and Ruby are playing dress-up. They have discovered their childminder's make-up bag and decide that some lipstick would really make them look like princesses.
>
> Source: author observation

Interactions in development

Increasingly, we are coming to understand the powerful role that children themselves play in their own development. Bruner (1996) identifies the goals of adult–child interactions as joint problem-solving, intersubjectivity, warmth/responsiveness and promoting self-regulation. He argues that if pedagogy is to empower young children to achieve their potential, it must transmit the tools of the society in which they live. This includes helping children to explore their own way of thinking and problem-solving. One of the critical features of children's developing identity and self-esteem is the extent to which they exhibit agency or consider themselves to be in control of their own actions. Agency can be observed when children take the initiative in their behaviour, form opinions or structure their experiences. To assist such positive development, Bruner stresses the importance of intense interactions in language-rich environments, reflecting the proximal processes proposed by Bronfenbrenner.

The 'turn taking' or 'serve and return' relationships commonly seen in the interaction between very young children and adults in games like 'peek-a-boo' seem to have a critical role in development through their influence on brain development. Effective interactions are positive and occur on a regular basis over extended periods of time. Young children benefit most from relationships when they occur within stable, caring and interactive learning environments. As previously explored, the quality of interactions is closely related to the development of generative dispositions (Bronfenbrenner and Morris, 2006). What seems to be most important to effective early years practice is the quality of the relationships between children, adults and learning environments. It facilitates 'created understandings' that flow across the 'in-between' – the physical and psychological gap between people, particularly in interpersonal interactions. Engagement across this gap provides critical spaces for learning. Everyday interactions in everyday contexts can be enriching and we should not underestimate the power of the ordinary. Studies on intersubjectivity have promoted a more respectful pedagogy, seeing the child as an active participant in the learning process. Bidirectional, transformational interactions facilitate children in explaining their ideas to others, negotiating and clarifying their thinking. Collaborative learning between peers is particularly important in early childhood where collaborative opportunities in safe environments enhance children's opportunities to refine their cognitive and metacognitive (thinking about thinking) skills (Hayes, 2007).

The importance of relationships and interactions for development is highlighted by research showing the powerful role that social context plays in the lives of young children. Support for the notion of collaborative learning derives from a theoretical stance recognising the social nature of learning and the social construction of meaning. It is based on the belief that participation in shared activities plays a key role in development. Working on problems together is particularly valuable in assisting young children to explain their thinking, to make their reasoning about things visible, even if it may not always result in enhanced performance, particularly if the more competent peer lacks confidence (Rogoff, 1998).

Children's capacity for intersubjectivity has developmental value, enabling participation in joint attention whereby an expert adult and novice child work together and develop a shared understanding (Bruner, 1996). Today, terms such as sustained shared thinking (Siraj-Blatchford, 2009), dialogic teaching (Alexander, 2004), nurturing pedagogy (Hayes, 2007) and extended purposive conversations (French, 2014) are used to describe such joint activity, and these ideas are recognised as being central to educationally supportive adult–child interactions. Sustained shared thinking is an interaction that "involves an adult being aware of the child's interests and understandings, and involves the adult and the child interacting together to develop an idea or skill" (Siraj-Blatchford *et al.*, 2008, p. 29). It has been linked to improved cognitive outcomes for children and is recognised as one key element of high-quality early years practice. Practitioners who are sensitive, attuned and responsive to children's cues, applying a nurturing pedagogy, are better able to engage in sustained shared thinking, assess what assistance children need, if any, and ensure their responses are respectful of the child.

Sustained shared thinking underpins a range of techniques for education of young children, such as constructing understanding, philosophising and scaffolding their learning, amongst others (MacNaughton and Williams, 2009). This view recognises the young social child as being capable of reasoning, making sense of the world and using higher-order functions such as thinking about thinking, connecting ideas through reflection or "going meta" (Bruner, 1996, p. 57). The process of sustained shared thinking is valuable beyond the early years setting, offering a blueprint for interactions with peers, teachers and work colleagues: "[i]n terms of competence, progression goes from mastering the very informal and strongly improvised *sustained and shared* interactions to more highly structured and much more formal *sustained and shared* interactions in adult life" (Siraj-Blatchford, 2009, p. 81, emphasis her own).

REFLECTION

Taking a recent experience you have had with young children, reflect on opportunities for sustained shared thinking. In what way did you extend the moment through your practice? Were there other learning/teaching opportunities? How best might they have been exploited?

The extent of development that typically occurs in the first six years of a child's life is striking. They develop physically from being tiny babes in arms at birth, unable to move from one place to the next, to crawling, then toddling and on to the competent physical child we see at six years of age. Language development is also visible as a child changes from a being with a limited range of sounds (the cry, the laugh, the coo) to a two-year-old making sentences to a six-year-old with a vocabulary of anything from 1,500 to 5,000 words or more. We see the influence of good food, exercise and language opportunities in the children we know and those we work with. What is less visible and even more amazing is the development of the brain; brain research notes "the extent to which the intervention between genetics and early experience creates either a sturdy or weak foundation for all learning, behaviour and health that follows" (National Scientific Council on the Developing Child, 2007, p. 3).

Thus, current research supports Bronfenbrenner's contention that proximal processes are the engines of development. It confirms that it is not simply the opportunity for interactions but also the *nature* and *quality* of the interactive process itself that is important. Research particularly highlights the value of dynamic, bidirectional social interactions as being crucial to early development. Early years programmes with a strong emphasis, both curricular (content) and pedagogical (practice), on the nurturing of affective development and support for social and emotional learning positively influence children's overall development, including their academic cognitive development. Good-quality social relationships are central to the positive wellbeing of both adults and children in early years settings. Positive learning environments provide secure relationships to facilitate children's exploration, play and learning. This is as true for the child of five months of age as it is for the child of five years. Practitioners who provide for these learning opportunities rather than focusing too closely on the development of academic skills are supporting the development of the fundamental, foundational aspects of learning. Positive and supportive adult–child interactions enhance children's security to explore and experience connectedness to peers and are important to wellbeing and flourishing as well as to the development of literacy and numeracy dispositions and skills. Blakemore and Frith highlight the danger of introducing academic training too early, noting that "there is no biological necessity to rush to start formal teaching earlier and earlier. Rather, late starts might be considered as perfectly in time with natural brain and cognitive development" (2005, p. 460).

Good-quality early years practice with children requires the attention of the adult *in context* to the whole child *in context*, highlighting the importance of being present in the now and not thinking of what you will be doing once the activity is over. Working professionally in the early years means being willing to recognise that there is always something more to learn about child development, learning environments and practice in general. A reflective practitioner monitors their practice and questions it: Why am I doing this? Why is this of value to the child, the group, my colleagues, parents, the community? A questioning approach to practice is key in sustaining quality. It challenges practitioners to evaluate the quality and relevance of early years practice to children. It is through asking and answering the 'why' questions that practitioners begin to consolidate a shared understanding and language of early years practice.

REFLECTION

Busy practitioners often find themselves planning for the next activity rather than fully attending to the activity they are engaged in or the child with whom they are engaged. Do you recognise this tendency in yourself? What can you do to help remind yourself to be present with children in the moment in spite of the pressures of a busy working life?

In reflecting on why early years experiences are so important to a child's development, research findings from a range of disciplines including developmental psychology, education and neuroscience are relevant, highlighting the connectedness between various experiences of young children in different developmental domains such as the physical, linguistic, cognitive, emotional and social. The cumulative knowledge of decades of research has contributed to a greater understanding of development in the early years and supports the complexity of development captured by Bronfenbrenner in his dynamic model of human development. The National Scientific Council on the Developing Child (2007) argue that research into early brain development confirms the importance of early life experiences and their impact on the basic architecture of the brain. They present evidence that brains are built up over time, beginning before birth and continuing into adulthood:

> Scientists now know a major ingredient in this developmental process is the "serve and return" relationship between children and their parents and other caregivers in the family or community. Young children naturally reach out for interaction through babbling, facial expressions, and gestures, and adults respond with the same kind of vocalising and gesturing back at them. In the absence of such responses—or if the responses are unreliable or inappropriate —the brain's architecture does not form as expected, which can lead to disparities in learning and behavior.
>
> (National Scientific Council on the Developing
> Child, 2007, pp. 1–2)

Infants particularly benefit from the undivided, uninterrupted attention of adults. A key ingredient in the process of brain development is the quality of early relationships between children and their parents and other significant adults. From the start, even very young children, infants, are equipped with the skills necessary to initiate and maintain communication. Reflect on the way in which Cillian, the baby in the vignette, is the central active component in the interactions, first engaging his two sisters and then his parents until all family members are participating in an activity which he initiated.

Ten-month-old Cillian is sitting on his mother's knee. The family are tired after a day out and are resting. Cillian, his mother and his sister Katie (seven) are watching television. His sister Saidbhín (three) is playing a game on the computer, and his father is tidying up. Cillian notices a strand of Katie's hair hanging down, reaches out and pulls it. Katie laughs, tickles Cillian's tummy and says, "You cheeky monkey, did you pull my hair?" Cillian giggles, and because Katie likes the sound, she tickles him again. Saidbhín moves away from the computer and joins her brother and sister in the fun. Soon the attention of the whole family is on Cillian's giggles, and instead of their solitary pursuits, they are all laughing together with the baby at the centre of their interactions.

Source: author observation

Responsive adults reply in kind with vocalisations and gestures of their own, and children then reward such adult attention by responding, smiling or mimicking behaviour, such as sticking out the tongue. This is why it is so important for adults working with children to give their full attention to them and not become distracted by, for example, checking their mobile phones.

We have long known that children who grow up in depleted environments such as some institutional settings or chaotic and impoverished homes show signs of developmental delay from very early on. We now know that this is, in part, because of the absence of close, stable relationships – the proximal processes described by Bronfenbrenner. Considering the brain as a 'social brain' strengthens our understanding of the importance of interactions and relationships to brain development. This may be a useful concept for those working directly with young children as it provides a clear link between the environment (the space, materials, people, time) and the learning, developing child. We also know that the brain is most flexible in early years and, therefore, more responsive to a range of environmental and interactional influences. As the child grows, this flexibility diminishes and it is more difficult to change existing brain circuitry. Take language development for instance. In the first months of life, the baby responds to a wide range of sounds and begins to differentiate and specialise in those sounds she is exposed to. At the same time as this discrimination and specialisation is happening, the brain is already starting to lose the sounds of other languages. "Although the 'windows' for language learning and other skills remain open, these brain circuits become increasingly difficult to alter over time" (National Scientific Council on the Developing Child, 2007, p. 2). For a rich example of the linguistic power of young babies, you may like to access the TED talk given by Patricia Kuhl (2010, October) entitled *The Linguistic Genius of Babies*.

In summary:

- *Brains are built over time from the bottom up*: early experiences strongly influence development of a child's brain architecture and this, in turn, can influence the strength or weakness of the foundation for future learning, development and behaviour.
- *The interactive influences of genes and experience shape the developing brain*: interactions are central to this developing architecture. The active agent of influence is the turn taking, 'serve and return' nature of interactive relationships. It is important therefore that adults are attuned and responsive to signals

from children. Young children need positive relationships, rich learning opportunities and safe environments in their early years settings.

- *The brain's capacity for change decreases with age*: the brain is most responsive to change during the early years, and so this is a crucial period. However, we still have a great deal more to learn about the brain, how it develops and what role the environment plays.
- *Cognitive, emotional and social capacities are inextricably intertwined throughout the life course*: as research grows, so too does our understanding of the complex, interrelated and dynamic nature of development. From a practice point of view, we need to be aware that everything we do with and for children may have an impact, so we need to be alert and present in our practice.
- *Toxic stress damages effective brain architecture, leading to lifelong problems in learning, behaviour and physical and mental health*: we know that children who grow up in poverty or in chaotic households need a great deal of support directly and indirectly to overcome the stresses they are living with. However, we must also recognise that while early years settings can provide a nurturing, safe and secure space for young children and a protective context within which they can develop and learn, such settings are only one of a number of supports that may be needed for children (National Scientific Council on the Developing Child, 2007).

Brain research has confirmed that the brain is complex and interconnected; social, emotional and cognitive (or thinking) capacities are intertwined. Positive early experiences contribute to wellbeing and the development of social skills. Both wellbeing and social competence contribute to a child's sense of self-confidence, which in turn contributes to learning and cognitive development. "The emotional and physical health, social skills and cognitive-linguistic capacities that emerge in the early years are all important prerequisites for success in school and later in the workplace and community" (National Scientific Council on the Developing Child, 2007, p. 5). The evidence also indicates that stress associated with poverty, neglect, abuse or poor parenting can compromise the positive brain development so essential to later achievement and success. In such cases, high-quality early years settings can counteract – to some extent – the impact of negative stressors and set the child on a more positive developmental path. This happens not only through direct impact on children but also indirectly through influences on parents and the home learning environment (Melhuish, 2014).

The basic principles of neuroscience indicate that early preventive intervention produces more favorable outcomes than remediation later in life. Supportive relationships and positive learning experiences begin at home and are also provided in high-quality early years settings. Babies and young children require secure, caring, interactive relationships with adults for healthy brain development. For babies and young children experiencing poverty, abuse or stress, additional specialised and supportive interventions may be needed to address, insofar as possible, the cause of stress and protect the child from its consequences. Bronfenbrenner (1985), writing about policy and the future of childhood, emphasises the need to counteract hectic or chaotic life experiences young children may have through the provision and support of good-quality early years services.

Thus, it is clear that the early years of children's lives are crucial to brain development, in turn influencing the trajectory of overall development and learning. Supportive relationships and positive learning experiences are key, and the role of early years practitioners cannot be overstated. Through good-quality practice, early years practitioners can provide learning environments that stimulate and challenge children and give them a sense of wellbeing and belonging within which they can explore, play, learn, develop and strive to reach their full potential.

Of course, there is a distinction between the brain and the mind. While the terms are often used interchangeably, there is a difference; the brain is a physical, observable organ, whereas the mind is a philosophical concept. The mind manifests in our thoughts and words and is unlocked within the social world. We are born into relationships and created through relationships. Our physical brain develops within our own individual skull but: "a mind only exists within a network. It is the result of inter-actions between brains, and it is important not to confuse brains with minds" (Brooks, 2011, p. 43). Although we know more about how relationships and interactions affect the architecture of the brain, we are still a long way from understanding how the brain actually works in the manifestation of mind and behaviour.

REFLECTION

Identify five key activities conducted within your early years setting on a daily basis, from play experience, care opportunities and social situations. Consider the role of social interactions in the value of these activities for education and development. How could you create further opportunities for social interaction and learning within these everyday activities?

Developing executive functions

Child development is a complex process involving the interrelationship between genes, the brain, the body, behaviour and the physical and social environment. The brain is only partially mature at birth and continues to develop over the first years of life. Why are proximal processes so important to development, and what is it about positive brain development that influences an individual's learning? For optimal development, babies and young children require calm, caring, interactive relationships, and healthy brain development depends on, and enables, complex social interactions. The quality of early experiences can determine how sturdy or fragile the foundations are for learning and behaviour over time.

The skills necessary to control and coordinate information, critical to success in life in general and school success in particular, are developed in the early years and provide the foundation for later learning and development. These skills are called the 'executive functions' and we use them to manage behaviour, emotions and attention (Diamond, 2013). 'Executive function' describes the set of mental processes that help us organise and order our actions; this involves both concrete behaviours and abstract concepts. Children who have good executive function and self-regulation do better both academically and socially. The development of executive function depends on the biological maturity of the child, but the process is heavily influenced by environmental experiences. Through their early learning experiences, children access opportunities to develop these functions, and the adults in their lives are of critical importance in facilitating this. These more recent understandings of the link between brain development and the experiences of children reflect Bronfenbrenner's bioecological argument that persons and environment, in and over time, work together to influence learning and development.

Different authors characterise the elements of executive function in different ways, but they generally include: (i) working memory and recall, (ii) activation, arousal and effort, (iii) mental flexibility and (iv) self-control (Diamond, 2013). According to Bronfenbrenner, the extent to which individuals develop these skills depends on the dynamic and quality of proximal processes and the influence of (and on) the person characteristics of the child – that is, their dispositions, resources and demand characteristics. We look more closely at these four elements below:

- *A working memory and recall* involve problem-solving, reasoning and planning. Through our working memory, we make sense of things over time. It requires that we hold in mind what has happened and relate it to what is happening now. It assists recall. In the HighScope model of early education, this is foregrounded through the *plan/do/review* process. Adults respond to children, give them time to talk about their ideas and plans, allow them space to actively explore their environment, create opportunities for them to review their plans and encourage their thinking and recall. Working memory is also necessary to connect ideas, to link what you have done, heard or read with what you are doing, hearing or reading right now, and to remember instructions and carry them out in the correct order. Additionally, our working memory helps us to understand cause and effect.
- *Activation, arousal and effort* refer to the child's willingness and ability to start something, to pay attention to the activity and to put in the effort necessary to complete it. Such skills only develop where the child is comfortable, secure and has a sense of belonging. Providing children with opportunities, materials, time and space to make choices in their activities while facilitating them in thinking about what they are doing is a key role for the early years practitioner – it is the essence of high-quality early childhood education and care.
- *Mental flexibility* includes being able to switch perspectives, to see things in a new light, to see opportunities and take advantage of them and to be willing

to change course if what you are doing is not working. This flexibility of mind allows people to think outside the box and be creative. It also helps us understand things from another person's viewpoint.

• *Self-control* is crucial to successful learning and development. It allows us to stay focused, avoid distraction, stay on task and limit impulsive behaviour. Where children are impulsive, they are less likely to persist at an activity or to pay attention, and this can lead to later difficulties in school and in adulthood. Moffitt *et al.* (2011) found that self-control, as measured by parents, teachers and self-report ratings during the first ten years of life, predicted physical and mental health, employment, financial security, substance use and criminal conviction (or lack of) in adulthood. Children with good self-control were less likely drop out of school, to smoke or to become teenage parents. Other studies have also linked settings where early years practitioners encouraged the development of self-control and self-regulation to later school success (Blair, 2002). Apart from these later impacts, children who have self-control are more likely to have enjoyable and satisfying everyday experiences; their childhoods are more likely to be happy and content than fractured and stressful (Hayes, 2013).

We know that development progresses through feedback loops. The messages we get back from the environment (social, cultural or material) inform the view we have of ourselves, which then influences the extent to which we see ourselves as masterful or helpless, trusted or mistrusted. Poor executive function can lead to troublesome behaviour, whereas good executive function leads to greater cooperation, caring and responsiveness in children. Through observation, adults can see executive function at work in children's play when they are talking themselves through an activity as they move objects around or place things in a particular order. Understanding the power of process and the *dynamic* dimension of individual development helps foreground interactions as a central aspect of development over time. It also highlights the complexity of development as there can be a developmental link between two dissimilar behaviours. Earlier in this chapter, we noted that children's make-believe play at three is related to word reading at five. So we see how important free pretend play is in any literacy strategy – even though pretend play rarely looks like reading!

Implications for practice

Viewing development as a dynamic and discontinuous process allows us to view behaviour and development in early childhood as being adaptive to the immediate demands of the child in context. This approach to early education is not tied to the age and stage of development of the child but, rather, to the sociocultural context of development for the child in the present. It is exemplified by the internationally recognised practices at Reggio Emila in Italy and the *Te Whāriki* early years curriculum of New Zealand in which pedagogy is directed by the connections, interactions and relationships between children and the wider world and by social, physical and emotional elements as opposed to any prescribed expectations of developmental outcome. There is increasing evidence from psychological research and neuroscience to support Bronfenbrenner's contention that proximal processes are crucial engines of development. Evidence also suggests that these interactive processes are particularly important in early childhood given the role of interactions in facilitating development of thinking skills (cognitive and metacognitive) and affective skills (dispositions); that is, their role in developing knowledge and skills, knowledge about knowledge and the inclination and readiness to apply knowledge.

Key concepts for early years practice

1   A feature of the final iteration of the bioecological model is its *focus on the role of the interactional, relational process in driving development.*

2   *The quality of proximal processes is mediated by social interactions* and provides a link between the structure (or biology) of development and the processes of development. It harmonises the view of the child as a biological reality and an 'agent', neither being sufficient in and of itself. This has implications for early educational practice.

3   Adults have a profound impact on the learning experiences of children. *Effective early years practitioners reflect on their practice and the quality of provision for young children* to create experiences in early years settings that are positive and affirming for all involved, children and adult alike.

4   *Sensitivity to both the normative and dynamic dimensions of development is critical in the early years.* The essence of 'being developmental' challenges early years practitioners to value the moment for its immediate developmental contribution to the individual whilst acknowledging (but not overemphasising) its potential in respect of the child's later development.

5   *Children's capacity for intersubjectivity has developmental value* as it enables them to participate in episodes of joint attention where an expert adult and novice child work together on a task and develop shared understanding (Bruner, 1996). Today, terms such as sustained shared thinking (Siraj-Blatchford, 2009), dialogic teaching (Alexander, 2004), nurturing pedagogy (Hayes, 2007) and extended purposive conversations (French, 2014) are used to describe such joint activity.

6   *A key ingredient in the process of brain development is the quality of early relationships* between children and their parents and other significant adults. Babies and young children require secure, caring, interactive relationships with adults for healthy brain development.

7   *Early preventive intervention produces more favorable outcomes than remediation later in life.* Supportive relationships and positive learning experiences begin at home and are also provided in high-quality early years environments.

8   The skills necessary to control and coordinate information, critical to success in life in general and school success in particular, are developed in the early years

and provide the foundation for later learning and development. These skills are called the *'executive functions' – the functions we use to manage behaviour, emotions and attention.*

9 *Children with good executive function and self-regulation do better both academically and socially.* Poor executive function can lead to troublesome behavior, whilst good executive function leads to greater cooperation, caring and responsiveness in children.

10 Understanding the power of process and the *dynamic* dimension of individual development helps foreground *interactions as a central aspect of changes in development over time.*

9

NURTURING CHILDREN'S LEARNING AND DEVELOPMENT

According to Rosa and Tudge, it "is easy to argue that persons and environments are mutually implicated in human development, but it is more difficult to explain how that functions" (2013, p. 255). In this chapter, we use the bioecological model to consider high-quality early years practice and the central role of early years practitioners in nurturing children's learning and development.

Concentrating more on dynamic development than on normative expectations highlights practices most beneficial to individual children at particular moments within particular contexts. Viewing development as a dynamic and discontinuous process facilitates a pedagogy attuned to the connections, interactions and relationships between children and the wider world while being sensitive to social, physical and emotional learning opportunities (Hayes, 2013). This particularly resonates in settings including children from diverse backgrounds who may be experiencing learning environments that do not reflect the expectations or experiences of their culture or family. This illustrates the multiple microsystems influencing development. To grasp why certain early years practices are more successful than others in facilitating children to achieve positive outcomes, researchers and practitioners seek to understand the mechanisms of development and learning. This is particularly important where investments are made to support early education as an intervention to counteract educational disadvantage.

The bioecological model introduces the new domain of process into the microsystems of development, emphasising the distinctive contribution of proximal processes to development – those close interactions that individuals have with other people, materials and ideas that occur in day-to-day life (Bronfenbrenner and Morris, 2006). For young children, the opportunity to experience and participate in these interactions is facilitated in calm, unhurried environments where adults are attuned to children's need for time and encouragement. Bronfenbrenner and Morris recognise the negative influences of limiting contexts, increasingly present in the lives of contemporary children, with "growing hecticness, instability and chaos in the principal settings in which human competence and character are shaped – in the family, child-care arrangements, school, peer groups and neighbourhoods" (1998, p. 995).

The potential of proximal processes for combatting such negative impacts has important implications for the early years, highlighting the power of interactions and the role of adults. Nurturing children's learning as part of a caring educative process requires adults to develop skills of observation and reflection, allowing for non-intrusive planning and provision of learning environments that support and extend children's learning and opportunities for good-quality interactions. To those outside early education, including parents, the complexity involved in early years practice may not be immediately obvious. There is a continuing tendency to underestimate the educative role of caring and the importance of high-quality early education to children's happiness and well-being (Wood, 2014). Hayes (2008), writing about the contested concept of care, proposes that there is a need for a significant shift towards explicit acknowledgement of the critical contribution of the interpersonal and relational aspects of early education.

Emphasising the often misunderstood educative role of care, Hayes (2008) argues for the reconceptualising of care as nurture so that its status as an educative dimension be enhanced. She introduces the concept of a 'nurturing pedagogy', recognising the educative role of care as nurture, the importance of relationships and the role of playful interaction, exploration, dialogue and collaborative learning in supporting young children's learning. Pedagogy provides a unique integration space for care and education and is, itself, a form of assessment and a guide to an emergent and responsive early years curriculum. Characterising good-quality early years practice as a nurturing pedagogy moves understanding of practice beyond simply minding children and watching them play. The role of the adult is one of low intervention and high response, conveying a more powerful level of interaction and requiring the early years practitioner to have specific skills, actively nourishing and educating the child. Effective, learning environments of a good quality are stimulating and challenging, risk-rich, respectful and reflective. The pedagogical process is relational, responsive and reciprocal, reflecting the importance of proximal processes as the engines of development, particularly in the early years.

Skills of observation and reflection are central to a nurturing pedagogy. They enhance practice and planning, are manifest in well-managed and yet reasonably flexible practice, and assist in providing learning environments that include children as active agents, supporting and extending learning. This allows for attention to the quality of interactions between children and the social, spatial and material learning environment. It also allows for planning by the adult for future opportunities to extend learning, taking the child, rather than prescribed curricular content, as central. Furthermore, reflective observation encourages movement away from traditional organisational/management roles, strengthening the educational, pedagogical role of the adult. Relationships and interactions are central to a nurturing pedagogy. There is a rich tapestry of relations across different microsystems, facilitated by enhanced communication and rich mesosystems, between children themselves, between adults and children, between adults and their colleagues and parents of the children they work with, and between learners and the environments where learning takes place. Interactions are the critical spaces for learning individually and in groups. To create a significant shift to understanding the educative role of care in practice, it is necessary to explicitly acknowledge the critical contribution of this interpersonal aspect of early education, to make it visible, to realise it as the practice of the everyday interactions, the proximal processes.

A nurturing pedagogy is a different style of practice to that many of us have experienced in our own education. It demands that adults let go of some traditional ideas about the educational relationship between adult and child where the adult was the source of knowledge and children were expected to passively receive this knowledge. Good-quality early years practice relies less on a content-led curriculum and direct instruction and more on a framework of values and principles, respecting the process underpinning an emergent or enquiry-based curriculum. An emergent curriculum is one that grows from the shared experiences of all participants in a learning environment. It is influenced by the layout and routines of the setting, the activities and materials available and the intentions of adults. It is also influenced by children's own background experiences, their dispositions and their individual characteristics, as discussed in Chapter 4. Thus, the content of curriculum derives from daily interactions with others and playful, meaningful interactions with materials, objects, symbols and ideas (Hedges, 2014). Many authors recognise the value of such a pedagogical approach, acknowledging that it "incorporates children's cultural practices, meanings and purposes" (Wood, 2013, p. 72).

In such interactive and integrated settings, children come to develop working theories about the world – material, social, physical and emotional. Children thereby make connections between everyday things and actions, forming the basis of knowledge relevant to different discipline areas – almost unaware that they are doing so (Fleer, 2010). It is the skill of an excellent adult that they can identify and exploit learning moments and draw children's attention to them or work in partnership with children to extend oral language and expression while enriching their knowledge base. Through reflecting on and engaging with children's working theories as they explore, play and create, the attuned early years practitioner can unlock curriculum content and expand children's knowledge and understandings.

A few four-year-olds were sitting together. Three of the children were wearing trainers that would light up when they stepped down on them.

Teacher:	Wow! Look at your shoes! That is so cool. They light up when you step down.
Child 1:	Yes, they do this. [Jumps up and down several times]
Teacher:	How does that happen? How does it light up?

Child 1:	Because they are new.
Teacher:	Um. Mine are new too but they don't light up.
Child 2:	No, because they light up when you step down on them [Steps down hard several times]
Teacher:	[Steps down hard several times] That's funny. Mine don't light up when I step down.
Child 3:	No, no, no, you have to have these holes. [Points to the holes]
Teacher:	[Pointing to the hole in her own shoe] But I have holes and mine still don't light up, and Josh has holes in his trainers too and his do not light up either. I wonder why?
Child 4:	I think you need batteries to make them work. [Thinks for a while] But I did not see batteries when I put my toes in.
Child 4:	I think they are under your toes.
Child 2:	I can't feel the batteries under my toes.
Teacher:	I wonder how we can find out about this?

Source: with thanks to the 'collector', Lilian Katz

Try to identify the key pedagogical moment in this vignette when the teacher moves the conversation about trainers into an educational conversation, extending the children's thinking. What moment do you select and why? Does she redirect the conversation or build on the children's contributions? (See note 1 for feedback on this task).[1]

Engaging children, respecting them and integrating learning opportunities across time and across the care and educational dimensions is central to effective practice. Traditionally, children were seen as adults-in-waiting, expected to be quiet in the presence of adults and the responsibility of their parents or guardians. Chapter 6 explored how our current understanding recognises children as full individuals with rights who should be consulted in matters affecting them. This image of children reflects many contemporary writings on the philosophy of education, including that underpinning Reggio Emilia. Using a rights-based lens to inform early years practice allows us to recognise children as being competent, strong, active and participatory, and as meaning-makers and fellow citizens. This approach to practice builds on the individual capabilities and dispositions of the child within the social context and emphasises close interactions, proximal processes, between children and their early learning environments, driving development and learning. Our understanding of early child development can guide us towards prioritising relationships and interactions over direct instruction as the cornerstone of early educational practice. Reflecting on practice thus provides a common language for discussing the central features that make early years practice unique and which are evident when observing skilled practitioners at work.

Respecting children as having rights makes demands on adults. It requires that adults trust children and empathise with them, which in turn requires understanding of children's cultural and developmental contexts. Manifesting trust in children translates in practice to providing, through nurturing environments, opportunities for them to recognise their own achievements and space for them to problem-solve and resolve conflicts. Throughout childhood, children experience disappointment, frustration, failure and disapproval. They may also experience exclusion by peers. In healthy development within supportive relationships, children recover from these experiences. When children, even very young children, learn through experience that their feelings and concerns will be appreciated and understood, their emotions become less urgent. In the security of predictability, children learn to regulate their emotions, confident that their feelings will be heard.

Children's curiosity and desire for knowledge and understanding is evident in their play, exploration, questions and behaviour. Young children need adults who trust that when provided with the opportunities, time and support, children will learn – adults who are excited, inspired and challenged by them. However, adults also need to set clear boundaries with rules that are sensible, understandable and consistent. Rules should not be extensive but, rather, few, fair and clearly explained; indeed, they are often most effective when developed with children themselves. Where the child is at the centre of early years practice, the day-to-day curriculum reflects this; adults actively include children in the regular experiences of the setting, engage with them and learn from them while also enhancing their learning opportunities. This approach to practice is informed by a belief in the dynamic nature of child development and reflects a shift away from more traditional didactic practice to more integrated, social and interactive approaches.

High expectations are also important; children learn best when we 'expect' them to succeed (Galinsky, 2010). High expectations enhance children's motivation, self-belief and resilience, whereas low expectations undermine self-confidence and compromise self-belief. Children who develop strong self-esteem, motivation and a sense of agency are more likely to achieve their potential at school and be resilient to risk factors throughout their education. Expectations that are high assist children to achieve a growth mindset rather than one that is fixed (Dweck, 2007). Mindsets refer to beliefs we have about ourselves and our abilities. In a growth mindset, children recognise that their abilities and talents can be developed by persistence and hard work, and they enjoy solving problems; in a fixed mindset, however, where children cannot succeed at a task, they see themselves as the problem. The role of adults is crucial here as self-image develops through feedback. Adults can create learning opportunities that enhance the development of a growth mindset and provide attractive and challenging opportunities for children. Where attuned to children, early years practitioners can extend learning moments created when the child needs a nudge to surmount a challenge.

Within the bioecological model, the processes mediating developmental pathways are influenced not only by the child's own interactions but also by features within the interacting individual, such as his beliefs and opinions. For high expectations to have meaningful effect, early years practitioners must believe that every child is capable of learning, take responsibility for encouraging learning and communicate their belief to the child and also to parents. This requires that they consider multiple ways of learning, value children's strengths and differences and use these in assessment and planning. They must find new ways to reflect on best practice and should employ a curriculum based on strengths and interests, allowing each child to experience success at his own level (Saffigna *et al.*, 2011). This means explicitly creating situations that build up children's resource characteristics so that they will be able to say, and believe, "I can".

Sustaining good-quality learning environments

While process and person(s) are key elements of development, so too is context – the early learning microsystem, including its activities, materials, relationships and roles. The quality of everyday experiences in early years environments has a profound influence on them. Young children are not merely recipients or consumers of a service but are deeply influenced, individually and collectively, by their early years experiences. Children learn in context; the ordinary spaces, places and people they encounter make up that context. Adults who are attuned, 'watchfully attentive' and mindful in their day-to-day practices with children can make important contributions to learning and development. There is no need to distance children from society in an effort to enhance their learning and development. Indeed, creating active and effective links between early years settings and other important environments in the lives and communities of young children (strengthening the mesosystem), carefully managing the various transitions they make, is an important dimension in quality early years practice. Early years practice is the curriculum made visible – even where the curriculum may not be readily definable.

Consider the dynamics in the vignette concerning the European Together Old and Young project. How might you create opportunities for children to link with community-based services? How can you create opportunities for cross-generational connections?

> We witnessed many examples of seniors teaching skills and sharing their hobbies in the initiatives studied: seniors introducing children to local history through examining artefacts or seniors teaching children gardening, food production and cooking skills. The destruction of the piazza, the traditional meeting and play space for all generations in Poggio Picenze, Italy and the heart of the town, prompted the instigation of a programme whereby old people passed on the collective cultural memory of the town [to young children] by demonstrating traditional crafts and telling stories from the past.
> Source: the European Together Old and Young project
> (The TOY Project Consortium, 2013, p. 18)

Exploring understandings of how early years practices impact on children's learning and development can act as a stimulus for reflection on the quality of provision for young children so that experiences in early years settings will be affirming for all involved. The adult, and their style of engagement, seems to have a significant impact on the learning experiences of children. The Australian Early Years Learning Framework introduced the idea of 'intentional teaching', which is thoughtful, informed and deliberate and "is the opposite to teaching by rote or continuing with traditions because things have always been done that way" (Commonwealth of Australia, 2009, p. 15). Intentional teaching must be consciously developed. It "requires wide-ranging knowledge about how children typically develop and learn . . . a repertoire of instructional strategies" (Epstein, 2007, p. 1). Furthermore, teachers must know when and how to use these strategies to benefit individual children in different content contexts. The intentional teacher is not only aware of the importance of proximal processes but also knows how to maximise the possibilities of those interactions. We must consider the rich and diverse nature of each child when planning early care and education, designing learning environments and providing learning opportunities. The adult sets the scene for engagement with the world and provides contexts within which children can be seen and valued for their own sake in the here and now. The contemporary view of children as active agents in their learning requires practitioners to respond to the reality that even the very youngest children contribute to the context and content of their own development. This is not to underestimate the dependence of the child or the very powerful, protective role of the adult. The earliest playful interactions are context specific and require supporting, intimate relationships (Parker-Rees, 2014).

The vignette involving Tony and Salima illustrates how early years practitioners can create opportunities for children to solve problems themselves and experience success. Report on two situations from your own practice where such opportunities were present.

Preschoolers Tony and Salima are sitting on the floor, playing with the acorns Salima collected outside. Salima divides the acorns evenly between them. Their teacher sits on the floor next to them. Tony piles his acorns together, while Salima forms a large circle with hers. Tony says, "Hey, you got more than me!" Salima responds, "No, I don't. We each got the same." The teacher wonders aloud how they could find out whether they have the same number, and the children suggest counting the acorns.

Tony: 1, 2, 3, 4, 5, 6, 7, 8, 9, 10, 11, 12, 13, 14. (He lines up his acorns in a row as he counts.)

Salima: 1, 2, 3, 4, 5, 6, 7, 8, 9, 10, 11, 12, 13, 14. (She also lines up her acorns in a row.)

Teacher:	You each have 14.
Tony:	Yeah. We got the same.
Teacher:	(Spreads Tony's acorns across the floor and puts Salima's in a pile.) Now who has more?
Tony:	(Smiles.) I do!
Salima:	No, you don't. We each got the same. See? (She counts her acorns and puts them in a row, then counts Tony's acorns and puts them in a row as well.)
Teacher:	(This time she puts Tony's in a pile and spreads Salima's out across the floor.) Now who has more?
Tony:	(Thinks for a moment.) Nobody's got more. We got the same!

Source: adapted from Epstein (2007)

How we consider the child in relation to the world impacts on how inclusive we are in our planning and practice. Our own history and experiences of learning – even (or perhaps especially) if we are largely unthinking about them – inform and influence our practice in ways that are not always useful. Fleer (2003) has written about the unintended constraints brought to our work by assuming a shared understanding of commonly used terms, references or constructs. She argues that we need to give more attention to our 'taken-for-granted', consider how it can impose on our practice and challenge it in order to enhance our day-to-day practice. To sustain good-quality pedagogy, it is important to adopt criticality in approaching language and take time to consider the assumptions we make. Unless we are willing to challenge, explore and reflect on our own assumptions, we may never really provide children with the rich learning environments they need. In her work, Fleer (2003) identifies four tacit assumptions that influence early years practice and are often thoughtlessly accepted rather than critically reflected upon. These assumptions have significant impacts on how we create and sustain learning environments and, thus, influence children's development and learning.

The first assumption relates to how we position the child – do we see the child as part of the wider world or essentially as part of the early years setting? How we view the child, discussed in Chapter 3 when considering the work of Carl Rogers, has important implications for early years planning and practice. Fleer suggests that practitioners should reflect on environmental organisation in early years settings and question it. Are we placing restrictions on children, limiting learning opportunities by creating 'corners' that we consider an essential element of the early years experience for those attending? Should we give children more freedom to circulate and choose their learning spaces and materials, placing less emphasis on these corners? Should we present a broader range of materials with a wider selection of objects representing more of what is ordinary and familiar to children?

The second assumption she considers relates to our view of children as learners – do we consider children as actively constructing knowledge or do they learn from being told? The meaning of 'active' needs careful consideration here. It is not simply about physical activity alone; it includes being actively engaged in whatever is happening, active listening and careful, active observation – from such focused behaviour children may expand what they are doing. Early years practitioners are models for learning here, showing rather than telling, listening actively to children. Understanding children's active engagement allows us to see where and how we might provide them with challenge and work with them.

The third assumption identified by Fleer relates to balance between the individual and the social orientation, the child alone or in a group. While it is important to understand the child as an individual, especially his particular learning style and needs, it is also important to recognise the child as a learner within a group. While individual development and learning are important, we know that children are social beings, social learners, that while they are independent they are also interdependent. Children like to be with other children, sharing knowledge and so extending it. They enjoy succeeding in groups, and there they learn how to cope with failure too (Kernan and Singer, 2011). As adults, we understand the value of working as a team. It is similar for even very young children, and so we should plan for both the individual developing child and for the interdependent child.

Finally, Fleer challenges us to question the assumptions underpinning how we consider communication and conversation. Children are embedded in the social world and are active in their communication through various verbal and non-verbal processes. Do we see both child and adult as partners together in learning or separate from each other with the adult in the powerful position? While there is of course inequity between the child and the far more experienced adult, this should not negate the value of considering children as partners and working to manifest this. The process of distancing children, of treating them as a separate 'other', is well embedded in Western society, and so there is a need for explicit consideration and for creating occasions, spaces and time for meaningful communication or what Fleer (2003) calls "conversational opportunities". Carefully planned child-friendly environments facilitate social and collaborative learning. Real communication, that is meaningful, between adults and children (and children and children) is not simple; it takes thoughtful planning and goes beyond reading stories or asking questions. Limiting conversation and dialogue to a question-and-answer style of communication is insufficient and also disrespectful to children. It runs contrary to the inclusive and respectful early years pedagogy that underlies a democratic approach to practice, which equips children with important developmental proficiency (Mitchell, 2011).

We referred earlier to the fact that children come to early years settings with "funds of knowledge" (Hedges, 2014). Similarly, we need to recognise what early years practitioners bring to their practice with regards to the taken-for-granted.

REFLECTION

Think about the four tacit assumptions that Fleer identifies. What might they mean to your practice in light of some recent example you can bring to mind? Discuss this with a colleague to identify if there is room for change.

Increasingly, families share the early care and education of their children with different types of early years settings. These settings are part of society and have links with other educational, social and cultural settings in local communities. They provide an important bridge for children and parents alike, from the seclusion of home through the early years setting and into the local community and wider society. Therefore, early years settings provide a particularly important connective or networking service for all families but particularly for minority or marginalised parents and their children. While the direct role of the practitioner is often characterised by their work with children attending their settings, it is important to recognise the indirect role they play, within the mesosystem, in creating these links. This becomes particularly important in supporting the home learning environment, which has a significant impact on the development of children (Siraj and Mayo, 2014). While encouraging close engagement with families is valuable and can sometimes lead to improvements in home learning environments, this is an issue to be handled with great cultural sensitivity and in real partnership with parents who are the experts of experience regarding their own children (Gaylor and Spiker, 2012).

Children are motivated to learn, to seek meaning in their world, and they depend on the adults they meet to assist them in this endeavour. It is within immediate, day-to-day experiences that children learn about the world around them; the ordinary things in their lives are often new and curious and have the potential to be extraordinary, to act as the foundation for new knowledge and understandings. Children have a right to expect that early childhood settings will challenge and excite them, provide safety and security, and enhance their overall development and learning. The adult can contribute by making experiences of the ordinary rich and meaningful through careful observation and reflection to inform their practice. Informed and attuned adults can expand children's language and thinking, fire curiosity, imagination and creativity, and extend skills through encouraging mastery and positive learning dispositions.

Children bring these funds of knowledge to and from different learning environments. Such knowledge is situated in children's everyday environments and provides a link across home learning and early years settings for both children and adults (Wood, 2013). Funds of knowledge are akin to the resource characteristics Bronfenbrenner identified as contributing to development, and they also echo Rogoff's (2003) idea that culture is embodied within us in terms of our beliefs, influencing the very way in which we approach making sense of the world. Adults can make these ordinary experiences rich and meaningful for children through tapping into their curiosity.

The importance of play

Bronfenbrenner wrote extensively about the important role of the child in his own development and about the centrality of proximal processes in particular. However, his writings focused mainly on the importance of interpersonal proximal processes, giving few examples of the developmental influence of individual interactions with materials, objects and symbols. It is in play that we see the power of this type of interaction in action. When exploring and playing, children make discoveries about the world and their place in it. Early years practitioners resource play in intentional ways to ensure that children encounter positive learning experiences rich in content, challenge and risk and in which learning is consolidated. Play is recognised as a key process through which children extend their learning and development during early childhood:

> [P]lay is about creating a world in which, for that moment, children are in control and can seek out uncertainty in order to triumph over it – or, if not, no matter, it is only a game . . . it is primarily behaviour for its own sake, for the pleasure and joy of being able to do it. Yet play is more than mere indulgence; it is essential to children's health and wellbeing.
>
> (Lester and Russell, 2010, p. x)

However, play suffers from being simultaneously over-referenced in early education yet poorly understood. It is often characterised as unimportant, trivial and lacking in serious purpose, especially when compared to work. Wood (2013) notes the ambiguous position of play in educational discourse, which is dominated by an outcomes agenda, particularly given that the outcomes of play are often not visible and certainly not measureable. Wood argues that "there is a general mistrust of play in educational contexts" (2003, p. 42) and reminds us that contemporary discourse on play in early childhood reflects little understanding of its powerful role in learning and development. Play continues to be seen as preparatory to the real learning that will occur when children transition to school. The distinction does a disservice to the important role of play in early years practice. In fact, play "is one of the highest achievements of the human species, alongside language, culture and technology" (Whitebread *et al.*, 2012, p. 3).

While children are, from birth, biologically equipped to play, they need sensitive adults to guide them through their frustrations and share in their satisfactions (Bruce, 2001). Generally, children are curious and interested in the world, and through play they become competent and confident learners, prepared to take risks and challenge themselves to learn more. However, children growing up in poverty or in stressful situations may be deprived of ordinary opportunities for play; here, the role of high-quality early years practitioners becomes more important and influential. Effective play is promoted and nurtured by adults who provide high-quality learning environments, objects, activities, time and encouragement. Through play, young children explore, create, imagine, experiment, manipulate, negotiate, problem-solve and consolidate their understandings. Play provides a safe 'magic circle' (Huizinga, 1950) within which they can struggle, strive and succeed; it is the space that allows them to explore feeling, to test their fears and find their own language of expression; it is through play that they come to experience the nature of materials, such as water and sand, and begin to explore the foundations of science and mathematics. Wood (2013) cautions against being too simplistic in considering play. Not everything children choose to do is play, and children can step in and out of play. We may consider children's activities in early years settings as following a continuum from pure play through to non-play (Broadhead, 2010).

While adults prepare environments to encourage play, there are times when it may also be appropriate for them to participate in play. Participating in play with children can provide valuable opportunities for early years practitioners to elaborate a particular theme through guidance or the introduction of new themes or new materials. Care needs to be taken, however; participating in play is most successful where practitioners are invited into a play situation and respect the direction of children in order to avoid intruding or interrupting the flow.

According to Lester and Russell (2007), common characteristics of play include being:

- based on a sense of free will and control, either individually or within the group;
- motivated for its own sake rather than any external reward;
- pleasurable and positively valued;
- flexible and adaptive, using objects and rules in a variety of changing ways;
- non-literal, 'as if' behaviour – it can rearrange or turn the world upside down;
- unpredictable, spontaneous, innovative and creative.

A long-standing challenge has been identifying more precisely what children learn through play and how that learning occurs. With careful support from attuned adults, children move through play from simplistic, sometimes magical, understandings of the world towards greater mastery of scientific concepts. Self-regulating functions fostered through play include working through ideas, surmounting obstacles, problem-solving and managing intense emotion. These facilitate careful, observant and scientific exploration of the world and objects therein. Play scenarios require children to devise and follow social rules. In enacting 'bedtime', 'school', or 'a rocket launch', children learn to overcome their immediate impulses and increasingly understand and commit to the rules of social life. Pretend play and role play provide particularly rich contexts through which children can develop self-regulation skills and socially responsible behaviour. Through playing with substitute objects in imaginary situations, children become adept at distinguishing symbols from real-life objects and better able to use words, gestures and other symbols as tools for controlling reality, including managing their own behaviour and attending to others. Pretend play is a rich context for learning to resolve differences of opinion, interact cooperatively and solve social problems while also facilitating curiosity, interrogation and scientific reasoning.

Play makes major contributions to developing regulation of emotion, building strong attachments and peer friendships, engendering positive feelings and enabling children to cope with stressful situations. Play also helps build resilience – the capacity for children to thrive despite adversity and stress in their lives. But not all play is positive. Young children's play can reinforce social and cultural divides and power inequalities, for example, through teasing, bullying, unkindness and isolating games. There are a number of reasons why children may be excluded or isolated by other children – gender, social class, ethnicity, disability, etc. (Grieshaber and McArdle, 2014). With support from adults who demonstrate inclusive values, children learn about playing fairly and how to build relationships within diverse groups.

Play also has a role in developing spatial reasoning or cognition, the type of reasoning used to judge where things are in relation to other things. Spatial reasoning is applied when making decisions about crossing a road or placing a kick for a goal, but it is also critical for more complex behaviours, such as reading and interpreting maps and graphs. The development of spatial reasoning contributes to children's mathematical ability, and the level of spatial skills children have may predict those who pursue STEM (Science, Technology, Maths and Engineering) careers (Newcombe et al., 2013). Through careful observation of play-based opportunities, adults can help children develop their spatial reasoning skills; for instance, in block play, giving children spatial language such as "show me the piece with the curved edge", or through encouraging children to draw simple maps from one place to another. Hiding things and giving directions for children to follow – 'over', 'under', 'up' and 'down' – encourages the development of spatial reasoning. We should also ensure that there are books and other materials available that use the images and language of space.

Children's play reveals their thinking to an observant adult whose guidance can support them in engaging with the forms of knowledge valued in the curriculum and society. Adult support for play allows children to develop new conceptual networks. Through observing play, adults can also see children's executive function at work when they talk themselves through an activity as they move objects around or place things in a particular order. The vignette involving Gabrielle is an illustration of a young child at play. If you follow closely, you will see the different elements of executive function in action and the early years practitioners' role in extending the opportunities presented.

At planning time, Gabrielle says, "I'm going to play with the doggies and Magnatiles in the toy area. I'm making a tall elevator." At work time, Gabrielle builds with the magnetic tiles while playing with the small toy dogs, as she planned. She stacks the tiles on top of one another in a tower-like form—her "elevator"—then places some dogs in it. The elevator then falls over. She repeats this several times but the elevator continues to fall over. Gabrielle then arranges the magnetic tiles into squares, connecting them to form a row. Gabrielle says to Shannon, her teacher, "I'm making doghouses because the elevator keeps falling down." Shannon says, "I was wondering what you were building, because you planned to make a tall elevator going up vertically, and now you are using them to make doghouses in a long horizontal row. You solved the problem by changing the way you were building." Gabrielle uses pretend talk while moving the dogs around. At one point she says, "Mommy, Mommy, we are hungry" and opens one of the doghouses and moves the dog inside where a bigger dog is placed. Gabrielle says, "Mommy says the food's not ready, so go play."

While moving the dogs around, Gabrielle says to herself out loud, "We have to find something to do until the food is ready." Gabrielle says to Shannon, "Let's pretend we are going to the park." Shannon agrees and says, "I'm going to slide down the slide three times and then jump off the climber." As Shannon pretends to do this with one of the dogs, Gabrielle watches then copies her and says, "My dog jumped higher than yours." She then says, "Mommy says we have to go home now. We need to move our dogs over there so they can eat." The pretend play continues.

At recall time, Gabrielle is using a scarf to hide some objects she played with. When it is her turn to recall, she gives clues about what is under the scarf. She shows the group a couple of magnetic tiles and dogs. Shannon asks her what she did with these materials during work time. Gabrielle talks about the problem with the falling "elevator" and then recounts the story about the doggies.

Lockhart (2010, pp. 1–2)

With the careful intervention of Shannon, the early years practitioner, Gabrielle was made aware of the fact that she had solved a problem. Later she was given the opportunity to see planning in action when Shannon talked through her plans for sliding on the slide. Finally we see Gabrielle being given the opportunity to recall and share her activity with others. Where playful everyday experiences are available in well-designed and interactive early years settings, children have the time, encouragement and context within which to develop the dispositions and skills necessary to function competently and effectively at their own level. The presence of observant, attuned and engaged practitioners enriches experiences, strengthening learning and development.

The design, organisation and resourcing of the early years setting is central to practice and the early learning process. Settings, both indoor and outdoor, should be safe whilst also providing rich and varied opportunities for exploration, play and risk-taking. However, while the planning and organisation of settings is important to early years practice, it is insufficient. Settings meeting the static requirements of quality may not be effective in enhancing children's learning and development. It is the process, what actually happens on a day-to-day basis, that is at the heart of good-quality early years practice. The most effective practice is found in settings with well-trained, well-informed staff, familiar with child development and subject material, who recognise and respond to the dynamic and individual nature of development in the early years and who can work with an emerging curriculum driven by the interests and experiences of children and the opportunities afforded by the environment (OECD, 2006). Curriculum frameworks such as *Te Whāriki* (Ministry of Education, New Zealand, 1996), Aistear (NCCA, 2009) and the Victorian Early Years Learning and Development Framework (Marbina *et al.*, 2011) provide a rich basis for effective practice. Cultivating positive learning dispositions in children leads to positive outcomes in social, linguistic and cognitive development and the skills necessary for later school success. It is a holistic, adaptive and, ultimately, more effective approach to early education. The process of good-quality practice is nurturing, dynamic and interactive, reflecting the dynamic and interactive nature of learning and development. Such a complex nurturing pedagogy requires that practitioners are responsive and reflective throughout both their planning for and their engagement with children.

Implications for practice

Implicit in good practice is a commitment to democratic principles that recognises the need to respect and engage meaningfully with children. This identifies early years settings as sites of democratic practice where children and adults can participate collectively in interpreting experiences and shaping decisions affecting children's own development and the nature of the context within which development occurs. Changing early years practice to meet this new vision is not an easy task. It requires ongoing practice, learning and reflection.

Key concepts for early years practice

1   Viewing *development as a dynamic* and discontinuous process facilitates a pedagogy attuned to the connections, interactions and relationships between children and the wider world while being sensitive to social, physical and emotional learning opportunities.
2   There is a continuing tendency to underestimate the *educative role of caring*. The concept of a *nurturing pedagogy* recognises the educative role of care as nurture, the importance of relationships and the role of playful interaction, exploration, dialogue and collaborative learning in supporting young children's learning.
3   Skills of *observation and reflection* are central to a nurturing pedagogy. They enhance practice and planning, are manifest in well-managed and yet reasonably

flexible practice, and assist in the provision of learning environments that include children as active agents.

4 Good-quality early years practice relies less on a content-led curriculum and direct instruction and more on *early years frameworks* of values and principles, respecting the process underpinning an emergent or enquiry-based curriculum.

5 An *emergent curriculum* arises out of the shared experiences of all participants in a learning environment. It is influenced by the layout and routines of the setting, the activities and materials available and the intentions of adults. It is also influenced by children's own background experiences and their dispositions and individual characteristics.

6 Using a *rights-based lens* to inform early years practice allows us to recognise children as being competent, strong, active and participatory, and as meaning-makers and fellow citizens.

7 When children, even very young children, learn through experience that their *feelings and concerns will be appreciated and understood*, their emotions become less urgent.

8 *High expectations* are important for positive development in young children. Children learn best when we 'expect' them to succeed.

9 *Mindsets* refer to the beliefs we have about ourselves and our abilities; in a growth mindset, children recognise that their abilities and talents can be developed; in a fixed mindset, however, children see themselves as the problem.

10 Creating *active and effective links* between early years settings and other important environments in the lives and communities of young children strengthens the mesosystem.

11 *Intentional teaching* is thoughtful, informed and deliberate and is a key dimension of an effective nurturing pedagogy.

12 Pay attention to the *tacit assumptions* unthinkingly brought to our practice.

13 *Play* suffers from being simultaneously over-referenced yet poorly understood.

14 Children's *play reveals their thinking* to an observant adult whose guidance can support engagement with the forms of knowledge valued in the curriculum and society.

15 *The most effective practice is found in settings with well-trained, well-informed staff, familiar with child development and subject material*, who recognise and respond to the dynamic and individual nature of development in the early years and who can work with an emerging curriculum driven by the interests and experiences of children and the opportunities afforded by the environment.

Note

1 The key pedagogical moment is when the teacher says – "Um. Mine are new too . . .", moving the focus beyond the specific and providing the opportunity to expand the discussion beyond the immediately observable.

10

REFLECTING THE BIOECOLOGICAL IN EARLY YEARS PRACTICE

Introduction

Bronfenbrenner developed his bioecological model to illustrate the complexity of human development within contemporary society. He was driven by a belief that we need to consider how society impacts on children and families and to present some solutions to improve the position of children in a world that he saw as increasingly challenging. He was an academic but also a scholar-activist, or public intellectual, using his scholarship to highlight social problems and influence policy solutions (Piven, 2010). It is through his advocacy work that the bioecological model of human development contributed to improved understandings of the factors that influence inequality and poverty and impact on human development. In his writings and his presentations, he provided possible mechanisms for enhancing quality of life, including contributing to the early years initiative Head Start. Throughout his life, Bronfenbrenner had a profound influence, nationally and internationally, on policy, practice and research across many disciplines.

In Chapter 2, we explored how Bronfenbrenner's bioecological model of human development provides a focus on the nested layers of influence which impact children's learning and development. We outlined how the model evolved over time to provide a greater emphasis on proximal processes, the close interactions which take place on a regular basis and over extended periods of time. We also reflected on the integrated nature of dynamic development, influenced by process, person, context and time (PPCT), and the implications for early years learning and development.

Ecological systems as nested and networked

As we have seen throughout the preceding chapters, one of the key strengths of Bronfenbrenner's bioecological model is that it helps us understand the complexity of a child's development. Specifically, the model reflects the interdependence of influencing factors and the multilayered levels at which these influences may operate, from the direct, proximal and immediate influences within the microsystem, such as family and school interactions, to more distant and less immediate influences, the exosysetm and macrosystem, in which the child may not participate directly. However, theorists have suggested recently that this 'nested' image may not adequately capture the precise relationship of the systems to one another and may, in fact, serve to obscure the relationship between these systems. One of the key arguments put forward by Neal and Neal (2013), for instance, is that in conceptualising systems as being nested within each other, we are placing emphasis on the importance of context or setting rather than focusing on the importance of interactions and relationships. They suggest that ecological systems or influences would be more accurately conceptualised as being 'networked', a term they suggest better reflects the way systems at different levels relate to one another in an overlapping rather than a nested manner.

Neal and Neal (2013) highlight key arguments in favour of re-envisioning Bronfenbrenner's model as being networked rather than nested. First, the illustration of the bioecological model of human development as a set of concentric circles tends to portray human development as being influenced concurrently by different settings, both immediate and more remote from the child. Such a portrayal of these systems suggests that each layer is a subset of the layer in which it is embedded. For example, the microsystem, which might involve the relationship and inter-actions between a child and parents, is represented as a subset of the mesosystem, which could involve the relationship between the child's parent and a teacher. However, it does not make sense to say that the child–parent relationship is a subset of the parent–teacher relationship, although it may well be influenced by it to a greater or lesser extent. No one system is a subset of another; rather, they all comprise the wider context within which humans develop. It enhances our practice in the early years to take account of the various systems impacting on our lives and the lives of the children and families we work with.

Second, placing greater emphasis on networked systems of influence foregrounds the actual patterns of social interactions within the child's life rather than presup-posing that these interactions will take place. In this way, we are foregrounding the processes of interaction that occur rather than the contexts in which they arise. As we have outlined in previous chapters and particularly in Chapter 8, early learning is a dynamic process. A greater emphasis on networks of interactions in Bronfenbrenner's bioecological model would generate the sense of a model that is more dynamic in nature, where each system is defined in terms of the social relationships surrounding the child. Let's take an illustration of how this might work in practice. A child may develop a close and trusting relationship with an early years practitioner within the microsystem of her early years setting. This relationship evolves over time, supported and fostered by interactions between the dispositions of the child and those of the practitioner with whom she is working closely. The relationship is also undoubtedly influenced by more distal influences and less visible influences beyond the microsystem, about which the early years practitioner may have little information and which may be difficult to determine. With another child, a positive, trusting relationship may develop with an early years practitioner, but in this case the quality of these interactions reflects a close and positive relationship between the child's parent and this early years practitioner in the mesosytem. The precise and quite distinct pathways to the quality of the relationship between practitioner and each of these children is to some extent obscured if we see both relationships as nested within the mesosytem. By placing more emphasis on the network of influences operating to build close and trusting interactions between children and adults working alongside them, we can identify more clearly the precise points of contact within these interactions, thus facilitating greater insight into the factors influencing children's development.

Neal and Neal (2013) show that if we perceive ecological systems as a series of settings that intersect and overlap to varying degrees, as the networked model does, we can ensure greater fluidity by not rigidly specifying that each system is wholly nested within the next. Such a perspective also facilitates a portrayal of the relationships between different systems that more closely mirrors reality, which is less static and predictable but, rather, characterised as dynamic and fluid when viewed "through the lens of a network of social interactions" (Neal and Neal, 2013, p. 726).

While considering the representation of the bioecological model as either a series of nested systems or a network of systems may seem somewhat disconnected from the day-to-day reality of early years practice, it is in fact quite an important consideration. In the decisions we make when working with children, individually or collectively, we are shaped by our awareness of the variety of interacting factors influencing those decisions. Being able to visualise as well as articulate the wide variety of influences and their various impacts on different elements of the systems within which we develop enriches the way we work with young children and their families.

Transformation versus reproduction

Some practitioners who read the work of Bronfenbrenner may become quite pessimistic about their ability to support the young children with whom they work. They may become overwhelmed by the idea of multiple influences on a child's development and wonder, with all that is out of their control, whether they can ever impact on the course a child's life will take. When early years practitioners feel this way, there is a danger that they will disengage from their responsibility to support children and avoid doing anything too novel or innovative because it is safer to just do what is always done. As classic work in psychology, such as that of Milgram[1] (1963) and Zimbardo[2] (1971), has shown, it may be that the default position of human beings is to go along with the status quo, regardless of moral or ethical concerns regarding institutional practice. In such circumstances, individual accountability gets lost within the totality of the system, and nobody is responsible for systems failure. As a result, the adults most responsible for protecting children and ensuring their wellbeing could fail to meet those responsibilities through a sense that either 'nothing can be done' or 'it's not my job to do it'. Certainly, systems tend to be slow to change, and Downes (2014) argues that systems can inculcate the mentality that 'it must be done this way because this is how it has always been done'. Downes calls this 'system blockage', and sociologists such as Pierre Bourdieu refer to the resulting outcomes as 'reproduction'.

However, the interpretation of Bronfenbrenner's systems model presented in this book is far more optimistic. Drawing on the emphasis on 'proximal processes' in the most recent versions of the bioecological model, we see that relationships matter in combatting such outcomes as system blockage and simple reproduction of the familiar. Chapter 3 showed how the bioecological model provides a framework within which to consider a variety of different theories, focusing on different aspects of development collectively. Within this framework, it is possible to draw linkages between, for instance, the concept of proximal processes and attachment theory and the humanist psychology of Carl Rogers, thus enhancing our understanding of the broad dynamic of human development. Relationships present a potential antidote to system blockage; if children are living 'linked lives' (Bronfenbrenner), 'securely attached' (Bowlby/Ainsworth) through strong 'proximal processes' (Bronfenbrenner) with the adults that populate systems, then the 'capacity' of both adults and children for positive action should be activated (Rogers). To put it simply, if the adults in a child's life are involved in caring, mutually supportive relationships with her, then they are more likely to be empowered to overcome the inertia inherent in systems blockage and act in the child's best interest, regardless of institutional norms. Equally, if children are on the receiving end of caring, mutually supportive relationships, they are more likely to be empowered to object when they experience unjust practices.

It may be that relationships have the power to overcome inertia and systems blockage, acting as a catalyst for change, even in difficult circumstances. To use bioecological terminology, in the most up-to-date versions of the model (Bronfenbrenner and Morris, 1998, 2006), 'process' is emphasised more than 'context'. In this way the adults who care most about children, including their parents and their early years practitioners, can work together through strong connections in the 'mesosystem' to ensure that early educational experiences provide the foundation for children's future academic, social and emotional well-being. The educational philosopher Paulo Freire refers to the changes this can lead to as 'transformation'. This belief in the transformative potential of education for profound change can begin with the provision and support for high-quality early years practice, something early years practitioners have to fight for in societies where mainstream education is privileged in terms of funding and status.

When we use the concept of proximal processes to make sense of other important psychological theories, it becomes obvious that relationships are vital for children's development emotionally, socially and cognitively, and building good relationships should be a central area of concern for early years practice. The analysis in Chapter 3 focused largely on process, but the bioecological model emphasises that such vital relationships are informed and shaped by the person characteristics of the children and adults involved, the context in which they take place and the time (both the time in the person's life and historically) in which those relationships are embedded. The bioecological model shows us that relationships do not happen in a vacuum and 'processes' are impacted by the 'person', 'context' and 'time' factors with which they interact.

Focusing on context, we saw in Chapter 4 and in Chapter 7 that Bronfenbrenner identified features of an optimally structured environment, or context, for child development, including the provision of "objects and environments that invite manipulation and exploration" (Bronfenbrenner and Morris, 2006, p. 815). As well as providing materials and planning learning environments, early years practitioners also have an important role in creating stability and consistency within settings, avoiding chaotic contexts, while at the same time maintaining a measure of flexibility to respond to individual needs. Supporting strong contact and mutual support between microsystems (e.g. home and school or different educational levels) through the concept of the mesosystem is also important.

According to the most up-to-date iteration of the model, strong proximal processes provide a buffer in less than ideal contexts. In fact, Bronfenbrenner draws on the work of Rutter (see Rutter, 1985; Rutter et al., 1998) to show that the impact of protective forces, such as strong, supportive proximal processes with an important adult, on the development of resilience in children is even greater in 'at-risk' contexts. As such, context factors are less emphasised than in earlier models, and now in Bronfenbrenner's work, the relationship (process) is foregrounded. This is consistent with the contemporary trends in developmental psychology generally and the move away from simple linear models of causality towards understanding of the interaction of risk and protective factors (Downes, 2014).

As further explored in Chapter 4, the integrated nature of the PPCT approach helps illustrate why we must understand issues of diversity and inclusion if we are to understand individual behaviours, perceptions and outcomes. Experiences and behaviour are influenced by factors such as socio-economic class, gender, disability and personal circumstances. Thus it becomes clear that individual choices around issues like how practitioners support children or how parents provide for their educational and developmental needs must be understood as stemming from a joint freedom–determinism base. What this means is that people make active choices, but only within the range of options they perceive to be available to them.

The bioecological model helps us to look beyond the individual person to the context in which they are developing and the relationships (processes) through which they do so, in and across time. This may help to avoid the emergence of a deficit narrative, characterising children and their families as responsible for difficulties and 'blaming' them for any potential educational difficulties, or the identification of certain groups of parents as 'not interested' in their children's education. It allows us to draw together a comprehensive picture of how individual characteristics interact with, are influenced by, and impact on the educational system in which they are present. The bioecological model recognises that no one cog in a system moves in isolation; experiences of context are influenced by the relationships or process within them, the person experiencing them and the time periods involved.

This emphasises the imperative on all, including early years practitioners, to interrupt negative cycles of alienation in order to give all children and families a fair chance in education and in life, reminiscent of the idea of scholar-activism. While educational interventions cannot be presented as the total solution for every problem that confronts society as a whole or the more localised school community, a bioecological perspective shows us the huge role that early education has to play in potentially changing lives for the better. The model highlights that if the design of educational interventions is based on a flawed expectation that all children and families are the same as each other, we run the risk of inadvertently reproducing the very inequalities we aim to address. For example, if we disregard the interaction of person factors with context and expect all children and parents to be similarly 'motivated' regardless of aspects such as socio-economic status, gender, age, linguistic and cultural background, and prior educational experiences, it is no surprise that deficit models result because we criticise those children and parents who, for whatever reason, do not appear to show the expected levels of motivation. Certain groups are then seen as being uninterested in education, devaluing them even further.

Since children's access to school is mediated through their parents and some parents are not in a position to actively promote their children's interests, we cannot argue that educational interventions that depend on all parents behaving similarly will provide equitable outcomes for all children. The reality of development and education for individual children, parents, teachers and schools is complex and contextual, and as a result, interventions must consider diversity and its potential impact on benefits of the intervention. On the other hand, educational interventions that look solely at individual person characteristics to explain why they succeed in education or not can run the risk that a deficit perspective will develop – one that sees the problem as located within the individual and, as a result, 'blames the victim' rather than considering the many other factors of influence.

What is important to note here is that contexts *can* be changed to support more healthy development, providing researchers and educationalists with a rationale and, in fact, a moral imperative to identify optimal environments for individual children and families. Bronfenbrenner's bioecological model imposes a responsibility on early years practitioners to acknowledge and act upon contextual knowledge, individual characteristics, environmental factors and processes in relationships while also taking account of the sociocultural time in which development takes place, thereby supporting the potential of all children and families to benefit from good-quality early years experiences. Through creating strong 'linkages' across early years settings, home and schools, practitioners can take account of the needs of diverse children and families to ensure the creation of an early childhood context where everyone feels welcome. Drawing on the 'funds of knowledge' that children and their families bring with them to an early years setting can enrich the context within which early learning occurs.

Understanding that our behaviour as early years practitioners has so profound an impact on children's development, and at such a crucial and deep level, can be daunting and even paralysing! The thing is that even without our understanding the influence of our practice, it has an impact on the children we work with – knowledge helps us to consider our practice a little more carefully; it challenges us to consider the implications such knowledge has for our practices, and it allows us to recognise that feedback and the form that such feedback takes has an influence on young children's confidence, mental flexibility and self-control.

In Chapter 5, we considered the research evidence showing how this can work in practice. Recognising the importance of positive proximal processes for children during educational transition, these can be supported through promoting friendships; developing a structured series of peer interactions with older students; supporting students to manage the logistical demands of the new setting; involving families and communities, particularly parents; avoiding jarring cultural shifts in educational approaches and behavioural expectations; and ensuring availability of supports for children with specific vulnerabilities such as special educational needs or behavioural difficulties. Through the provision of opportunities, materials, times and space to explore, play, take risks and rise to social and physical challenges in a setting that is secure and comfortable, children develop a sense of belonging and they feel that they are trusted participants in the learning environment, and this in turn facilitates healthy development and learning.

The analysis presented in this book, and summarised in this chapter, opposes any interpretation of the bioecological model that presents the functioning of systems as static, immutable and deterministic. The most up-to-date version of the model certainly leaves much room for dynamic change within systems, given certain circumstances. In fact, the idea of human beings as potential change agents in their world is flagged from the start of Bronfenbrenner and Morris' seminal chapter:

> [W]e are the only species that . . . has developed the capacity to engage successfully in scientific inquiry, and thereby, in many respects, has been able to change the nature of the world in which we live. As a result, within certain limits, we humans have altered the nature and course of our own development as a species.
>
> [. . .] Our primary emphasis . . . is on the role of developmental processes and outcomes in producing large scale changes over time in the state and structure of the broader society over time, and the implications of those changes for the society's future.
>
> (2006, pp. 793–794, 796)

Bronfenbrenner and Morris (2006) provide an imperative for educators at all levels to identify and implement optimal conditions for human development, warning that otherwise children will not be free to reach their full potential, to their detriment and the detriment of society as a whole. While allowing for Downes' point that generally systems tend to develop inertia and resistance to change in those who are a part of them, the bioecological model highlights research, policy and practice "committed to transforming experiments" (2014, p. 37). As Bronfenbrenner tells us, "no society can long sustain itself unless its members have learned the sensitivities, motivations and skills involved in assisting and caring for other human beings" (1979, p. 53). Quite simply, relationships matter, and with careful attention, these relationships can be empowering and enabling and lead to transformation.

At the conclusion of each chapter, we have provided key concepts to consider for early years practice. Below we outline a series of key points to remember in considering the bioecological model as a totality. These points provide the broad theoretical framework guiding the model within which early years practice can be considered, reviewed and transformed.

'Process' in the microsystem

The bioecological model yields the strong recommendation that practitioners must emphasise the creation of supportive contexts through which positive relationships can develop. Early years settings ought to focus strongly on relationship-building between children, parents, teachers and educational settings. While contextual supports for families are vital in early childhood, these supports should be aimed at facilitating strong proximal processes rather than tick-box or politically motivated systems with false models of 'quality'. An ethos of respectful consideration and caring for children and families is vital for the protection of potentially vulnerable children and adults, as is support for agency and capacity that fosters positive social, emotional and educational outcomes. Such an ethos can be hard to measure and requires proactive efforts and ongoing reflection to achieve and maintain. As predicted by the bioecological framework, this *can* be successful and can make all the difference to individual experiences.

The importance of engaging with children and families as individuals with their own needs and strengths cannot be overestimated. Brooker's recommendation of "a serious and respectful listening, and not . . . a home school dialogue that assumes the school is always right" (2005, p. 128) is relevant here. Settings must consider issues of diversity such as language, culture, religion, socio-economics, gender, disability and family structure in developing support systems for children and families. Uni-cultural approaches may be doomed to failure and may actually widen pre-existing gaps in experience and understanding, leading to damaging levels of disjuncture at the mesosystem level. We cannot assume that one 'truth' exists for all human beings.

'Process' in the mesosystem – the creation of 'linkages'

The emphasis on relationships in the bioecological framework highlights the importance of considering the nature and quality of interactions in the mesosystem.

We saw in Chapter 5 that minimising differences between educational levels can support positive experiences. This echoes Bronfenbrenner's ideas on linkages in the mesosystem so that children can 'drag' (Slesnik *et al.*, 2007) their skills across settings. In creating linkages in practice, transition programmes should focus on 'soft skills' such as independence, concentration and organisational skills rather than academic skills to prepare children to move on to the next educational level. Early years settings could prioritise mastering the skills of looking after one's self and one's belongings, sharing, active listening, problem-solving and persistence, while primary schools could continue to develop their mindfulness of the developmental needs of young children for self-direction and play.

In terms of meso-level recommendations, one of the strongest outcomes of a bioecological approach relates to the importance of including and supporting parents and families. As explained by the bioecological model, outcomes such as 'behaviour' or 'motivation' are not solely a function of individual child factors, but result from complex interactions with contexts and relationships experienced. Parents can act as the interpretive bridge between home and the early years setting for children. It is important that early years practitioners realise that expecting all parents and families to behave in the same way or to hold the same values, beliefs and capacities regardless of background or personal circumstances may be futile. The onus is on the settings to be proactive on these issues because previous experiences of education can leave some children and adults vulnerable to marginalisation and intimidation.

'Process' in the exosystem and the macrosystem

Those involved in early education at every level, from research to policymaking to practice, must recognise the impact of diversity and the need to be vigilant in supporting and maintaining inclusive practice, incorporating this recognition into all initiatives. Development of a 'one-size-fits-all' approach can feed into the very problems we aim to address through the development of deficit models and alienation of traditionally marginalised groups.

In spite of financial pressures, significant direct investment and support is required for the early years sector in many countries; too often there is investment in regulation and monitoring without sufficient support or improvement for those working directly with children and families 'on the ground'. Good-quality systems in the early years tend, in some countries, to depend on crude indicators of quality of provision. Good-quality systems sometimes emphasise structural, contextual ratings using a tick-box – for instance, whether there is a fridge and bottled water in an early years setting – rather than asking more difficult questions regarding relationships and interactions (process) between children and those who care for them. There is urgent need for research into the quality of early years provision and practice through examination of genuine nurturing, educative and caring practices and processes rather than simply examining contexts in isolation from the social nature of that context and the elements comprising it.

Guiding practice bioecologically

Bronfenbrenner's bioecological model of human development provides a powerful argument for reflective and dynamic early educational practices. In chapters 6 to 9, we have provided detail on how we might use the learning through exploring the real potential of the bioecological model in early years practice. We have seen that the model necessitates a view of behaviours and learning within the dynamic social and historical contexts in which they occur. For instance, in Chapter 6, we saw how Bronfenbrenner's model positions the child at the centre of her learning and development in early years practice. The unique constellation of dispositions and characteristics that individual children bring to their early years settings influences and shapes the experiences they will have within these settings. Early years practitioners play an important role in facilitating and supporting children's agency and participation in their learning and development. Working closely alongside children in the early years, we soon become familiar with and tune in to the particular and distinct characteristics of each individual child, and the extent to which we succeed in doing this is undoubtedly influenced by the characteristics of individual practitioners and their associated responses to individual children.

Consistent with Bronfenbrenner's bioecological model, we support children's autonomy by providing them with opportunities to explore and develop their own particular interests and competencies rather than prescribing learning aims and objectives which do not reflect their individual talents and interests. Those curricula which emphasise presumed and prescribed learning objectives for children tend typically to benefit a small number of children while serving to impede or restrict the potential for other children to thrive. Ideally, early years practitioners should aim to support children to become agents and constructors of their knowledge of the world around them. As Cooper (1998) points out, knowledge of the social world occurs when an interaction is a shared vehicle for thought. Individuals who are teaching and individuals who are learning can both make meaning from their activities. Through such engagement, there is true participation in the learning process when learners and early years practitioners are mutually involved. While locating the child at the centre of practice, Bronfenbrenner's bioecological model also acknowledges children's vulnerability, their need for protection and their dependence on adults as well as their need for space for self-development, greater autonomy and independence (Tomanovic, 2003).

The model also provides a valuable conceptual space within which to consider other important theoretical insights into education and learning, including those provided by John Dewey, who suggested that individuals interacted and cooperated with one another in ways that could only be explained with reference to the entire social context, and Lev Vygotsky, who proposed a cultural-historical theory of human development. It is a model that also incorporates more contemporary thinking such as the work of Bourdieu on social and cultural capital, Brooker on transitions, and Fleer, Wood and others on the complex role of play in early learning and development. The important unifying feature of Bronfenbrenner's model is the priority placed on the central role of process and context as integrated and integrating mechanisms in the development of the young child across time and setting.

In Chapter 7, we focused on the importance of creating a welcoming learning environment where children encounter invitations to learn in a space that not only provides them with a sense of security and belonging but also offers them a space with dynamic and stimulating opportunities to explore and discover new experiences and concepts. A rich learning environment in the early years provides opportunities for children to explore and discover meanings in a manner that is characterised as emergent rather than prescribed. Learning is informed and guided by the child's interest, and consistent with the bioecological model of human development, the emphasis is on the processes that are generated through careful observation and documentation of children's interests and skills in order to provide meaningful and rich learning experiences.

Guided by the PPCT structure, we explored the concept of 'rich learning environments' through a focus on the process, person, context and time factors that may influence and shape their development. Consistent with the concept of a learning environment that evokes the sense of emergent rather than prescribed learning opportunities, the importance of providing opportunities for children to change and transform their environments is highlighted in Chapter 7 and throughout this book with an emphasis on flexibility – opportunities for children to transform their environments and to experience a sense of autonomy and control within these environments. In considering key features of a rich learning environment, we emphasised the value and significance of creating invitations for children to learn. We highlighted the importance of designing and developing environments rich in affordances for children to engage in joint activities and tasks, providing opportunities to work together and negotiate shared meanings with other children and adults in early years settings. Rich learning environments do not require sophisticated tools or equipment but will be enhanced through innovative and creative inputs from both children and adults working together, consistent with the bioecological model's emphasis on the interaction between process, person and context. Rich learning environments also ensure that time is available to allow for reciprocal, meaningful interactions between those who share early learning spaces.

In Chapter 8, we saw that viewing development as a dynamic and discontinuous process, or as a 'to-ing and fro-ing' process, allows us to see behaviour and development in early childhood as being adaptive to the immediate demands of the child in context. Such an approach to early education is not tied to the age and stage of development of the child but, rather, is linked to the sociocultural context of development for the child in the present. It is exemplified by the internationally recognised practices at Reggio Emila in Italy and in the *Te Whāriki* early years curriculum of New Zealand where pedagogy is directed by the connections, interactions and relationships between children and the wider world and by social, physical and emotional elements rather than by any prescribed expectations of developmental outcome. There is increasing evidence from psychological research and neuroscience to support Bronfenbrenner in his contention that the proximal processes of daily life are crucial engines of development. Evidence also suggests that these interactive processes are particularly important in early childhood given the role that interactions (their quality, bidirectionality and content) play in facilitating the development of thinking skills (cognitive and metacognitive) and affective skills (dispositions).

Finally, Chapter 9 considered how best to provide a nurturing learning experience for young children. Despite recognising the powerful framework for early practice provided by Bronfenbrenner's bioecological model, working ecologically in day-to-day practice is not simple. In fact, there are many cases where, despite an expressed commitment to a rich, dynamic and relational pedagogy, more traditional practices dominate. Implicit in early years practices consistent with the bioecological approach to human development, which we have characterised as a 'nurturing pedagogy', is a commitment to democratic principles that recognise the need to respect and engage meaningfully with children. This approach is reflective of an understanding of early years settings as sites of democratic practice where children and adults can participate collectively in interpreting experiences and shaping decisions affecting their own development and the nature of the context within which development occurs.

Bronfenbrenner's model of human development provides an impetus for responding to contemporary understandings of child development. Changing early years practice to incorporate this new knowledge, based on scientific understandings of development, is not an easy task. Such transformation rests with all those concerned with good-quality early years practice and requires ongoing reflection and a commitment to learning and change. As Bronfenbrenner puts it:

> Human beings create the environments that shape the course of human development. Their actions influence the multiple physical and cultural tiers of the ecology that shapes them, and this agency makes humans – for better or for worse – active producers of their own development.
>
> (2005, p. xxvii)

Notes

1 Stanley Milgram found that two-thirds of people were willing to electrocute and potentially murder another human being simply because someone in authority had told them to do so. You can find out more about the Milgram experiments at: http://psychology.about.com/od/historyofpsychology/a/milgram.htm

2 Zimbardo showed the negative impact of authority on human behaviour through the infamous 'Stanford Prison experiments'. A group of students were randomly assigned as guards or prisoners in a mock prison, and the experiment had to be ended after only six days because the 'guards' became so sadistic and the 'prisoners' became so depressed. You can find out more about the Stanford Prison experiments at: www.prisonexp.org/

GLOSSARY

Active learning The idea of the child as curious, meaning-making and doing everything possible to understand the world.

Agency A quality allowing the child to engage in intentional action to achieve particular valued goals.

Attachment Bond formed by an infant with the primary caregiver, thought by attachment theorists to form the basis of all future relationships and of psychological well-being for the rest of the individual's life.

Bioecological model Model of human development conceptualised by Urie Bronfenbrenner and colleagues. Central features include emphasis on relationships and interactions with other human beings and objects/symbols, and the importance of context in understanding development.

Chronosystem A level of context within Bronfenbrenner's bioecological model. The patterning of environmental events and transitions over time.

Cultural capital Bourdieu's idea that the taken-for-granted behaviours and ways of being of certain groups are valued by the dominant culture, whereas other groups may be devalued.

Demand characteristics Characteristics of the child inviting or discouraging reactions from the social environment that can foster or disrupt the operation of proximal processes.

Directive belief systems Beliefs developed through internalisation of experience whereby children begin to conceptualise a sense of agency within the world. Such belief systems may direct behaviour, thereby impacting on future experiences and, in turn, reinforcing directive belief systems in a two-way process. This concept is evident in many theories, such as social cognitive theory and bioecological theory.

Dispositions Characteristics of the child that may be 'generative', inviting positive responses from others, or 'disruptive', inviting negative responses from others.

Educational transition May refer to multiple transitions. In the current work, educational transition refers to the move from preschool to primary school.

Exosystem The level of context within the bioecological model that the child may never enter but which may, nevertheless, affect what happens to them.

Head Start American programme initiated by Bronfenbrenner and others, incorporating a range of early interventions for disadvantaged young children and their families.

Internal working model A concept from attachment theory. Internalisation of the quality of attachment with the primary caregiver, which forms the basis of a child's concept of self and directs future relationships.

Internalisation Interweaving of cultural, relational and biological influences to determine the characteristics and behaviour of the child.

Intersubjectivity Interactions in which there is dynamic and engaged input from both adults and children.

Linkages Experiences, structures and processes that tie various systems together and encourage individuals to apply learning from one setting to events in another.

Macrosystem The level of context within the bioecological model reflecting the wider pattern of ideology and organisation of social institutions common to a particular social class or culture.

Mediated learning A sociocultural concept. Acknowledges biological inheritance as the basis for subsequent development, but maintains that higher-order functioning develops through social activity that is embedded in the cultural values of particular communities.

Mesosystem The level of context within the bioecological model accounting for interconnections between two or more settings, such as school, peer group and family. The mesosystem is a system of two or more microsystems.

Microsystem The level of context within the bioecological model of which the individual has direct experience on a regular basis.

Nurturing pedagogy An approach to early educational practice. Emphasises the educative value of care and the caring nature of education.

Proximal processes Progressively more complex reciprocal interaction between an active, evolving, biopsychological human organism and the persons, objects and symbols in its immediate environment.

Resilience Complex interaction of protective and risk factors with the personal characteristics of the child, leading to positive or normative outcomes in spite of challenging circumstances.

Resource characteristics Experience, knowledge and skills required for effective functioning of proximal processes at a given stage of development.

Scaffolding A sociocultural concept capturing the gradual removal of adult support as a child becomes more competent.

Self-efficacy A concept from social cognitive theory. A person's self-efficacy beliefs reflect the level of competence they believe themselves to have in a given domain.

Synaptic pruning The process by which the brain adapts to experience. Synapses are brain connections. Those that have been reinforced through repeated experience in early life tend to become permanent. Synapses that are not used in the early years are eliminated. In this way, experiences (positive or negative) that children have in their early lives influence the ways their brains will be wired into adulthood.

System blockage   The tendency for systems to instil inertia in those within them.

Temperament   The child's tendency to respond to the environment in characteristic ways, reflecting energy levels, persistence, and tolerance of frustration.

Zone of proximal development   A sociocultural concept. The gap between what a child can achieve alone and with support from a 'more expert other'.

ABBREVIATIONS

DAP	developmentally appropriate practice
EPPE	Effective Provision of Pre-school and Primary Education
PPCT	process–person–context–time
UNCRC	United Nations Convention on the Rights of the Child
USSR	Union of Socialist Soviet Republics
ZPD	zone of proximal development

REFERENCES

Aguiar, A. and Baillargeon, R. (1999). 2.5 month old infants' reasoning about when objects should and should not be occluded. *Cognitive Psychology*, *39*(2), 116–157.

Aguiar, A. and Baillargeon, R. (2002). Developments in young infants' reasoning about occluded objects. *Cognitive Psychology*, *45*(2), 267–336.

Ahn, J. (2011). I'm not scared of anything: Emotion as social power in children's worlds. *Childhood*, *17*(1), 94–112.

Ahnert, L., Pinquart, M. and Lamb, M. E. (2006). Security of children's relationships with nonparental care providers: A meta-analysis. *Child Development*, *77*(3), 664–679.

Ainsworth, M. D. S., Blehar, M., Waters, E. and Wall, S. (1978). *Patterns of Attachment*. Hillsdale NJ: Erlbaum.

Alexander, R. (2004). Still no pedagogy: Principles, pragmatism and compliance in primary education. *Cambridge Journal of Education*, *34*(1), 7–33.

Ames, C. (1993). How school-to-home communications influence parent beliefs and perceptions. *Equity and Choice*, *9*(3), 44–49.

Anastasi, A. (1958). Heredity, environment, and the question "how?" *Psychological Review*, *65*(4), 197–208.

Armitage, M. (2011). Risky play is not a category – it's what children do. *ChildLinks: Children's Risky Play*, *3*, 11–14.

Bae, B. (2009). Children's right to participation: Challenges in everyday interactions. *European Early Childhood Research Journal*, *17*(3), 391–406.

Balbernie, R. (2007). *What About The Children? Cortisol and the Early Years* [pdf file]. Available at: www.whataboutthechildren.org.uk/downloads/research-summaries-2006-to-2010/summary_watch_2007_cortisol.pdf (accessed 10 October, 2016).

Bandura, A. (2001). Social cognitive theory: An agentic perspective. *Annual Review of Psychology*, *52*(1), 1–26.

Baumrind, D. (1971). Current patterns of parental authority. *Developmental Psychology Monographs*, *4*(1), 1–103.

Baumrind, D. (1978). Parental disciplinary patterns and social competence in children. *Youth and Society*, *9*(3), 239–276.

Baumrind, D. (1996). The discipline controversy revisited. *Family Relations: An Interdisciplinary Journal of Applied Family Studies*, *45*(4), 405–414.

Belsky, J. (1984). The determinants of parenting: A process model. *Child Development, 55*(1), 83–96.

Belsky, J. (1988). The "effects" of infant day care reconsidered. *Early Childhood Research Quarterly, 3*(3), 235–272.

Bergen, D. (2002). The role of pretend play in children's cognitive development. *Early Childhood: Research and Practice, 4*(1) [online]. Available at: http://ecrp.uiuc.edu/v4n1/bergen.html

Berk, L. E. (2009). *Child Development*, Eighth Edition. New York: Pearson.

Bertram, T. and Pascal, C. (2002). What counts in early learning. In O. N. Saracho and B. Spodek (Eds), *Contemporary Perspectives in Early Childhood Curriculum* (pp. 241–256). Greenwich, CT: Information Age.

Blair, C. (2002). School readiness: Integrating cognition and emotion in a neurobiological conceptualization of children's functioning at school entry. *American Psychologist, 57*(2), 111–127.

Blakemore, S. J. and Frith, U. (2005). The learning brain: Lessons for education: A précis. *Developmental Science, 8*(6), 459–471.

Bourdieu, P. (1990). *The Logic of Practice*. Cambridge: Polity Press.

Bourdieu, P. and Passeron, J. C. (1977). *Reproduction in Education, Society and Culture*. London: Sage.

Bowlby, J. (1973). *Attachment and Loss: Vol 2. Separation, Anxiety and Anger*. New York: Basic Books.

Bowlby, J. (1988). *Attachment and Loss: Vol 4. A Secure Base: Clinical Applications of Attachment Theory*. London: Routledge.

Bowlby, R. (2007). Babies and toddlers in non-parental daycare can avoid stress and anxiety if they develop a lasting secondary attachment bond with one carer who is consistently accessible to them. *Attachment and Human Development, 9*(4), 307–319.

Boyd, J. W., Barnett, S., Bodrova, E., Leong, D. J. and Gomby, D. (2005). *Promoting Children's Social and Emotional Development through Preschool Education. Preschool Policy Brief*. New Brunswick, NJ: National Institute for Early Education Research.

Bradford, H. (2012). *The Wellbeing of Children Under Three*. Abingdon: Routledge.

Bredekamp, S. and Copple, C. (Eds) (1997). *Developmentally Appropriate Practice in Early Childhood Programmes*. Washington, DC: National Association for the Education of Young Children.

Brennan, M. A. (2005). *"They Just Want to Be with Us." Young Children Learning to Live the Culture: A Post-Vygotskian Analysis of Young Children's Enculturation into a Childcare Setting* (Unpublished doctoral dissertation). Wellington, New Zealand: Victoria University of Wellington.

Brewster, S. (2004). Insights from a social model of literacy and disability. *Literacy, 38*(1), 46–51.

Broadhead, P. (2010). Cooperative play and learning from nursery to year one. In P. Broadhead, J. Howard and E. Wood (Eds), *Play and Learning in Early Years: Research to Practice* (pp. 43–60). London: Sage.

Bronfenbrenner, U. (1942/2005). Social status, structure, and development in the classroom group. In U. Bronfenbrenner (Ed.), *Making Human Beings Human: Bioecological Perspectives on Human Development* (pp. 22–26). London: Sage.

Bronfenbrenner, U. (1967/2005). The split-level American family. In U. Bronfenbrenner (Ed.), *Making Human Beings Human: Bioecological Perspectives on Human Development* (pp. 201–209). London: Sage.

Bronfenbrenner, U. (1970). *Two Worlds of Childhood: US and USSR*. New York: Russell Sage Foundation.

Bronfenbrenner, U. (1970/2005). Minority report of Forum 15: 1970. White House Conference on Children. In U. Bronfenbrenner (Ed.), *Making Human Beings Human: Bioecological Perspectives on Human Development* (pp. 210–214). London: Sage.

Bronfenbrenner, U. (1975). Reality and research in the ecology of human development. *Proceedings of the American Philosophical Society, 119*(6), 439–469.

Bronfenbrenner, U. (1977). The ecology of human development in retrospect and prospect. In H. McGurk (Ed.), *Ecological Factors in Human Development* (pp. 275–286). Amsterdam: North Holland.

Bronfenbrenner, U. (1979). *The Ecology of Human Development: Experiments by Nature and Design.* Cambridge, MA: Harvard University Press.

Bronfenbrenner, U. (1985). The future of childhood. In V. Greaney (Ed.), *Children: Needs and Rights* (pp. 167–186). New York: Irvington Publishers, Inc.

Bronfenbrenner, U. (1986a). Ecology of the family as a context for human development: Research perspectives. *Developmental Psychology, 22,* 723–742.

Bronfenbrenner, U. (1986b). Recent advances in research on the ecology of human development. In R. K. Silbereisen, K. Eyferth, and G. Rudinger (Eds), *Development as Action in Context: Problem Behavior and Normal Youth Development* (pp. 287–309). New York: Springer-Verlag.

Bronfenbrenner, U. (1988/2005). Strengthening family systems. In U. Bronfenbrenner (Ed.), *Making Human Beings Human: Bioecological Perspectives on Human Development* (pp. 260–273). London: Sage.

Bronfenbrenner, U. (1989a). Ecological systems theory. In R. Vasta (Ed.), *Annals of Child Development,* Vol. 6 (pp. 187–249). Greenwich: JAI Press.

Bronfenbrenner, U. (1989b). *Who Cares for Children?* Paris: UNESCO.

Bronfenbrenner, U. (1992/2005). Ecological systems theory. In U. Bronfenbrenner (Ed.), *Making Human Beings Human: Bioecological Perspectives on Human Development* (pp. 106–173). London: Sage.

Bronfenbrenner, U. (1993). The ecology of cognitive development: Research models and fugitive findings. In R. Wonziak and K. Fischer (Eds), *Development in Context: Acting and Thinking in Specific Environments* (pp. 3–44). Hillsdale, NJ: Erlbaum.

Bronfenbrenner, U. (1995). Developmental ecology through space and time: A future perspective. In P. Moen, G. H. Elder Jr and K. Lüscher (Eds), *Examining Lives in Context: Perspectives on the Ecology of Human Development* (pp. 619–647). Washington, DC: American Psychological Association.

Bronfenbrenner, U. (Ed.) (2005). *Making Human Beings Human: Bioecological Perspectives on Human Development.* London: Sage.

Bronfenbrenner, U. and Ceci, S. J. (1993). Heredity, environment and the question "how?": A first approximation. In R. Plomin and G. E. McClearn (Eds), *Nature, Nurture and Psychology* (pp. 313–323). Washington, DC: APA Books.

Bronfenbrenner, U. and Ceci, S. J. (1994). Nature–nurture reconceptualised in developmental perspective: A bioecological model. *Psychological Review, 101*(4), 568–586.

Bronfenbrenner, U. and Morris, P. (1998). The ecology of developmental processes. In W. Damon and R. M. Lerner (Eds), *Handbook of Child Psychology: Vol 1, Theoretical Models of Human Development* (pp. 993–1028). New York: John Wiley and Sons.

Bronfenbrenner, U. and Morris, P. A. (2006). The bioecological model of human development. In R. M. Lerner and W. E. Damon (Eds), *Handbook of Child Psychology: Vol 1, Theoretical Models of Human Development,* Sixth Edition, (pp. 793–828). Chichester: John Wiley and Sons.

Brooker, L. (2005). Learning to be a child: Cultural diversity and early years ideology. In N. Yelland (Ed.), *Critical Issues in Early Childhood Education* (pp. 115–130). Maidenhead: Open University Press.

Brooker, L. (2008). *Supporting Transitions in the Early Years*. Maidenhead: McGraw-Hill.

Brooker, L. (2015). Cultural capital in the preschool years. In L. Alanen, L. Brooker and B. Mayall (Eds), *Childhood with Bourdieu* (pp. 13–33). Basingstoke: Palgrave Macmillan.

Brooks, D. (2011). *The Social Animal: The Hidden Sources of Love, Character and Achievement*. New York: Random House.

Bruce, T. (2001). *Learning Through Play: Babies, Toddlers and the Foundation Years*. London: Hodder Stoughton.

Bruner, J. (1996). *The Culture of Education*. Cambridge, MA: Harvard University Press.

Buckingham, D. (2008). *Youth, Identity and Digital Media*. Cambridge, MA: MIT Press.

Burchinal, M. R., Peisner-Feinberg, E., Pianta, R. and Howes, C. (2002). Development of academic skills from pre-school through second grade: Family and classroom predictors of developmental trajectories. *Journal of School Psychology, 40*(5), 415–436.

Burck, C. (2005). *Multilingual living: Explorations of language and subjectivity*. Houndmills: Palgrave Macmillan.

Burman, E. (2008). *Developments: Child, Image, Nation*. London: Routledge.

Byrne, D. and Smyth, E. (2010). *No Way Back? The Dynamics of Early School Leaving*. Dublin: The Liffey Press in association with The Economic and Social Research Institute.

Carr, M. A. (1999). Being a learner: Five learning dispositions for early childhood. *Early Childhood Practice, 1*(1), 81–99.

Carr, M. (2004). *The Marsden Learning Dispositions in Social Context (DISC) Project: Some Thoughts about the Framework*. Unpublished discussion for the Marsden DISC Project, Waikato University, Hamilton, New Zealand.

Carr, M. and Claxton, G. (2002). Tracking the development of learning dispositions. *Assessment in Education: Propositions, Policy and Practice, 9*(1), 9–37.

Carr, M. and Lee, W. (2012). *Learning Stories: Documenting and Constructing Learner Identities in Early Education*. London: Sage.

Chen, X. and French, D. C. (2008). Children's Social Competence in Cultural Context. *Annual Review of Psychology, 59*, 591–616.

Chess, S. and Thomas, A. (1991). Temperament and the concept of goodness of fit. In J. Strelau and A. Angleitner (Eds), *Explorations in Temperament* (pp. 15–28). Boston, MA: Springer US.

Christensen, P. and Prout, A. (2005). Anthropological and sociological perspectives on the study of children. In S. Greene and D. Hogan (Eds), *Researching Children's Experience: Methods and Approaches* (pp. 42–60). London: Sage.

Clark, A. and Moss, P. (2001). *Listening to Young Children: The Mosaic Approach*. London: National Children's Bureau/Joseph Rowntree Foundation.

Clark, A., Kjorholt, A. T. and Moss, P. (Eds) (2005). *Beyond Listening: Children's Perspectives on Early Childhood Services*. Bristol: Policy Press.

Coldsmith, H. H., Buss, A. H., Plomin, R., Rothbart, M. K., Thomas, A., Chess, S., Hinde, R. A. and McCall, R. B. (1987). Roundtable: What is temperament? Four approaches. *Child Development, 58*(2), 505–529.

Commonwealth of Australia (2009). *Belonging, Being and Becoming: The Early Years Learning Framework for Australia*. Canberra: Council of Australian Councils.

Cooper, D. M. (1998). More law and more rights: Will children benefit? *Child and Family Social Work, 3*(2), 77–86.

Corsaro, W. A. (2005). Collective action and agency in young children's peer cultures. In J. Qvortup (Ed.), *Studies in Modern Childhood: Society, Agency, Culture* (pp. 231–247). Houndmills: Palgrave Macmillan.

Corsaro, W. A. (2010). *The Sociology of Childhood*. London: Sage.

Covington, M. V. and Müeller, K. J. (2001). Intrinsic versus extrinsic motivation: An approach/avoidance reformulation. *Educational Psychology Review*, *13*(2), 157–176.

Crouch, S. R., Waters, E., McNair, R., Power, J. and Davis, E. (2014). Parent-reported measures of child health and well-being in same-sex parent families: A cross-sectional survey. *BMC Public Health*, *14*:635.

Cummins, J. (2000). *Language, Power, and Pedagogy: Bilingual Children in the Crossfire* (Vol. 23). Clevedon: Multilingual Matters.

Cummins, J. (2001). Bilingual children's mother tongue: Why is it important for education? *Sprogforum*, *19*, 15–20.

Cummins, J. (2005). A proposal for action: Strategies for recognizing heritage language competence as a learning resource within the mainstream classroom. *Modern Language Journal*, *89*(4), 585–592.

Cummins, J., Bismilla, V., Chow, P., Cohen, S., Giampapa, F., Leoni, L., Sandhu, P. and Sastri, P. (2005). Affirming identity in multilingual classrooms. *Educational Leadership*, *63*(1), 38–43.

Curtis, D. (2001). Strategies for enhancing children's use of the environment. *Child Care Information Exchange*, *142*, 42–45.

Dahlberg, G. and Moss, P. (2005). *Ethics and Politics in Early Childhood Education*. Abingdon: RoutledgeFalmer.

Dahlberg, G., Moss, P. and Pence, A. (1999). *Beyond Quality in Early Childhood Education and Care: Postmodern Perspectives*. London: Falmer Press.

Daoust, L. M. (2007). The importance of play in early childhood education. *TRENDS*, *1*, 34–43.

Diamond, A. (2013). Executive functions. *Annual Review of Psychology*, *64*, 135–168.

Dockett, S. and Perry, B. (2007). Children's transition to school: Changing expectations. In A. W. Dunlop and H. Fabian (Eds), *Informing Transitions in the Early Years: Research, Policy and Practice* (pp. 92–104). Maidenhead: Open University Press.

Dockett, S. and Perry, B. (2013). Siblings and buddies: Providing expert advice about starting school. *International Journal of Early Years Education*, *21*(4), 348–361.

Dockett, S., Perry, B. and Kearney, E. (2012). Family transitions as children start school. *Family Matters*, *90*, 57–67.

Downes, P. (2014). *Access to Education in Europe: A Framework and Agenda for System Change*. London: Springer.

Downes, P., Maunsell, C. and Ivers, J. (2007). The jolt between primary and post-primary. In P. Downes and A. L. Gilligan (Eds), *Beyond Educational Disadvantage* (pp. 407–417). Dublin: Institute of Public Administration.

Drotner, K. (2008). Leisure is hard work: Digital practices and future competences. In D. Buckingham (Ed.), *Youth, Identity, and Digital Media* (pp. 187–211). Cambridge, MA: Heinemann. (The MacArthur Foundation series on digital media and learning).

Duncan, J., Jones, C. and Carr, M. (2008). Learning dispositions and the role of mutual engagement: Factors for consideration in educational settings. *Contemporary Issues in Early Childhood*, *9*(2), 107–117. London: Sage. DOI: 10.2304/ciec.2008.9.2.107. http://cie.sagepub.com/content/9/2/107.full.pdf+html

Dunphy, E. (2008). *Supporting Early Learning and Development through Formative Assessment, A Research Paper*. Dublin: National Council for Curriculum and Assessment.

Dweck, C. S. (2007). *Mindset: The New Psychology of Success*. New York: Ballantine Books.

Early Childhood Matters (2013). *Learning Begins Early*. The Hague: Bernard Van Leer Foundation.

Educational Transitions and Change Research Group (2011). *Transition to School: Position Statement*. Albury-Wodonga: Research Institute for Professional Practice, Learning and Education, Charles Sturt University.

Ellis, R. J. (2012). *The Study of Second Language Acquisition*. New York: Oxford University Press.

English, H. B. and English, A. C. (1958). *A Comprehensive Dictionary of Psychological and Psychoanalytical Terms: A Guide to Usage*. New York: David McKay Company, Inc.

Epstein, A. S. (2007). *The Intentional Teacher: Choosing the Best Strategies for Young Children's Learning*. Washington, DC: National Association for the Education of Young Children.

Fitzpatrick, S. (2015). From sectoral to systemic solutions in educational policy. Proceedings from Education Studies Association of Ireland annual conference, *Educational Research and Practice in Times of Transition: Looking to the Future*, 9–11 April, Maynooth University and Carton House.

Fjortoft, I. (2001). The natural environment as a playground for children: The impact of outdoor play on pre-primary school children. *Early Childhood Education Journal*, *29*(2), 111–117.

Fleer, M. (2003). Early childhood education as an evolving "community of practice" or as lived "social reproduction": Researching the "taken-for-granted". *Contemporary Issues in Early Childhood*, *4*(1), 64–79.

Fleer, M. (2010). *Early Learning and Development: Cultural-historical Concepts in Play*. New York: Cambridge University Press.

French, G. (2007). *Children's Early Learning and Development: A Background Paper*. Dublin: National Council for Curriculum and Assessment.

French, G. (2014). *Let Them Talk: Evaluation of the Language Enrichment Programme of the Ballyfermot Early Years Language and Learning Initiative*. Dublin: Ballyfermot/Chapelizod Partnership.

Frønes, I. (1993). Changing childhoods. *Childhood*, *1*(1), 1–2.

Galinsky, E. (2010). *Mind in the Making: The Seven Essential Life Skills Every Child Needs*. New York: Harper Collins.

Gaylor, E. and Spiker, D. (2012). Home visiting programs and their impact on young children's school readiness [pdf file], *Encyclopedia on Early Childhood Development*. Available at: www.child-encyclopedia.com/sites/default/files/textes-experts/en/912/home-visiting-programs-and-their-impact-on-young-childrens-school-readiness.pdf (accessed 9 October, 2016).

Gergen, K. J. (1973). Social psychology as history. *Journal of Personality and Social Psychology*, *26*(2), 309–320.

Gergen, K. J. (1997). Social psychology as social construction: The emerging vision. In C. E. McGarty and S. Haslam (Eds.), *The message of social psychology: Perspectives on mind in society* (pp. 113-128). Oxford: Blackwell Publishing.

Gerhardt, S. (2004). *Why Love Matters: How Affection Shapes a Baby*. Hove: Brunner-Routledge.

Goleman, D. (1996). *Emotional Intelligence: Why it Can Matter More than IQ*. London: Bloomsbury.

Good, T. L. (1987). Teacher expectations. In D. C. Berliner and B. V. Rosenshine (Eds), *Talks to Teachers: A Festschrift for N. L. Gage* (pp. 157–200). New York: Random House.

Good, T. L. (1993). New direction in research on teacher and student expectations. *Mid-Western Educational Researcher*, *6*(1), 7–10, 17, 33.

Greene, S. and Moane, G. (2000). Growing up Irish: Changing children in a changing society. *Irish Journal of Psychology*, *21*(3–4), 122–137.

Greene, S. and Hill, M. (2005). Researching children's experience: Methods and methodological issues. In S. Greene and D. Hogan (Eds), *Researching Children's Experience: Methods and Approaches* (pp. 1–21). London: Sage.

Greene, S., Williams, J., Layte, R., Doyle, E., Harris, E., McCrory, C., Murray, A., O'Dowd, T., Quail, A., Swords, L., Thornton, M. and Whelan, C. T. (2010). *Growing Up in Ireland: National Longitudinal Study of Children: Background and Conceptual Framework*. Dublin: Office of the Minister for Children and Youth Affairs.

Greeno, J. (1994). Gibson's affordances. *Psychological Review, 101*(2), 336–42.

Gregory, A., Cornell, D., Fan, X., Sheras, P., Shih, T.-H. and Huang, F. (2010). Authoritative school discipline: High school practices associated with lower bullying and victimization. *Journal of Educational Psychology, 102*(2), 483–496.

Grieshaber, S. and McArdle, F. (2014). Ethical dimensions and perspectives on play. In L. Brooker, M. Blaise and S. Edwards (Eds), *The Sage Handbook of Play and Learning in Early Childhood* (pp. 103–114). London: Sage.

Guerrettaz, A. M. and Johnston, B. (2013). Materials in the classroom ecology. *The Modern Language Journal, 97*(3), 779–796.

Hall, K., Conway, P. F., Rath, A., Murphy, R. and McKeon, J. (2008). *Reporting to Parents in the Primary School: Communication, Meaning and Learning*. Research Report No. 9. Dublin: National Council for Curriculum and Assessment.

Halpenny, A. M. and Pettersen, J. (2014). *Introducing Piaget: A Guide for Practitioners and Students in Early Years Education*. Abingdon: Routledge.

Halpenny, A. M., Greene, S. M. and Hogan, D. M. (2008). Children's perspectives on coping and support following parental separation. *Child Care in Practice, 14*(3), 311–325.

Halpenny, A. M., Nixon, E. and Watson, D. (2010). *Parents' Perspectives on Parenting Styles and Disciplining Children*. Dublin: Office of the Minister for Children and Youth Affairs.

Hayes, N. (2004). Towards a nurturing pedagogy – reconceptualising care and education in the early years. In N. Hayes and M. Kernan (Eds), *Transformations: Theory and Practice in Early Education*, Proceedings of the annual OMEP conference, University College Cork, 5 April 2003 (pp. 140–152). Cork: OMEP, Ireland.

Hayes, N. (2007). *Perspectives on the Relationship Between Education and Care in Early Childhood – A Background Paper*. Dublin: National Council for Curriculum and Assessment.

Hayes, N. (2008). Teaching matters in early educational practice: The case for a nurturing pedagogy. *Early Education and Development, 19*(3), 430–440.

Hayes, N. (2013). *Early Years Practice: Getting it Right from the Start*. Dublin: Gill and Macmillan.

Hayes, N. (2015). Troubling outcomes: A challenge for early childhood education. *An Leanbh Óg. The OMEP Ireland Journal of Early Childhood Studies, 9*, 13–29.

Hedges, H. (2014). Children's content learning in play provision: Competing tensions and future possibilities. In L. Brooker, M. Blaise and S. Edwards (Eds), *The Sage Handbook of Play and Learning in Early Childhood* (pp. 192–203). London: Sage.

Heft, H. (1988). Affordances of children's environments: A functional approach to environmental description. *Children's Environments Quarterly, 5*(3), 29–37.

Hornby, G. and Lafaele, R. (2011). Barriers to parental involvement in education: An explanatory model. *Educational Review, 3*(1), 37–52.

Huizinga, J. (1950). *Homo Ludens: A Study of the Play Element in Culture*. New York: Harper Row.

Irish National Teachers' Organisation (INTO) (2009). *INTO Consultative Conference on Education, 2008: Transitions in the Primary School*. Dublin: INTO.

James, A., Jenks, C. and Prout, A. (1998). *Theorising Childhood*. Cambridge: Polity Press.

Katz, L. G. (1988). What should young children be doing? *American Educator, 12*(2), 28–33, 44–45.

Katz, L. G. (1993). *Dispositions: Definitions and Implications for Early Childhood Practices.* Perspectives from ERIC/EECE: A Monograph Series, No. 4. Urbana, IL: ERIC Clearinghouse on Elementary and Early Childhood Education.

Katz, L. and Chard, S. C. (1994). *Engaging Children's Minds: The Project Approach*, Second Edition. Norwood, NJ: Ablex Publishing.

Kavanagh, L. and Hickey, T. (2013). An exploration of parents' experiences of involvement in immersion schooling: Identifying barriers to successful involvement. In F. Farr and M. Moriarty (Eds), *Language Learning and Teaching: Irish Research Perspectives* (pp. 65–86). Bern: Peter Lang.

Kernan, M. (2007). *Play as a Context for Learning and Development: A Research Paper.* Dublin: National Council for Curriculum and Assessment.

Kernan, M. (2010). Space and place as a source of belonging and participation in urban environments: Considering the role of early childhood and care settings. *European Early Childhood Education Research Journal, 18*(2), 199–213.

Kernan, M. (2015). Learning environments that work: Softening the boundaries. A paper prepared for the symposium, *Early Educational Alignment: Reflecting on Context, Curriculum and Pedagogy*, Trinity College Dublin, 15 October.

Kernan, M. and Devine, D. (2010). Being confined within? Constructions of the good childhood and outdoor play in early childhood education and care settings in Ireland. *Children and Society, 24*(5), 371–385.

Kernan, M. and Singer, E. (Eds) (2011). *Peer Relationships in Early Childhood Education and Care.* Abingdon: Routedge.

Kraftsoff, S. and Quinn, S. (2009). Exploratory study investigating the opinions of Russian-speaking parents on maintaining their children's use of the Russian language. *Irish Journal of Applied Social Studies, 9*(1), 65–80.

Kuhl, P. K. (2010). Brain mechanisms in early language acquisition. *Neuron, 67*(5), 713–727.

Kuhl, P. (2010, October). *Patricia Kuhl: The Linguistic Genius of Babies.* Available at: https://www.ted.com/talks/patricia_kuhl_the_linguistic_genius_of_babies?language=en (accessed 24 October, 2016).

Lantolf, J. and Thorne, S. (2006). *Sociocultural Theory and the Genesis of Second Language Development.* Oxford: Oxford University Press.

Lave, J. and Wenger, E. (1991). *Situated Learning: Legitimate Peripheral Participation.* Cambridge: Cambridge University Press.

Ledger, E., Smith, A. B. and Rich, P. (2000). Friendships over the transition from early childhood centre to school. *International Journal of Early Years Education, 8*(1), 57–69.

Lester, S. and Russell, W. (2010). *Children's Right to Play: An Examination of the Importance of Play in the Lives of Children Worldwide.* Working Paper 57. The Hague: Bernard van Leer Foundation.

Lippman, P. C. (2010). *Evidence-based Design of Elementary and Secondary Schools: A Responsive Approach to Creating Learning Environments.* New York: Wiley.

Little, H. and Sweller, N. (2015). Affordances for risk-taking and physical activity in Australian early childhood education settings. *Early Childhood Education Journal, 43*(4), 337–345.

Llamas, C. and Watt, D. (Eds) (2010). *Language and Identities.* Edinburgh: Edinburgh University Press.

Lockhart, S. (2010). Play: An important tool for cognitive development. *Extensions, 24*(3), 1–8.

Lynch, H. and Hayes, N. (2015). An affordance perspective on infant play in home settings: A "just-right environment". *Childlinks, 2*, 17–22.

Machowska-Kosciak, M. (2013). A language socialization perspective on knowledge and identity construction in Irish post-primary education. In F. Farr and M. Moriarty

(Eds), *Language Learning and Teaching: Irish Research Perspectives* (pp. 87–110). Bern: Peter Lang.

MacNaughton, G. and Williams, G. (2009). *Techniques for Teaching Young Children: Choices in Theory and Practice*, Third Edition. French's Forest, NSW: Longman.

MacRuairc, G. M. (2009). "Dip, dip, sky blue, who's it? NOT YOU": Children's experiences of standardised testing: A socio-cultural analysis. *Irish Educational Studies, 28*(1), 47–66.

Malaguzzi, L. (1993). For an education based on relationships. *Young Children, 49*(1), 9–12.

Marbina, L., Church, A. and Tayler, C./Department of Education and Early Childhood Development (2011). *Victoria Early Years Learning and Development Framework. Evidence Paper: Practice Principle 6: Integrated Teaching and Learning Approaches.* Melbourne: University of Melbourne.

Margetts, K. (2003). Children bring more to school than their backpacks: Starting school down under. *European Early Childhood Education Research Journal, Themed Monograph I: Transitions,* 5–14.

Margetts, K. and Kienig, A. (Eds) (2013). *International Perspectives on Transition to School.* Abingdon: Routledge.

Markstrom, A. M. and Hallden, G. (2009). Children's strategies for agency in preschool. *Children and Society, 23*(2), 112–122.

Mashford-Scott, A. and Church, A. (2011). Promoting agency in early childhood education. *Novitas-Royal (Research on Youth and Language), 5*(1), 15–38.

Masten, A. and Reed, M.-G. J. (2002). Resilience in development. In C. R. Snyder and S. J. Lopez (Eds), *Handbook of Positive Psychology* (pp. 117–132). Oxford: Oxford University Press.

Melhuish, E. (2014). The impact of early childhood education on improved wellbeing. In British Academy, *"If You Could Do One Thing. . .": Nine Local Actions to Reduce Health Inequalities* (pp. 32–43). London: British Academy.

Melhuish, E., Phan, M., Sylva, K., Sammons, P. and Siraj-Blatchford, I. (2008). Effects of the home learning environment and preschool center experience upon literacy and numeracy development in early primary school. *Journal of Social Issues, 64*(1), 95–114.

Mhic Mhathúna, M. (2011). *An Traein: Ag Aistriú ón Naíonra go dtí an Bhunscoil: Eolas agus Moltaí do Stiúrthóirí Naíonraí agus do Mhúinteoirí Gaelscoileanna.* Baile Átha Cliath: Forbairt Naíonraí Teo.

Milgram, S. (1963). Behavioral study of obedience. *The Journal of Abnormal and Social Psychology, 67*(4), 371–378.

Ministry of Education, New Zealand (1996). *Te Whāriki: Early Childhood Curriculum.* Wellington, New Zealand: Learning Media Limited.

Mitchell, L. (2011). Enquiring teachers and democratic politics: Transformations in New Zealand's early childhood education landscape. *Early Years,* iFirst Article, 1–12. doi: 10.1080/09575146.2011.588787

Mitchell, L., Wylie, C. and Carr, M. (2008). *Outcomes of Early Childhood Education: Literature Review.* Wellington, New Zealand: Ministry of Education.

Moffitt, T. E., Arseneault, L., Belsky, D., Dikson, N., Hancox, R. J., Harrington, H., Houts, R., Poulton, R., Roberts, B.W., Ross, S., Sears, M. R., Thomas, W. M. and Caspi, A. (2011). A gradient of childhood self-control predicts health, wealth and public safety. *Proceedings of the National Academy of Science, 108*(7), 2693–2698.

Morss, J. R. (2013). *Growing Critical: Alternatives to Developmental Psychology*, Third Edition. London: Routledge.

Mosier, C. E. and Rogoff, B. (2003). Privileged treatment of toddlers: Cultural aspects of individual choice and responsibility. *Developmental Psychology, 39*(6), 1047–1060.

Mullin, A. (2007). Children, autonomy, and care. *Journal of Social Philosophy, 38*(4), 536–553.

Murray, C. and O'Doherty, A. (2001). *Éist. Respecting Diversity in Early Childhood Care, Education and Training.* Dublin: Pavee Point.

National Council for Curriculum Assessment (NCCA) (2009). *Aistear: The Early Childhood Curriculum Framework.* Dublin: National Council for Curriculum Assessment.

National Scientific Council on the Developing Child (2007). *The Science of Early Childhood Development: Closing the Gap Between What We Know and What We Do.* Cambridge, MA: Center on the Developing Child, Harvard University. Available at: http://developing child.harvard.edu/resources/the-science-of-early-childhood-development-closing-the-gap-between-what-we-know-and-what-we-do/ (accessed 10 October, 2016).

Neal, J. W. and Neal, Z. P. (2013). Nested or networked? Future directions for ecological systems theory. *Social Development, 22*(4), 722–737.

Neugebauer, R. (2010). The start of Head Start. *Exchange,* May/June, 20–21.

Newcombe, N. S., Uttal, D. H. and Sauter, M. (2013). Spatial development. In P. D. Zelazo (Ed.), *Oxford Handbook of Developmental Psychology. Volume 1: Body and Mind* (pp. 564–590). Oxford: Oxford University Press.

Ntelioglou, B. Y., Fannin, J., Montanera, M. and Cummins, J. (2014). A multilingual and multimodal approach to literacy teaching and learning in urban education: A collaborative inquiry project in an inner city elementary school. *Frontiers in Psychology,* 5:533, 70–79.

Nutbrown, C. and Clough, P. (2009). Citizenship and inclusion in the early years: Understanding and responding to children's perspectives on "Belonging". *International Journal of Early Years Education, 17*(3), 191–205.

O'Connor, A. (2013). *Understanding Transitions in the Early Years: Supporting Change through Attachment and Resilience.* Abingdon: Routledge.

O'Donoghue Hynes, B. and Hayes, N. (2011). Who benefits from early childhood education and care policy tool design in Ireland? *Journal of Poverty and Social Justice, 19*(3), 277–288.

OECD (2006). *Starting Strong II: Early Childhood Education and Care.* Paris: Organisation for Economic Co-operation and Development.

Ofsted (2014). Research and analysis: Ensuring a smooth transition from nursery to school [online] *GOV.UK.* Available at: https://www.gov.uk/government/publications/ensur ing-a-smooth-transition-from-nursery-to-school (accessed 10 October, 2016).

O'Kane, M. (2015). Multiple Transitions. A Paper prepared for the symposium *Early Educational Alignment: Reflecting on Context, Curriculum and Pedagogy,* 15 October, 2015, Trinity College Dublin.

O'Kane, M. and Hayes, N. (2006). The transition to school in Ireland: Views of pre-school and primary school teachers. *International Journal of Transitions in Childhood, 2,* 4–16.

O'Kane, M. and Hayes, N. (2013) "The child snapshot": A tool for the transfer of information from preschool to primary school. *International Journal of Transitions in Childhood, 6,* 28–36.

O'Toole, L. (2014). Cooperative learning in initial teacher education: Student experiences. *Problemy Wczesnej Edukacji/Issues in Early Education, 10*(2), 7–20.

O'Toole, L. (2015). Student-centred teaching in initial teacher education. *International Journal for Cross-Disciplinary Subjects in Education, 6*(1), 2111–2119.

O'Toole, L. (2016). *A Bio-ecological Perspective on Educational Transition: Experiences of Children, Parents and Teachers.* (Unpublished Doctoral Dissertation). Dublin Institute of Technology, Dublin, Ireland.

O'Toole, L., Hayes, N. and Mhic Mhathúna, M. (2014). A bioecological perspective on educational transition. *Procedia – Social and Behavioural Sciences, 140,* 121–127.

Panken, J. (2005). *Behind the Mirror Image: Urie Bronfenbrenner in the Soviet Union*. (Unpublished Doctoral Dissertation). Cornell University, Ithaca, New York.

Parker-Rees, R. (2014). Playfulness and the co-construction of identity in the first years. In L. Brooker, M. Blaise and S. Edwards (Eds), *The Sage Handbook of Play and Learning in Early Childhood* (pp. 366–377). London: Sage.

Parrish, M. (2014). *Social Work Perspective on Human Behaviour*. London: McGraw-Hill Education.

Pellegrini, A. D. and Bjorklund, D. F. (1998). *Applied Child Study: A Developmental Approach*, Second Edition. Hillsdale, NJ: Lawrence Erlbaum Associates.

Penn, H. (1997). *Comparing Nurseries*. London: Paul Chapman Publishing.

Perkins, D. (1995). *Smart Schools: Better Thinking and Learning for Every Child*. New York: The Free Press.

Piaget, J. (1951). *The Child's Conception of the World*. Lanham, MD: Littlefield Adams Quality Paperbacks.

Piaget, J. (2001). *The Psychology of Intelligence*. Abingdon: Routledge.

Pinker, S. (1994). *The Language Instinct: The New Science of Language and Mind*. London: Penguin UK.

Piven, F. F. (2010). Reflections on Scholarship and Activism. *Antipode*, *42*(4), 806–810.

Pramling-Samuelsson, I. and Asblond-Carlsson, M. (2008). The playing learning child: Towards a pedagogy of early childhood. *Scandinavian Journal of Educational Research*, *52*(6), 623–641.

Reay, D. (2005). Mothers' involvement in their children's schooling: Social reproduction in action? In G. Crozier and D. Reay (Eds), *Activating Participation: Parents and Teachers Working towards Partnership* (pp. 23–33). Stoke on Trent: Trentham.

Resnick, L. B. (1987). *Education and Learning to Think*. Washington, DC: National Academy Press.

Rich, A. (1986). *Blood, Bread, and Poetry: Selected Prose, 1979–1985*. New York: W. W. Norton.

Riley, P. (2011). *Attachment Theory and the Teacher–Student Relationship*. Abingdon: Routledge.

Ring, E., Mhic Mhathúna, M., Moloney, M., Hayes, N., Breatnach, D., Stafford, P., Carswell, D., Keegan, S., Kelleher, C., McCafferty, D., O'Keefe, A., Leavy, A., Madden, R. and Ozonyia, M. (2015). *An Examination of Concepts of School Readiness among Parents and Educators in Ireland*. Dublin: Department of Children and Youth Affairs.

Robinson, K. and Jones-Diaz, C. (2006). Diversity and difference in early childhood education: Issues for theory and practice. *British Journal of Educational Studies*, *54*(4), 496–498.

Robinson, K. and Harris, A. L. (2014). *The Broken Compass*. Cambridge, MA: Harvard University Press.

Rogers, C. R. (1974). Questions I would ask myself if I were a teacher. *Education*, *95*(2), 134–139.

Rogers, C. R. (1995). *Client-Centered Therapy: Its Current Practice, Implications and Theory*. London: Constable.

Rogoff, B. (1998). Cognition as a collaborative process. In W. Damon, D. Kuhn and R. S. Siegler (Eds), *Handbook of Child Psychology, Vol. 2: Cognition, Language and Perceptual Development* (pp. 679–744). New York: Wiley.

Rogoff, B. (2003). *The Cultural Nature of Human Development*. New York: Oxford University Press.

Rosa, E. M. and Tudge, J. R. H. (2013). Urie Bronfenbrenner's theory of human development: Its evolution from ecology to bioecology. *Journal of Family Theory and Review*, *5*(6), 243–258.

Runions, K. C. (2014). Does gender moderate the association between children's behaviour and teacher-child relationship in the early years? *Australian Journal of Guidance and Counselling, 24*(2), 197–214.

Rutter, M. (1985). Resilience in the face of adversity. *British Journal of Psychiatry, 147*(1), 598–611.

Rutter, M. and the English and Romanian Adoptees (ERA) Study Team (1998). Developmental catch-up, and deficit, following adoption after severe global early privation. *Journal of Child Psychology and Psychiatry, 39*(4), 465–476.

Sabol, T. J., Soliday Hong, S. L., Pianta, R. C. and Burchinal, M. R. (2013). Can rating pre-K programs predict children's learning? *Science, 341*(6148), 845–846.

Saffigna, M., Church, A. and Tayler, C./Department of Education and Early Childhood Development (2011). *Victoria Early Years Learning and Development Framework. Evidence Paper: Practice Principle 3: High Expectations for Every Child.* Melbourne: University of Melbourne.

Sandseter, E. B. H. (2007). Categorizing risky play – how can we identify risk-taking in children's play? *European Early Child Education Research Journal, 15*(2), 237–252.

Santer, J. and Griffiths, C. with Goodall, D. (2007) *Free Play in Early Childhood: A Literature Review.* London: Play England and the National Children's Bureau.

Santrock, J. W. (2007). *Child Development,* Eleventh Edition. New York: McGraw-Hill Companies, Inc.

Saskatchewan Ministry of Education (2009). *Creating Early Learning Environments: Into Practice Booklet* [pdf file], *Government of Saskatchewan.* Available at: http://publications.gov.sk.ca/documents/11/82950-Creating%20Early%20Learning%20Environments.pdf (accessed 10 October, 2016).

Sayeed, Z. and Guerin, E. (2000). *Early Years Play: A Happy Medium for Assessment and Intervention.* London: David Fulton Publishers.

Singer, E. (2013). Play and playfulness, basic features of early childhood education. *European Early Childhood Education Research Journal, 21*(2), 172–184.

Singer, E. (2015). Play and playfulness in early childhood education. *Psychology in Russia: State of the Art, 8*(2), 27–35.

Siraj, I. and Mayo, A. (2014). *Social Class and Educational Inequality: The Impact of Parents and School.* Cambridge: Cambridge University Press.

Siraj-Blatchford, I. (2009). Conceptualising progression in the pedagogy of play and sustained shared thinking in early childhood education: A Vygotskian perspective. *Educational and Child Psychology, 26*(2), 77–89.

Siraj-Blatchford, I. and Clarke, P. (2000). *Supporting Identity, Diversity and Language in the Early Years.* Buckingham: Open University Press.

Siraj-Blatchford, I., Sylva, K., Muttock. S., Gilden, R. and Bell, D. (2002). *Researching Effective Pedagogy in the Early Years.* Research Report RR365. London: Department for Education and Skills.

Siraj-Blatchford, I., Taggart, B., Sylva, K., Sammons, P. and Melhuish, E. (2008). Towards the transformation of practice in early childhood education: The Effective Provision of Pre-school Education (EPPE) project. *Cambridge Journal of Education, 38*(1), 23–36.

Slesnick, N., Prestopnik, J. L., Meyers, R. J. and Glassman, M. (2007). Treatment outcome for street-living, homeless youth. *Addictive Behaviors, 32*(6), 1237–1251.

Smidt, S. (2013). *Introducing Vygotsky: A Guide for Practitioners and Students in Early Years Education.* Abingdon: Routledge.

Smith, A. B. (2013). *Understanding Children and Childhood.* Wellington, New Zealand: Bridget Williams Books.

Smyth, E., Darmody, M., McGinnity, F. and Byrne, D. (2009). *Adapting to Diversity: Irish Schools and Newcomer Students*. Dublin: The Economic and Social Research Institute.

Sommer, D., Pramling-Samuelsson, I. P. and Hundeide, K. (2013). Early childhood education and care: A child-perspective paradigm. *European Early Childhood Education Research Journal*, *21*(4), 459–475.

Strong-Wilson, T. and Ellis, J. (2007). Children and place: Reggio Emilia's environment as third teacher. *Theory into Practice*, *46*(1), 40–47.

Sylva, K., Melhuish, E., Sammon, P., Siraj-Blatchford, I. and Taggart, B. (2004). *The Effective Provision of Pre-School Education (EPPE) Project: Final Report*. London: Institute of Education/SureStart.

Taylor, P., Rietzschel, J., Danquah, A. and Berry, K. (2015). Changes in attachment representations during psychological therapy. *Psychotherapy Research*, *25*(2), 222–238.

The TOY Project Consortium (2013). *Reweaving the Tapestry of the Generations: A Guide to Community-based Intergenerational Initiatives in Europe*. Leiden: The TOY Project.

Thomas, A. and Chess, S. (1956). An approach to the study of sources of individual differences in child behavior. *Journal of Clinical and Experimental Psychopathology*, *18*(4), 347–357.

Thomas, A. and Chess, S. (1977). *Temperament and Development*. Oxford: Brunner/Mazel.

Tobin, J., Arzubiaga, A. and Adair, J. K. (2013). *Children Crossing Borders: Immigrant Parent and Teacher Perspectives on Preschool for Children of Immigrants*. New York: Russell Sage Foundation.

Tomanovic, S. (2003). Negotiating children's participation and autonomy within families. *International Journal of Children's Rights*, *11*(1), 51–71.

Tovey, H. (2010). Playing on the edge: Perceptions of risk and danger in outdoor play. In P. Broadhead, J. Howard and E. Wood (Eds), *Play and Learning in the Early Years* (pp. 79–94). London: Sage.

Townsend-Cross, M. (2004). Indigenous Australian perspectives in early childhood education. *International Journal of Equity and Innovation in Early Childhood*, *2*(2), 2–11.

Trevarthen, C. (2011). What young children give to their learning: Making education work to sustain a community and its culture. *European Early Childhood Education Research Journal*, *19*(2), 173–194.

Tudge, J. R. H. (2008). *The Everyday Lives of Young Children: Culture, Class, and Child Rearing in Diverse Societies*. New York: Cambridge University Press.

Tudge, J. R. H., Mokrova, I. L., Hatfield, B. E. and Karnik, R. B. (2009). Uses and misuses of Bronfenbrenner's bioecological theory of human development. *Journal of Family Theory and Review*, *1*(4), 198–210.

Tzuo, P. W., Yang, C. H. and Wright, S. K. (2011). Child-centered education: Incorporating reconceptualism and poststructuralism. *Educational Research and Reviews*, *6*(8), 554–559.

United Nations (1989). *Convention on the Rights of the Child*. Geneva: United Nations. Available at: www.unhcr.org/uk/4aa76b319.pdf (accessed 10 October, 2016).

Valentine, K. (2009). Accounting for agency. *Children and Society*, *25*(5), 347–358.

Van Ijzendoorn, M. H. and Sagi-Schwartz, A. (2008). Cross-cultural patterns of attachment: Universal and contextual dimensions. In J. Cassidy and P. R. Shaver (Eds), *Handbook of Attachment: Theory, Research and Clinical Applications* (pp. 880–905). New York: Guilford Press.

Vygotsky, L. S. (1978). *Mind and Society: The Development of Higher Psychological Processes*. Cambridge, MA: Harvard University Press.

Warger, T. and Dobbin, G. (2009). *Learning Environments: Where Space, Technology, and Culture Converge*. ELI White Paper 1. Washington, DC: EDUCAUSE.

Wenger, E. (1998) *Communities of Practice: Learning, Meaning and Identity*. Cambridge: Cambridge University Press.

Whitebread, D., Basilio, M., Kuvalja, M. and Verma, M. (2012). *The Importance of Play: A Report on the Value of Play with a Series of Policy Recommendations.* Brussels, Belgium: Toy Industries of Europe.

Wood, E. (2013). *Play, Learning and the Early Childhood Curriculum.* London: Sage.

Wood, E. A. (2014). Free choice and free play in early childhood education: Troubling the discourse. *International Journal of Early Years Education, 22*(1), 4–18.

Woodhead, M. (1999). Reconstructing developmental psychology: Some first steps. *Children and Society, 13*(1), 3–19.

Woodhead, M. (2000). Towards a global paradigm for research into early childhood. In H. Penn (Ed.), *Early Childhood Services: Theory, Policy and Practice* (pp. 15–33). Buckingham: Open University Press.

Woodhead, M. (2006). Changing perspectives on early childhood: Theory, research and policy. *International Journal of Equity and Innovation in Early Childhood, 4*(2), 1–43.

Zigler, E. and Muenchow, S. (1992). *Head Start: The Inside Story of America's Most Successful Educational Experiment.* New York: Basic Books.

Zimbardo, P. G. (1971). *Stanford Prison Experiment.* Redwood City, CA: Stanford University Press.

INDEX